IT'S A QUEE

Mark Simpson is the author of *Male Impersonators*. He is a critic and journalist.

Dear Nick,
Thanks for making
me laugh a lot!
Love Jues.

Mark Simpson

IT'S A QUEER WORLD

V

VINTAGE

Published by Vintage 1996

2 4 6 8 10 9 7 5 3

First published in Great Britain by
Vintage, 1996

Vintage
Random House, 20 Vauxhall Bridge Road, London SW1V 2SA

Random House Australia (Pty) Limited
20 Alfred Street, Milsons Point, Sydney
New South Wales 2061, Australia

Random House New Zealand Limited
18 Poland Road, Glenfield,
Auckland 10, New Zealand

Random House South Africa (Pty) Limited
PO Box 337, Bergvlei, South Africa

Random House UK Limited Reg. No. 954009

A CIP catalogue record for this book
is available from the British Library

ISBN 0099597519

The author and publishers wish to thank the following publications for
permission to reproduce articles included in this book: the *Independent*, the
Guardian, *Attitude*, the *Observer*, *Time Out*, and *Homme Plus*

Papers used by Random House UK Ltd are natural,
recyclable products made from wood grown in
sustainable forests. The manufacturing processes
conform to the environmental regulations of the
country of origin

Typeset by Deltatype Ltd, Ellesmere Port, Cheshire

Printed and bound in Great Britain by
The Guernsey Press Co. Ltd., Guernsey, Channel Islands

ACKNOWLEDGEMENTS

THANKS ARE DUE to Rudolph Bakker, James Collard, Pas Paschali, Ian Tucker and all the staff at *Attitude*. Thanks also to Susie Aikin-Sneath, Dave Arias, Claire Armitstead, Simon Audley, Helen Birch, Simon Blow, Michael Blighton, Dan Borras, Jonathan Burnham, Paul Burston, Tristan Davies, Lorraine Gamman, Nick Haeffner, Steve Howard, John Lyttle, Tim Nicholson, Lisa O'Kelly, Dick Peach, Ray Purtee, Meirion Todd and Steven Zeeland.

For M. (whether he wants it or not)

CONTENTS

II
Hollywood

TV

Pop Stars

Shopping

Men

Introduction: The Gay Nineties

IT'S A QUEER old world and getting jolly queerer all the time. Instead of cosmetic tips and boy-meets-girl story-lines, something called 'lesbian chic' is used to promote women's magazines and soap operas. Instead of practising their karate, Hollywood male box-office paramours and action heroes scratch each other's eyes out to play bisexual bloodsuckers and screaming drag queens. Instead of images of big-breasted, submissive blondes being used to whet our appetites, billboards and commercial breaks are filled with images of big-breasted, submissive *blonds*. Instead of offering teen girls real men to lust after, pop music parades hairless boy-bands with unbroken voices in leather chaps and nipple rings. Any red-blooded heterosexualist would be forgiven for thinking the world turned upside down, as cross-dressing and cross-over turns inversion into the (dis-)order of the day in the giddy, topsy-turvy and not a little pervy Nineties.

Truly, the times are out of sorts when this kind of deviation is deemed the 'popular' part of culture. Once upon a time, not so very long ago, homosexuality was kept out of sight and mind. As a result, 'Out of the closets on to the streets!' became the rallying cry of gay libbers in the late 1960s and early 1970s determined to end the dark, suffocating silence which surrounded homosexuality – a silence which nowadays can seem slightly charming and nostalgic. Not even the wildest eyed gay radical of that era, for all their

1

propaganda about homosexuality's potential to change the world, would have dared believe then that homosexuality would, within just a quarter of a century, became the object of noisy, brightly lit, videotaped fascination that it is today. Homosexuality has left its closet, but instead of the streets it has headed straight for the media. The love that once dared not speak its name now won't shut up and is followed everywhere by a TV crew, a fashion photographer, a Hollywood agent and millions of screaming girls. In the Gay Nineties, homosexuality, once a passport to obscurity if you were lucky and to infamy if you weren't, is now a form of celebrity.

Such is the public's fascination with homosexuality that a word has even been coined to describe it. Bishops, MPs and even silly TV entertainers whose preference happens to be for the same sex and who were remiss enough to withhold this fact from the world are now 'outed' against their will by tabloids or gay rights groups. Although originally a neologism invented to describe the naming, by vengeful homosexuals, of public homophobes who were privately homosexual, 'outing' actually describes a process that is beyond the control of any gay activist or tabloid editor. 'Outing' is the spirit of the age; an age with an insatiable appetite for the exposure of homosexuality – insatiable because it is an irresolvable mixture of repulsion and attraction, rejection and recognition.

How did this very funny-peculiar state of affairs come about? Why, in the last decade of the twentieth century, when estimates of the actual numbers of homosexuals in the population are being rapidly revised downwards, from the famous Kinsey 10 per cent (really a distortion of Kinsey) to the 2.5 per cent of recent surveys, is interest in homosexuality going through the roof? What is it about 'perversion' that is now so 'sexy' to straights?

The usual answers don't quite add up. Undoubtedly the efforts of the gay movement to bring gay rights into the arena played a part. AIDS, which turned obituary columns into posthumous coming out lists and put anal sex into the news, also played a part. And, yes, of course, 'changing attitudes' – a popular phrase which begs more questions than it answers – have had their effect. But while this helps to explain why people's tolerance levels of homosexuality might have been raised, none of these factors explains why in the last few years shirt-lifting should have achieved nothing short of stardom.

No, the real answer to the *fin-de-siècle* obsession with same-sex desire and its trappings, strangely enough, has little to do with homosexuals, or even homosexuality. The plain truth is that homosexuality is such a preoccupation of the 1990s because *heterosexuality* is in such a bad way. In the past, when heterosexuality was beyond criticism, when it was a faith that everyone believed in (including homosexuals), no one spoke of 'heterosexuality' except psychiatrists trying to cure homosexuals. Heterosexuality was just 'normality'. This explained the taboo status of homosexuality. Since the term was created to define, categorise and pathologise what was not permissible, not 'normal', the silence around homosexuality was just a function of the sacredness of heterosexuality. Homosexuality was just as awful as heterosexuality was wonderful. Heterosexuality was beyond reproach; homosexuality was beyond the pale.

It hardly needs pointing out that heterosexuality is no longer beyond reproach. Even if it is still rarely named (although now homosexuals and the politically correct have joined the ranks of psychiatrists), it is in trouble and in the news. Normality is not so normal any more. The rise in divorce, single-parent families, the challenge to gender roles encouraged by consumerism, changing productive practices and employment patterns that increasingly favour women have seen to that. Meanwhile the advances of feminism and its relentless exposure of the injustices perpetrated against women – rape, wife battering, sexism and more – by a world ordered according to sexual difference, i.e. a life-script written according whether you possess a penis or not, have shaken practically everyone's faith in the magical ability of

3

the conjunction of penis and vagina in holy wedlock to bring happiness and fulfilment.

It isn't that opposite-sex attraction is going out of fashion or is in any danger of being supplanted by homosexuality, rather it is that the system of prohibitions and proscriptions that cluster around it called heterosexuality no longer provides people with the reassurances they expected in return for obedience. When 'normality' brings with it so many upheavals and uncertainties, when it no longer delivers to you the sense of security and self-affirmation it was synonymous with, what is the point of striving for it? Why, in other words, should one keep to the straight and narrow when it seems barely better going than deviating through the undergrowth?

Deprived of their comforting notions of who and what they were, based on how they were plumbed and who they were plumbed by, people have begun, if not to explore it themselves, at least to look in a queer direction. Of course, many are curious merely because they expect the cold shiver that homosexuality produces in them when they gaze upon its ghastly features will confirm their own identity – I'm definitely not *that* so I must be normal, after all, in spite of my chaotic, unpredictable, confusing life. Like the wives in Bluebeard's castle, opposite-sexers are trying the one door that was forbidden them by their previous master, hoping that behind it lies some secret that will tell them who they are and what their fate is – or at the very least titillate them. But there are others who try the previously barred door because they seriously wonder whether homosexuals have any better answers to the new life-problems which beset them. Gay cross-over into the mainstream is all the rage these days because now the sexual shibboleths of yesteryear are being dispensed with, there is nothing to lose and perhaps a world to gain by hanging around with 'one of them' or, more usually, watching them on telly.

This about-turn in attitudes towards homosexuality is most apparent in regard to the toppling of those once all-powerful idols: masculinity and femininity, whose fall is reverberating throughout our culture. One of the reasons homosexuals were reviled in the past was because they represented an *uncertainty* about masculinity and femininity, a repellent confusion of the divine law of sexual difference which insisted that male (penis-bearer) must map on to masculine which in turn must map on to active, while female (penis-envier) must map on to feminine which must map on to passive.

Worse, queers embodied a scepticism about sexual difference which became a dangerous heresy by advertising male passivity and female activity. In the hellish world of the homosexual, penis-bearers not only offered their bottoms to each other but also trivialised the phallus, its powers and its responsibilities (to impregnate and subjugate women), by turning this God-given answer to the otherwise overwhelming curse of feminine power into just a plaything, a realistic (i.e. more modestly proportioned) sex toy. Female inverts displayed the same irreverence and irresponsibility by chasing one another instead of waiting for Prince Charming's magic lance to make them into a Woman. The answer to this, naturally, was to place a quarantine on these people and decree that such perverse creatures weren't *really* men and women. Hence homos were dubbed 'cruel tricks of nature' whose very 'freakish' interior androgyny – a woman trapped in a man's body/a man trapped in a woman's body – shored up the old order by being the laughable/punishable treatable exception that proved the rule.

But the old order is breaking down; the active/passive gender split doesn't work the kind of voodoo it used to. As male employment opportunities continue to fall and female employment continues to rise, men are no longer always bringing home the bacon to demure wifey waiting at home. As female sexual desire grows in confidence, men are no longer always sweating away masterfully on top. As images of naked male narcissism are used to sell everything from jeans to ice cream, men are transparently no longer always lusting, never lusted after. And as we move further and further away from a time when there was no pill and consequently no mass culture of sex-as-recreation except prostitution, the power of the phallus continues to shrink and diminish.

These inescapable changes have led to a growing acceptance that 'masculine' and 'feminine', 'active' and 'passive', and even 'male' and 'female' are not, after all, adamantine in their relationships, that instead they are increasingly 'free floating', and that they are at some level a kind of performance which anyone can 'do'. It isn't that 'masculine' and 'feminine' are being dispensed with – they have merely become more self-conscious; people are beginning to wear gender instead of it wearing them.

This 'performativity' of gender and the discovery that anatomy need not be destiny after all, that at the very least a little irony can be a spanner in Fate's grinding cogs, is what has made homosexuality so famous and so inspirational today. Homosexuality itself stands for a certain kind of irony about sex and sexuality (although homos can be very un-ironic about the actual *business* of sex). Nowadays, the 'joke' of homosexuality is one that speaks to more and more people. The 'cruel trick of nature' has become a cool trick of gender; the 'interior androgyny' of homosexuals has become the exterior androgyny of our times – what would once have been a suitable case for treatment and the subject of earnest late-night TV documentaries, is now a suitable case for celebrity. Hence the phenomenon of 'lesbian chic', in which otherwise heterosexual women are encouraged to celebrate the possibility of active female desire, independent of men and their penises, and enthusiastically explore their 'masculine potential' – without being 'men-hating'. Hence the crop of media features on the exploits of 'drag kings': women who dress up as men, complete with moustache and stuffed crotch, take classes in how to sit and spit 'like a man' and then spend a day trying to fool the world into believing they have a penis – without wanting to change sex. Hence also the current 'drag chic' where macho Hollywood stars like Patrick Swayze can't wait to jump into taffeta and 'do' femininity – without, and here's the true irony, wanting to 'take it like a man'.

Of course, the men are a long way behind the women in celebrating the cool trick of gender through gay-play. For most men, homosexuality still stars in their lives as an anxiety rather than an aspiration; they believe that the queer currents around them will unman them if they acknowledge them and so are locked into a kind of sulky denial, further handicapping the male sex in general in a rapidly changing world. However popular dragging up right now might be with the guys, it is usually adamantly presented as something that is *not* homosexual, and in fact proof of their heterosexuality – I'm so secure in my masculinity that . . . This despite the fact that a man in woman's clothes is undoubtedly *the* popular image of male homosexuality, since it removes queers from the milieu of real men (See – I told ya he really wanted to be a girl!). In contrast to the gay-play of the women, men can only talk about 'getting in touch with their feminine side' on the sensible condition that we accept this doesn't actually mean, of course, that they want to do anything *really* 'feminine' – like being penetrated by another man.

It is, however, in another kind of drag that homosexuality makes its Big Entrance in the sleepless dreams of the heterosexual male these days. Khaki drag. The gay male in uniform (and he is always male; lesbians are hardly ever mentioned) has become one of the most fraught and fought-over symbols of the Nineties. By 'dressing up as a man' he threatens to reveal that all soldiers are in fact dressing up as men and that being a soldier – the most manly of occupations – might just be another kind of performance after all, ironising what is supposed to be a deadly serious business (masculinity as much as soldiering). This, of course, regardless of how seriously the individual gay soldier takes his job or masculinity. After all, as a homosexual he is only a symbol.

Thus, to permit 'out' gay men in the showers of the straight male psyche is to acknowledge that the world really has changed, that the old idols have fallen, that previous prejudices are no longer valid even for me whose job it is to kill other men. In other words, ending the ban on gays in the military would mean ending the mollycoddling of trained killers which consists of playing along with their pretence that they have already spent their lives living, sleeping and scratching their balls around men who liked to check out their tackle in the washroom, and feigning horror at their stories of the terrors of taking their pants down within fifty miles of a known homosexual. But most of all it means ending the segregation of homosexuality from heterosexuality and an end to playing along with the disavowal of the possibility of male passivity. Permitting gay men to serve would be going some way to permitting all men to think the unthinkable thought: that, to paraphrase Freud, dropping the soap is something they are all capable of and in fact is something they have already done in their unconscious.

But for all this, men in Britain do have their own counterpart to lesbian chic -- New Lad. The fashion for celebrating manliness, which began in the late Eighties as a masculinist reaction to the female-dominated, wimpish 'new man' (usually pictured holding babies), has unwittingly blurred the distinction, as important as it was incoherent, between an interest in manly things and an interest in *men*. Just as lesbian chic was used by straight women to celebrate a female sexuality independent of men, New Lad celebrates a male sexuality not dependent on women (unless they are decorative 'babes' who look like transsexuals). Both sexes are increasingly less inclined and less able to depend on the opposite sex for their sexual identity and more inclined to look to their own. Homosexuality, inevitably, occupies the nexus-point here. It may, as shown earlier, represent gender non-conformity, but paradoxically it also increasingly offers a form of gender reassurance. Especially in the case of men, since (post-feminist) women and the (integrated) workplace no longer do. However, in the case of New Lad this reassurance is still dependent on an implicit repudiation of homosexuality; hence it dictates an exhausting schedule of boozing, shagging babes and fighting over football scores which is, in part, a hysterical attempt to ward off any suggestion of poovery and keep the homo tag at bay. New Lad may well be a male counterpart to lesbian chic, but so far it appears to have rather less in the way of balls.

The homosexual male made another recent top of the bill appearance in another national male psycho-drama, this time in the House of Commons, when the British Parliament debated lowering the age of consent for male homosexual acts to sixteen, the age of consent for heterosexual relations. Once more, what was really at stake had little or nothing to do with homosexuals themselves. What was at issue was, again, a desperate 'rearguard' action to disavow the increasingly apparent phenomenon of masculine passivity and maintain the quarantine on homosexuality by keeping the legal discrimination against it in place. The House voted to maintain an unequal age of consent (eighteen as compared with sixteen) to ensure the continued protection of male orifices by the majesty of the law longer than the female variety, sending a frankly not very surprising message to the country that its mostly middle-aged, male Members were horrified by the idea that young men should be treated the way many of them like to treat young women.

Some MPs also took this occasion to draw attention to the mortal peril that homosexuality presented to the family and explain why Parliament should continue to persecute it for the good of the nation and mothers' milk. Homosexuality is looked to by these people not as something that may offer the beginnings of an answer to the new uncertainties that face us all but rather as the cause of them. They accept completely that traditional heterosexuality, or 'family values' as they brand it (so that those who oppose them are 'anti-family'), is in crisis. The solution to this crisis is to close down the alternatives: if you lock people in church they will have nothing to do but pray. The 'family values' or Retrosexuality Movement is deeply unhappy with the separation of sex from reproduction which contraception and late consumer capitalism has brought about and the

9

gender revolution that all this has made possible. Interestingly, the Retrosexuality Movement, despite drawing people from all parts of the political spectrum, is usually supported by those whose natural political home has been Republican/Conservative parties, the parties most closely identified with consumerism, the parties who have governed most since its advent in the post-war period and the parties who were exclusively in power during the Eighties when this process accelerated dramatically.

So it's hardly surprising, then, that these Retrosexualists are deeply nostalgic about a heterosexuality they see as 'timeless' ('the family is the basic building block of society' is a favourite phrase), so 'timeless' it never really existed except in 1950s advertising for frozen food. Paradoxically the Retrosexuality Movement resembles nothing so much as the Romantics and Christian Socialists who reacted against the upheavals brought about by the arrival of early capitalism and urbanisation by idealising rural idiocy.

Needless to say, Retrosexualists don't blame consumer capitalism for all the woes that trouble them, but a decade – the Sixties. The break-up of the nuclear family is seen to proceed from people having more choices as a result of 'free love' and 'permissiveness' in the Sixties and thus being able to escape from their reproductive/familiar responsibilities. And homosexuality, which is about as non-reproductive and therefore as irresponsible as you can get, is the clearest alternative to heterosexuality, and one which became, according to legend, freely available in the Sixties, if not actually on the Welfare State.

The answer is, of course, to undo the legacy of the Sixties. Hence it is the state's duty to maintain the legal proscriptions against homosexuality (and maybe introduce some more) and continue turning a blind eye to discrimination in areas such as the workplace and housing, and thus send out the clear message that homosexuality is most definitely not equal to heterosexuality and is indeed a second or even third-rate life that decent, respectable people will have nothing to do with.

10

The homo-segregationist strategy of the Retrosexualists is not, however, likely to achieve anything except make homosexuality even more famous. The whole point of the segregation of homosexuality in the past was so that you didn't have to think about or talk about it very much. Trying to banish homosexuality into the margins again, whether or not it is possible, involves a great deal of thinking and talking about it. Not surprisingly, the Retrosexually inclined are obsessed with homosexuality even more than the media they despise. Putting cats back into bags because you don't like cats involves, unavoidably, a lot of thinking and talking about – not to mention handling of – cats.

But the leading role of homosexuality in this production of The Death of the Nuclear Family does not end there. Homosexuality is not just the cause of family ruin, it is also the consequence – you reap what you sow. 'The chances that your marriage will end in DIVORCE is even greater than ever,' a *Daily Mail* strap-line for a double-page feature recently shouted. 'If it does, you know to expect anguish and pain. We reveal how it can also make your sons GAY.' Homosexuality behind us; homosexuality before us. What kind of world are we making for the *Daily Mail* reader!

But, again, there is a certain truth behind this slightly paranoid scenario – which reveals yet another reason why homosexuality is such an overdetermined symbol these days. Gay men *are* fatherless – either literally or more often metaphorically, in the sense that there are no examples for the homosexual to follow, no archetypes to introject, no role models to imitate, no ego ideals to worship. The male homosexual grows up alone, with no ancestral map to navigate the world by and no paternal shoes to step into; he grows up, in other words, in the way that more and more straight boys are growing up. As more and more mothers elect to raise their children without a father and the function of the fathers who remain and the relevance of the 'heritage' masculinity they represent and want to pass on to their sons becomes increasingly unclear, the world is becoming more and more 'fatherless'. Gay or straight, more and more boys

11

are being 'fathered' by popular culture – the telly, cinema, video games, pop music – and look for their masculine identity not through imitating Dad but in wearing commodities advertised through that medium that 'accessorise' masculinity: Nike trainers as worn by Ryan Giggs, jeans as worn by James Dean. In this sense, the future is decidedly homosexual.

At the same time that homosexuality seems to be looming large on the horizon, it is breaking free of the public/private distinction on which its toleration/segregation was based in the recent past. Since homosexuality was, unlike skin pigmentation, something that could be hidden, homosexuals were permitted to go about their business on the understanding that they would be 'discreet' and keep their 'private' sexuality private; toleration was conditional, in other words, on how well the homosexual 'passed' as a heterosexual. Interestingly, the Pentagon's 'don't ask; don't tell' compromise formula devised to head off President Clinton's attempts to overturn the military ban on lesbians and gays is nothing more or less than an explicit formulation of this implicit understanding: we won't persecute you as long as you don't force us to acknowledge your homosexuality. Like the homo-segregationist approach of the Retrosexualists (who are strongly represented in the armed forces), this strategy of discretion is doomed precisely because it now has to be explicit. But perhaps this is just a function of the general indiscretion of our media-saturated times.

In our astonishingly mediatised age, where there is an endless appetite for information in all its formats, an appetite grows with what it feeds on. So there is a terrible shortage of that sexiest of gaps between knowledge and reality – scandal. Too much is known; too few secrets remain. The line between public and private has been erased by what Jean Baudrillard has called 'the ecstasy of communication'. The dirty linen of the rich and famous has been washed in public so many times that it is no longer dirty. And as the career boost such 'scandals ' give personalities these days shows, shame isn't a serious condition any more; everyone, even and especially the sanctimonious reader of the Sunday scandal-sheets, recognises it for what it is: a priceless PR opportunity.

Naturally, since he knew that his survival depended upon it, the homosexual was once the principal guardian of the public/private demarcation; consequently he was also likely to be the greatest believer in shame. Nowadays, emboldened by the general noseyness and the corresponding frankness of our times, and spurred on by the disaster of AIDS (Silence= Death), the homosexual has become the greatest detonator of that demarcation and the most famous practitioner of shamelessness, by bringing his sexuality out of the private closet into the public limelight. Even to the extent of outing other homosexuals, once the ultimate crime, in the name of shamelessness. This is what reduces so many liberals to incandescent rage about outing when practised by other gays; the refusal of homosexuals to check the locks on each other's closets any more is the final proof that the public/ private system of tolerance has vanished and with it the fond hypocrisies with which liberals are so at home. Outing is so 'controversial' merely because it represents more clearly than anything else the consequences of the invasion of privacy that necessarily goes with a modern, mediatised world.

It was, of course, the distinctly illiberal tabloid press which helped bring this process about. The liberal press, if left to its own devices, might still be printing sad euphemisms about 'life-long bachelors' in the obituary columns, while privately gossiping about the expired 'bachelor's' taste in men, along with their exact proportions, in the local wine bar. It took the plebeian, saloon-bar instinct of the tabloid press to be honest about the public's interest in that kind of gossip and their feverish fascination with homosexuality in general.

And it was the tabloid outing of British TV entertainer Michael Barrymore that demonstrated just how the public expects and even requires homosexuals to be indiscreet

13

about their sexuality these days. Initially hounded by the tabs when they got wind of a scandal, Barrymore did the now customary trick of turning the tables and appealing to the tabloid readership over the heads of the tabloids. How? By out-tabbing the tabs and providing the public with even more personal information by coming out through a radio interview. This performance won him applause from almost every section of the auditorium and tributes to his courage and character. But only because Barrymore was giving the audience what they wanted; he was just fulfilling the contemporary expectation of the homosexual as pall-bearer to the public/private distinction.

In this age of fewer and fewer secrets, the 'secret of sex' is sought after more and more, and confessed more and more, through pornography and its related industry of sex surveys, magazine questionnaires and ten-page 'how-to' features, agony aunt columns, 'Better Sex' videos, books and TV chat shows discussing sexual problems. This climate of open fascination with sex has undoubtedly helped changed public attitudes towards homosexuality from fear and loathing to intrigue and curiosity. Since homosexuality represents 'sex' in its purest, or rather its most abstract and indulgent form, neither reproductive nor institutionalised like hetero-sexuality – just sex for sex's sake – public opinion on homosexuality is bound to be a reflection of attitudes towards sex itself. When sex was a filthy, sniggersome thing, homosexuality was the filthiest, most sniggersome thing of all. Now that everyone is 'outing' sex, and trying to unlock its mysteries, homosexuality takes on the solemn, sacred significance of the Rosetta Stone.

And the 'secret of sex' which everyone is searching for is more and more looked to as somehow holding within itself another, even more precious secret – the secret of who we are and the secret of liberation from the slavery of inauthentic-ity. Along with this tendency goes the increasing move towards finally separating sex from reproduction (with all its nasty obligations) and seeing it as more of a form of personal therapy/self-expression. This may be nothing more

14

than a function of the vanity and self-absorption of our times, or it may be, as Michel Foucault has suggested, the culmination of an historical discourse on sexuality which has led us to believe that it is through the ritual telling, confessing and categorising of sexuality that we somehow set free something truly unique and individual about ourselves – when in fact all we are really doing is tracking down the lines of power already laid out. Sexuality is itself a system of control and, contrary to the sexual liberationist dream that everyone under forty seems to share nowadays, saying 'yes' to sex is not saying 'no' to power, it's just learning to enjoy the chafing of the manacles around your wrists.

Whatever the truth behind the sex-confessional imperative of the late twentieth century, homosexuals are, more than anyone else, creatures of this 'secret of sex' narrative. It is taken as given that it is *their* 'secret of sex' – so much more secret because it was so much more shameful – which holds the key to their identity; their sexuality is what defines them and is, indeed, how they choose to define themselves when they 'come out'. In fact the coming out narrative is a myth for our time, a myth in which the homosexual takes on the status of a modern religious hero who, through a process of testing sexual self-inquiry, soul-searching and self-examination arrives at the answer to the question 'Who am I?' in terms of the sex-confessional question 'Whom do I desire?' and then shares that discovery with the world. Or, more succinctly, the homosexual learns to say 'yes' to sex and *thus to himself*. And saying 'yes' to oneself is by far the most virtuous thing anyone can do these days; saying 'no' the worst possible crime. In short, the homosexual is the existential, expressive star of our modern, individualistic, introspective universe.

Unsurprisingly, the heroic, not to say dramatic, narrative of coming out has increasingly attracted people whose natural bent is to be in the public eye and who are apt to want to associate the 'star quality' of homosexuality in these times with their own person. Coming out is essentially a script which places the individual at the centre of world history, offering everyone their fifteen nanoseconds of fame; homosexuality represents within itself the most truly democratic interpretation of celebrity. It can be no coincidence that two of the most famous gay activists in Britain today are both actors, and both arguably more famous for coming out than for treading the boards.

Which is a curious reversal considering that the limelight was something homos often sought as consolation for being homo; a variation of the theory that the best way to hide is to place yourself somewhere where you can't be missed. To an extent, the stardom aspect of homosexuality is a by-product of its marginalisation. Homosexuals have no proper place within the family and are told, implicitly and explicitly, they are ugly/disgusting/unlovable, so it is hardly surprising that they colonise the arts, where they can fashion a more hospitable, more attractive world for themselves and, if they are sufficiently talented, win approval and adoration from the society that exiled them in the first place (homos with less opportunity or imagination are generally found in large numbers in the church and the army).

So, historically, culture has been full of homos; and in a sense, that's what they are 'for': to entertain, educate and inspire, to serve and protect. And now we can add 'innovate' to that list. With the explosion of consumer culture homosexuals have found another place to be: the market place. And once again, their apparent 'at-homeness' in the world of boutiques, salons and out-of-town Swedish furniture hypermarkets is a result of them making a virtue out of a necessity. A homosexual man was (and still is, last time I checked) a contradiction in terms; an absence instead of a presence. So gay men literally had to re-invent (and 'de-castrate') themselves – out of accessories, clothes and a subculture of styles. All of which placed them at the heart of consumerism. Feeling alienated/depressed/empty/worthless? Looking for self-validation? Then go shopping! There is more than a grain of truth in the old joke: 'My mother made me a homosexual.' 'Really? If I gave her the pattern would she

16

make me one too?' In a sense, late capitalism has already made perverts of us all, blocking the 'natural aim' of desire and turning it into a commodity – capitalism as fetishism. After all, consumerism is inherently 'unnatural', encouraging the reproduction of the self through commodities rather than the 'free' route of biology, and is much more interested in 'infantile' pleasures, such as orality, than 'adult' genital ones (compare the turnover of, say, the cream cake or beer industry with that of Durex).

Excluded from the family, deprived of the consolation of the ready-made identities that heterosexuals employed, the poor gays recast themselves in the Seventies as sovereign consumers, who were very happy, thank you very much, to seek their identity through pleasure. When the Eighties came along, the hedonism, commodity fetishism and proud-to-be-shallow attitude of gays set them up as aspirational figures. This was partly because post-modernism was rapidly stripping everyone of their consoling determinacies fragmenting identities as more and more people were exposed to market forces and the maelstrom of consumerism. Consequently the survival techniques of gays, their styles and sensibilities, became highly prized commodities themselves. The fuss in the early Nineties over the so-called 'pink economy' and 'pink pound' was really a form of displacement activity. It wasn't the alleged spending power of gays that interested so much as the fact that spending was something they had turned into a full-time activity, if not vocation. This is the cross-over success of the 'gay lifestyle'. Serial monogamy? Shopathons? Cruising in supermarkets? Sex toys? Gays have been there, done that and made a lifestyle out of it. This is why they have become not just avant-garde consumers but pioneering lifestylers, whose experiments in living, shopping and loving (though not necessarily in that order) offer heterosexuals inspiration and deterrence in equal measure. Truly, if homosexuals didn't exist it would be necessary to invent them – if only so that heterosexuals didn't have to be the first to wear see-through mesh T-shirts or tinted eyelashes.

So guys, once the ultimate underdogs, have come to represent a certain victory over and mastery of the post-modern genie that threatens to atomise everyone. Victim status has been exchanged for fashion victimhood – an ironic reversal. What is a lifestyle if it isn't a way of fashioning something personal out of the impersonal forces of consumption? A (marketing) niche to shelter from the storm? Style is itself a certain holding together of certain contradictions; an ability to rise above them. Gays have held together more contradictions than anyone else and have consequently risen faster and further than any group in history.

Little wonder, then, that many young people today look to gays for style leadership. This is because gays are bourgeois without being bourgeois and consumerist without being like your mum and dad. And also because young people are the most open to experiments in living and are also, alas, most intimately acquainted with the contemporary shortcomings of that traditional lifestyle, the family and its dependent sex roles. So-called rave culture, initially a gay innovation, is a clear example of a gay lifestyle crossing over to young people in general. Nor are 'the kids' unaware of the origins of rave – many of the best rave clubs describe themselves as 'gay' although the majority of punters are straight. The gayness is an aspiration, a party-party, touchy-feely lifestylism which naturally excludes the sort of lad who would be more inclined to accuse you of looking at his bird than discuss your crystal energy with you.

Further evidence, if it is needed, of the cross-over of gayness into the mainstream is shown by the panty-dampening success of boy bands such as Take That, whose look was taken straight from gay clubs in the late Eighties. In fact, Take That, with their nipple rings and shaved bodies, represent one of the most successful commodifications of gayness yet. An entire generation of young girls are being raised to lust after archetypes of masculinity which are anything but heterosexual. But the success of Take That, which is based not just on appeal to teen girls but their mums as well, also demonstrates the vitality of a consumer-political alliance that seems destined to take over the world, if it hasn't done so already: gay men and straight women fed up with straight men.

While it may be true that the basis of this relationship relies upon a certain emasculated toy boy appeal of gay men, it is also true that women are increasingly looking towards gay men for leadership on how to combine an active sexuality with narcissism – passivity into activity again. It may even be the case that lesbian chic is something that straight women learnt from gay men rather than lesbians. Certainly its earliest practitioners, such as Madonna, liked to describe themselves as 'a gay man trapped in a woman's body'. These days girls don't just want to be fag hags, they want to be fags. Another reason why *Daily Mail* readers should worry about the future sons of our nation.

But this peculiar interior androgyny of balls-out female superstars, a modern ironic variation on the old-fashioned pathological formula for homosexuality, also spells out an increasingly prevalent condition affecting more and more heterosexuals, a condition in which they feel themselves trapped in the wrong body and their desires being mocked by their anatomy; in other words, more and more people are experiencing nature's cruel joke. And perhaps this is not such a bad thing, since this condition is probably nearer the truth of the preposterous nature of desire and identity. There is a certain kind of poetic justice here too. Once upon a time homosexuality was always explained as failed or confused heterosexuality. Now heterosexuality is increasingly likely to be explained as failed or confused homosexuality.

Inevitably the end result of all this fascination with all things homosexual and the cross-over of gayness into the mainstream is that heterosexuality has changed unrecognisably. Straight ain't so straight any more – at least not in a way in which your grandma and probably even your mother would recognise. What, pray, is 'straight' these days? Roseanne? Keanu Reeves? Tom Cruise? Ren and Stimpy? Please. Which is, of course, the whole point. Old-fashioned

I-have-a-penis-you-don't-therefore-you-are-my-slave hetero-sexuality was faced with the ultimatum: adapt or die; or, put another, more pointed way: lighten up or we axe your next movie/TV series. So, in a world where images are everything, it *has* adapted and livened up. Heterosexuality has been recommissioned, but the scriptwriters have been changed.

Meanwhile, freed of some of the fond, sleepy nostrums of yesteryear, people are beginning to rub their eyes and notice that, wouldn't you know it, heterosexuality never was quite what it was supposed to be; that if you looked long enough and hard enough you'd have noticed there was always a lot of queer business going on, even if it was under the table or on the sexual black market. But few people saw it and even fewer people wanted to hear about it simply because it wasn't supposed to happen. Now, in the Gay Nineties, as I hope my journalism collected in this volume shows, the reporting restrictions are being lifted and the stories are beginning to come in. The new above-board regime, with its assimilation of homosexualness, is quite literally the return of the repressed.

But all this contains mixed messages for homosexuals themselves. Homosexualness may be big business but homosexuals are still discriminated against. Perhaps, though, it is not too naïve to hope that the cross-over boom may ultimately liberate homos from being homos in the way it has begun to liberate heteros from being heteros. The extraordinary metamorphoses of heterosexuality – albeit far from complete – are necessarily transforming what we mean by homosexuality; when the master-code changes, so do all its subject codes. The quarantine on same-sex desire is in the process of being raised, but this may not be good news for homosexuality as an identity. Ghettos are only warm and inviting because the outside world is so cold and hostile. When the revulsion felt for same-sex passion recedes Gaytown may turn into a ghost town as people leave it to make their lives around something other than their sexual preference. The Gay Nineties just might prove to be a closing-down sale for the gay identity.

It remains to be seen, however, whether it will come to pass that Gore Vidal's famous dictum, that 'heterosexual' and 'homosexual' are adjectives not nouns, that they describe only acts and not people, will cease to be a piece of wishful thinking. Even in the unlikely event of all persecution ending, the gay identity is likely to continue to provide consolation and affirmation – not to mention business opportunities – for many of those whose preference is for the same sex. Compared to the uncertain alternatives, the gay womb-world (a.k.a. the gay community) will continue to look inviting to many.

Nevertheless, it's difficult not to relish an adjectival future and the possibility that history, the force that made the homosexual and has recently made him into a superstar, is now intent on consigning him to oblivion. The queerest irony of all would be a queer world that had no place for queers.

Relishing aside, I make no predictions, and leave it to the reader to decide what the future holds. And if nothing else, the journalism collected in the second part of this book will give him/her some clues as to the outlandish shape it is taking and some of the 'outrageous' frocks it's already trying on. Consisting mostly of feature articles written for the *Guardian* and the *Independent*, national newspapers who have recently discovered homosexuality, it documents the crossover of gayness into the mainstream and the breath-taking, kinky transformation of straightness in the Gay Nineties. It is thus, aptly enough, part of the process it purports to describe.

Meanwhile, the sideways, snideways, *perverse* look on the world that is offered in the 'It's A Queer World' columns in the first part of this volume represents a kind of vindictive table-turning. While the mainstream media is increasingly obsessed with what were once 'marginal' sexualities, these columns take apart the *mainstream* from a marginal perspective, researching the twilight world of the heterosexual. These columns, originally published in *Attitude* magazine, Britain's first gay male style publication, are a kind of voyage

21

of exploration, a captain's Log detailing truly bizarre and scary encounters with Planet Normal.

In their humorous critiques of such 'naff' institutions as bingo and boxing, daytime TV and football, shopping centres and stag nights, I hope these columns don't merely score cheap shots against ordinariness (although they certainly do that), but instead illustrate how things are frequently never quite as settled, quite as unambiguous as they seem – or would like to be seen. That nothing is more funny-peculiar or funny ha-ha than normality if you only look closely and uncharitably enough. 'It's a Queer World' sets out to decode what did not at first appear coded, bring out the strange in the familiar, the odd in the ordinary, the uncanny in the canny. A kind of Barthes' *Mythologies*, if you will, but with a few more gags.

I hope too that this mischievous impulse is not mistaken for some kind of banner-waving homosexual chauvinism. It should become apparent that I have no home to be patriotic about. Any reasonably attentive reader will note that the author of this collection obsessively navigates the national boundaries between 'straight' and 'gay', only to blur and betray them whenever possible. Identitism is not my cause. Hence the 'queer world' of this collection is not a world of homosexuality – God forbid – but rather a world put out of order, out of sorts, out of joint; a world of queasy dislocation and general indeterminacy; a drunken world of wayward fun that can be had when you refuse to recognise the sovereignty of sexual identity.

Maybe this sounds too much like glamorisation of mundane misanthropy. Perhaps that's all it is. But, this sexual 'outsiderdom', this sense of watching the wife-swapping party from the wrong side of the B&Q windows, is not such a lonely romantic place to be these days. In fact, it's getting rather crowded out here. If the changes I document and attempt to explain actually exist and are not just figments of my by turns bitter and over-optimistic imagination, there must be an ever-increasing number of people who feel their sexual identity something of a fraud perpetuated on them – a one-zone bus pass, bearing an I.D. photo you don't want to recognize, that takes you nowhere and costs you your dreams.

I

What is a homosexual? . . . he is a man . . . who by his nature is out of step with the world, who refuses to enter into the system that organises the entire world. The homosexual rejects that, denies that, shatters that whether he wants to or not . . . to live with surprises, changes, to accept risks, to be exposed to insult, it's the opposite of social constraint, of the social comedy.

Jean Genet

THE COST OF LOVING

'IT'S ONLY £5, darling. Lots of lovely girls. There's a show starting any minute. Go on, you'll really enjoy yourself.' The woman behind the desk is very persuasive – all the women around here are very persuasive. You feel like you have to have a good reason to say no. Preferring men isn't enough. I'm still dithering when she lowers the price to £3 and that clinches it – now it would be just plain rude not to go in. I hand over my money and head down the stairs.

I'm in Soho, home of LIVE NUDE GIRLS. Soho may be turning pink and filling up with gay bars full of boys in sheer T-shirts and goatees, but tonight I'm leaving all that behind and taking in the authentic Soho experience – that's the Soho of the Sixties and Seventies, the Soho of hetero sleaze (as opposed to homo tack), where sex is SEX (i.e. big boobies not pert pecs) and where business is about GIRLS rather than Boyz. And like any punter, I want to get as much for as little as possible.

Downstairs in the LIVE EROTIC REVUE BAR there's a dimly lit room with a tiny stage in one corner and a bar in the other. A few miserable men in suits are scattered around on grimy sofas. Before I can sit down I'm politely but very, very firmly accosted by an attractive young woman in lace. 'Good evening, I'm Marie and I'm your hostess for the evening.' She informs me sweetly that I have to pay a £20 'cover charge'. 'But I just paid an entrance fee,' I whine. Marie looks at me like a very skilled, very patient special needs

27

teacher might look at a particularly special pupil. I must be
the last punter in the world not to know that in Soho, SEX is
more about emptying your wallet than about emptying your
prostate gland.

Back upstairs, the persuasive woman on the desk per-
suades me that she's actually quite right not to refund my
money and that she's really doing me a big favour giving me
a slip that allows me to return later in the evening when I'll
be too drunk and too desperate to care about being ripped
off.

I try my luck with a PEEP SHOW next door. '£1 Only' it
promises. 'Yessir, only £1, no extra charges,' the helpful but
hideous man on the door confirms. The place looks (and
smells) exactly like a toilet – a woman's toilet. There's no
urinal, just some stalls. There's a line of shifty, uneasy men
waiting for a stall to become vacant so they can spend a
pound. Romance and femininity is added by a pink light
bulb. Finally my turn comes and I squeeze into a stall, trying
not to touch anything, knowing that it's bound to be covered
in crusty bits and worse. There's a bright light on in here and,
in front of me, a slot in the wall with '£1' pencilled above it.
Above that is a letter box with some kind of mirror in it. I
dutifully insert my £1. The light goes out and the mirror
becomes a window. I peep gingerly through it.

The glass is dirty and the room on the other side is not well
lit. Finally I make out some flesh. A young woman in a black
bikini is leaning towards my window (she's raised up so that
her hips are at eye level). She's saying something to me; I
can't hear her. 'Can you speak up, please?' I say like some
old fart at a bank teller's window. She repeats herself. I still
can't hear her. She's getting pissed off. She jiggles her tits
impatiently – I imagine this usually speeds matters up.
Finally, she shouts, 'If you put £5 through the slot then I'll
take my clothes off and . . .'

I miss the final, most important detail. I signal that I still
couldn't hear her and she evidently decides that my 'thing' is
wanking to the sound of young women repeating themselves
and that I'm getting it for only £1. The light comes on and

the window turns into a mirror again. *Paris Texas* wasn't like this. It dawns on me that this is a kind of straight cottaging – where the glory hole is operated by money.

Outside I'm accosted by a short, fat, balding middle-aged man who is clearly the original model for the 'Psst! Seen any good films lately?' spiv – a character I thought went out of circulation shortly after penicillin was introduced. But round Soho way, no one seems to mind if they're an anachronism. 'Want to see a show, mister?' he asks, conspiratorially. 'No,' I say, and move off. But no sooner am I out of range than another man, equally ugly and equally conspiratorial, asks me the same question. Then before I can move away he asks me, 'Would you like a girl?'

'How much?' I ask in the most casual way I can muster.

'Thirty quid. You can see her before you pay. You shouldn't get a girl off the street, y'know – you might catch something.'

'How long do you get for that?'

'An hour. You look first. No need to pay anything if you don't like.'

'How far away?'

'Two minutes. Follow me.'

And I do. I'm so fed up of the rip-off voyeurism SEX that I want to try some of the 'hands-on' stuff. Around the corner, up some stairs and into a room with a double bed and again the aroma of cheap disinfectant (would I be able to recognise expensive disinfectant?). It was last decorated around the time of Profumo. An elderly woman greets me. She must be the maid – just like *Personal Services* (when you're in territory as unfamiliar as this you clutch at any reference points available). 'Julie'll be out in a minute, love,' she says like she's Julie's mum and I've been courting Julie for years.

In less than a minute, and in less time than it takes for me to start wondering what Julie is like and what the hell I'm going to do when she gets here, Julie bounds into the room. She's gorgeous. She doesn't look anything like what a prostitute is supposed to look like – whatever happened to that word 'whorish'? She looks like the girl that might have made me straight. Suddenly I'm frightened – it's been a long, long time.

'What would you like?' she asks. 'I think that I'm going to chicken out,' I mumble, like some public schoolboy talking about a dare to break the out-of-bounds rule. She looks genuinely disappointed – but how can you tell? 'Come back any time you like,' she calls after me as I hurry out. And, exiting onto the street, I catch myself seriously thinking about coming back. She really was nice. Am I developing a Gladstone complex?

Shaken, I decide to find some SEX to watch from a safe distance. At an EROTICA CINEMA I ask the guy if the films are EXPLICIT. 'Oh yes. They're all hot porno films.' No more charges once I pay the £5? 'No more charges.'

Downstairs again. The cinema is a medium-sized room, reeking of that eau de Soho antiseptic, stifling hot and decorated in that fake red velour you always imagined Soho sex cinemas had. A few men are ranged around the room watching the large video screen at the far end. The film is American. It is not EXPLICIT. There are lots of slapping sounds and groaning, but no willies or fannies – instead heads and legs block the view or the camera cuts away at the key moment. It is unutterably dull. As if acknowledging this, the makers of the movie have inserted that universal postmodern excuse for crap – ironic humour. One guy says to a girl before 'fucking' her, 'If Rico knew I was with his best friend's uncle's first cousin's girl he'd kill me.'

The story line seems to be based around a guy who makes men's fantasies come true – for a price. It may be my depraved (deprived?) imagination but there seems to be an almost erotic tension between the men talking business. The scenes between them where they haggle seem to be inordinately long.

Some of the punters, meanwhile, are spending inordinately long in the gents while the others are moving almost imperceptibly closer to one another, like iron fillings subjected to a weak but persistent magnetic force, eyes fixed all the time on the bouncing silicone on the screen. I suspect that most of the men here are looking for the very thing they'll never be shown on this screen – dick.

Up the stairs, outside and into an ADULT VIDEO CENTRE, I brush gingerly past the flyscreen which all these places have in their doorways (to protect casual passers-by from a non-consenting glance at the merchandise). Unlike the cinema, there are dicks aplenty. There are dicks of all sizes, from gargantuan to just large: black, white, curved, curly (I kid you not). Most of them are gripped by the hands/mouth/vagina/anus of some woman with blonde highlights, lip gloss and scarlet nail polish (the word 'whorish' is back in business).

With titles such as *Maximum Perversion to the Third Degree* (one for the Queer Studies crew), *Cute Blond Cocksuckers* and my favourite, *Anal Academy*, they all offer what, according to the Obscene Publications Act (1956), you're not supposed to be able to purchase in Soho or anywhere else in this country – 'hardcore'. In fact, this stuff is so unashamedly explicit that it isn't SEX – this is the lower-case casual continental variety.

Fortunately the unkempt, contemptuous state of the store and the shopkeeper is very SEX. He's wearing the clothes he first turned up for work in twenty-eight years ago, a glazed seen-it-all (if not done-it-all) expression on his shiny face. Even the cigarette dangling from his lower lip seems to mock the upright virility on display. 'How do you get away with selling this stuff?' I ask, 'We don't,' he replies in a lazy south London accent. 'Like everyone else, we get raided every few months, taken to court and fined and then it's back to business. It's like a kind of taxation.'

Judging by a survey of the stock, it seems the most popular pose is a young woman positioned between two oversized penises. There's a big poster on the wall showing this scene, with two very fat, ugly men staring at one another while a young woman on her knees services them. The French feminist Luce Irigary would like that poster – it confirms her theory that women are just goods to be exchanged between

31

men in a phallocentric, 'homosexual' heterosexual economy.

But the phallocentric economy seems to be a bit depressed tonight. 'They're all watching the World Cup on telly,' sighs the porn merchant. 'Sounds funny, I know, but most men would just as soon as watch football as porn.' The man is now playing me some videos on his monitor in fast foward – a kind of Keystone Kops with no clothes. The idea is to get me worked up enough to part with the £20 he wants for a video. 'What do you like: anal, oral or straight penetration?' he asks with the banality that can only come from decades of over-exposure.

I'm saved by a punter who asks if *Babes Who Love Big Black Cocks* is any good. 'Depends whether you like big black cocks,' replies the shopkeeper in perfect deadpan. I decide to buy the tape he's previewing. It's German with Dutch subtitles ('Neuk me! Neuk me!' is a popular one – and judging by the size of the weaponry involved quite appropriate). It features the first attractive men I've seen all evening.

Clutching my authentic Brown Paper Bag I step out into the street. But before I can make my getaway, a pleasant-looking thirtyish woman tells me she's called Joanne and she knows some very nice girls that she'd like me to meet. 'We have all kinds of girls: black, white, even Chinese – although you have to reserve them, they're very popular. There's no obligation – you can pull out any time you like.' She's not very SEXY but she's very nice; saying no would be unkind. Nevertheless I chose interruptus instead of coitus: 'I don't think so,' I mutter.

'Why not?' she asks, full of sincere concern.

'Well, you see, I think I might be gay.'

'Oh no, dear,' she chides me. 'Of course you're not. You're just a bit shy. Trust me, I know what men like.'

September 1994

AWAY WITH THE LADS

IT'S BRASS MONKEY weather this evening in Bolton and I've been standing in it for two hours. But I'm warm to the cockles. You see I'm on the visitors' terrace of Bolton FC with about a thousand Arsenal fans watching the Gunners play the Wanderers. In an era of New Lad chic, football features in men's style magazines extolling the aestheticism of the game and televised national cry-ins over the death of football heroes like Matt Busby, the Beautiful Game is simultaneously alarmingly now and reassuringly yesterday – a masculine fashion accessory *and* a return to a better, more authentic time when men were men and they became 'legends'.

Actually, I lied. I've never felt so uncomfortable or depressed in my life. For a non-fan like me this is not just boredom, this is mental cruelty. Once you enter a football stadium there is no escape from football; there is no bar to slink away to, no chance of a quick snooze, nor even a mild daydream. I search in vain for any distraction in the architecture of the Spartan stadium – all sissy form and pansy design has been squeezed out of this cattle shed. Those who were shocked by the grimness of Ceauşescu's public buildings clearly never saw a British football stadium. Even the advertising hoardings seem determined not to catch your eye.

There is decidedly no glamour and no national salvation here – everything about this place shouts 'naff'. Unlike

33

American football which is a crazy blend of show-business and sadism executed with the ruthless precision of the invasion of Grenada, British football is a strange brew of puritanism and castor oil and executed with . . . well, just executed. And then there are the fans. Overwhelmingly male, mostly young and all working-class (if you believe their accents – and I do), they are so uniform in their appearance – whether long hair, short hair, casual clothing or Arsenal colours – they all have studiously achieved one sartorial statement: we are *lads*. Their concentration upon the game is so intense, so straining, so, I have to say, *anal*, that to look at them while they stare ahead unawares seems almost indecent.

So I survey in a glazed way the muddy young men on the pitch in front of us as they pass, punt, 'knob' and slam the wretched ball back and forth across the shredded turf and can't help myself thinking that at least on TV you get a better view of their legs. Then a noise like a lawnmower overhead; ten thousand eyes raise heavenwards and there's someone on the end of what looks like a wing parachute with a propeller engine strapped to his back buzzing the stadium while waving to us. Is it Anneka Rice? (Given my state of cultural deprivation I'd be willing to believe that it was Oscar Wilde on a mercy mission to save my sensibility.) The game stops while the players and spectators watch this loon circling above the stadium. The Unidentified Flying Eccentric finally leaves and the dismal game resumes.

Of course, the New Lad school of football fans, those chiefly responsible for football's renaissance, would assert that the beauty of football lies not in its surfaces but in its soul – an essential, deep and graceful masculine mystery of flesh, sweat, skill and leather which non-believers cannot possibly comprehend. But who are these New Lads? Why, chaps whose role it is to deal with *appearances*! As the name suggests, an oxymoronic combination of 'New' with the determindedly timeless 'Lad', they are contradictions in terms. Almost to a man the leading New Lads are media luvvies like David Baddiel, Terry Christian and Danny

Baker, men whose chosen career has taken them further away from virile working class authenticity than hairdressing.

In fact football to the New Lads is just a signifier – of regular blokishness A (constantly) declared passion for football helps ward off any suspicion that you might be an effete middle-class wanker despite your mincing profession or lah-dee-dah education or background. So free-floating is the football signifier that even plummy members of the Tory cabinet like Chelsea supporter David Mellor, ex-Minister for the poncy arts, can attach it to themselves; the *Sun* cartoonist's portrayal of Mellor in a Chelsea strip jumping on top of Antonia de Sancha is probably the most apt image of the New Lad you could wish for.

The marvellous irony in all this desperate search for authenticity is that 'real' football no longer exists – football is just an apparition of images controlled by TV companies. Hence the 'Super League' hype and hence I and the loyal Arsenal fans had to flog our arses all the way to Bolton on a weekday rather than a Saturday as originally fixed because Sky TV ordained it. Like the game they follow, the 'real' fan and the 'old' lad are anachronisms. Even the grounds are now being turned into living rooms: all-seater covered stadia are soon to be the norm.

On the terrace before the kick-off I asked a 27-year-old printer from Mill Hill called Dave why he bothered to come all this way. 'I follow them everywhere,' he says, shrugging. 'So do my mates.' Why? He ponders this for a moment, as if he's never thought of this before, and finally replies, 'Because Arsenal are my team.'

What's the appeal of football? I ask another lad, who is unemployed. 'You just can't explain it,' he says. 'A lot of the time it can be really disappointing and boring, but when your team scores it's like sex – only better.' Am I the only person unkind enough to wonder what this common habit of comparing goals favourably to copulation says about the quality of football fans' sex lives?

In case you hadn't noticed, football is a game in which

men are permitted, nay compelled, to express passion for other men; 'Ars-sen-al we lahve yoo!' Within the sacred walls of the football ground, men can kiss and hug and blub over one another in a way which would, outside those walls, require a minimum of ten pints – because, naturally, it's the *game* they all love, not one another. The obliqueness of this expression of passion for men and manly things may well satisfy the fans that there's nothing queer going on here but to the more cynically inclined, those pursers of lips and archers of eyebrows – men, in short, who cannot be relied upon to 'play ball' by the rules – this doesn't (white) wash.

The British habit of attributing homosexuality exclusively to the upper classes because they send their sons to single-sex public schools, and the clichéd contrast of bourgeois decadence with vigorous proletarian heterosexuality has always struck me as bizarre. Public schoolboys eventually leave school and are expected to become men. Working-class boys, on the other hand, become 'lads' and never leave the homosocial world of male working-class culture: the factory, the pub, the football club. Public schoolboys at least try homosexuality, usually abandoning it later; working-class boys apparently spend their lives postponing it.

Bolton 'bang home' the first goal of the match and the Arsenal fans hang their heads in shame. Bolton fans, meanwhile, go berserk, jumping up and down, grabbing one another and throwing confetti and toilet rolls in the air (I told you there was something anal about this game). But for many of them their joy at their team scoring seems to consist mainly of an opportunity to give us the finger. Suddenly I understand why we are separated from our 'hosts' by an empty section of stand, some iron spikes, barbed wire and a number of policemen. Looking on this scene, it crosses my mind that if football has a soul it is an ugly one. Now the Arsenal fans give their witty riposte to Bolton's *bon mot*, making a 'wanker' motion with their right hand held in the air. Later Arsenal equalise and then lead by one point; on both occasions the Arsenal fans return with interest the jeering and gloating that Bolton offered them.

No doubt my being a middle-class wanker myself (and a queer to boot) is what prevents me seeing the humour, the fun, the *sport* in this. But it seems to me that the pantomime of hatred and the verbal violence are what many men relish most about football, even if actual violence has waned. There is so much ill will here that even several thousand Bolton fans can't soak it all up, and so beloved Arsenal also get it in the neck when they don't come up to expectations (which seems to be most of the time): 'Faackin' 'ell! What are those faackin' cahnts playin' at, for Chrissakes!'

But the most startling thing is not the language or the malevolence but the dun uniformity of these voices, not just the way the sounds are forced out of the back of throats like phlegm or the mandatory dropping of soft, poovey vowel sounds like 'h' at the beginning of a word and 'g' at the end, but the easy way in which these thousand voices become an homogeneous sound: 'Caaam on yoo rehds!' No one here wants to be a man – they want to be *lads*. They want to belong and in that belonging forget themselves and their personal frailties. They want to be more and less than they are. They want to be a team in a world where men now play alone.

The inhuman but poignant – almost wistful – sound of men chanting on the football terrace 'Ars-en-al we lahve yoo' is an echo of a patriotic age that has already vanished, an age of working-class *regimentation*. The factory and mine enlisted men by the thousand and set them to work in battalions. The heyday of football (and football violence) was the Seventies – that decade was the high watermark of mass production. Now those days have gone and with them the certainties about what a man should be. Mass consumerism has replaced mass production, Thatcherism triumphed over social democracy, demand over supply and, as the service industries have grown while the heavy industries have shrunk, woman over man.

On the coach back to London you would be forgiven for thinking that the last twenty years had never happened. The only woman on the coach serves up an endless supply of sandwiches and tea to the lads.

The end result was a two-all draw; no one happy, but no one sad either. Or so I think. Before we leave, a brick hits the side of the coach and bounces off. A farewell gift from the lads of Bolton. Later, on the motorway, a car with go-faster stripes and spoilers overtakes us. As it does so, two men in their late twenties lean recklessly out of the car's passenger windows, their faces writhing with an almost sexual hatred, a violent arousal neatly illustrated by their jabbing, erect index fingers. The Beautiful Game.

May 1994

SEVENTH HEAVEN

SOMEWHERE IN BRITAIN there's a paint factory, opened circa 1948, producing colours exclusively for bingo halls and municipal leisure facilities. Sad colours that think they're gay; despondent hues all the more depressing because they're intended to be distracting. Those unhealthy reds, those sighing blues, those suspicious creams and that eerie salmon pink – the colour all bathroom furniture came in when you were little. A good proportion of that factory's sorry output has ended up on the walls of this Top Rank bingo hall in London's Camden Town.

On a wet Wednesday afternoon this pleasure palace is full of BHS cardies in the very same colours, hunched over their sheets, crossing off numbers as quickly as the nice young man in the jacket and tie (who introduced himself as Stuart) can call them out. Like *les tricoteuses*, the women of the French Revolution who knitted while watching Madame Guillotine in action, these women are cool but enthusiastic witnesses to Fate.

'Two fat ladiees – eightee-eight,' Stuart croons in his best Seaside Special voice, apparently oblivious to the fact that most of the women in here are themselves fat. Those who aren't are wizened by old age. But for all the bakelite quality of this place, there is an intensity and communal atmosphere in this fug-filled converted cinema that you don't often come across in churches. Except for Stuart's game-show vowels and the occasional hacking cough, the silence is absolute and

39

worshipful. Compare this with the thoroughly unpleasant, anxious urinal silence of the world of all-male betting shops, and the whole effect is rather awe-inspiring.

A group of ladies in their late fifties – the average age here today – have taken me to their ample bosoms. Kindly overlooking the fact that I'm the wrong sex and generation to be here for legitimate reasons, they have already arranged my sheets in the right order for me and instructed me on how to cross off my numbers. 'First you need a line, then two lines and then a whole block,' Joyce, the leader of the group, explained patiently. 'That's what we call a house. Do you get it, love?' 'Yes, yes,' I lied, not listening because everyone knows that bingo is a cinch, a time-filler for those with nothing left to do but tick off the days till their last number is called.

In fact I've already wasted my first sheet because I haven't got a clue what I'm doing. The caller calls those numbers bloody fast. 'Seven and one – seventee-one, four and six – fortee-six, all alone – seven . . .' babbles Stuart who, with his round, slightly rosy cheeks (just perfect for pinching) is every granny's dream grandson. I'm working up a sweat looking for those blasted numbers on my sheet. What was the last number he called? Fourteen or forty-six? Oh shit, now he's called another one. These old bats, meanwhile, cross the numbers off with uncanny and unnatural speed, all the while maintaining icy, don't-fuck-with-me, poker-game expressions as they draw on their Silk Cuts.

The funny thing about bingo is that it requires quick reflexes, rapid eye movement, long concentration – the very things that you're not supposed to have when you're a crumbly. Actually, they're all the things I don't have as a twentysomething.

At last someone calls 'House!' and the first session ends. I feel like I've just emerged from an exam. During the break I get up and have a wander round to walk off the adrenalin. Every single woman in the hall lights up. At the back I come across some one-armed bandits played by women who appear to be cut from a different cloth from your usual bingo-goer. There's a real hunger and aggression here which isn't very attractive. Perhaps the lights, electronic fanfares and pound signs attract those women not satisfied with the rather passive pleasures of bingo.

One very large and slightly demented 'lady' is jabbing those buttons as if they were the shoulder of a woman she suspects of carrying on with her husband, all the while taking vicious, slitty-eyed drags on her fag. She looks like a docker in drag. No, she makes a docker look like *he's* in drag. In fact, she looks like a good case for reinforcing gender roles. If this is what these women are like *after* they've been conditioned to be 'feminine', then God help men if women are allowed to grow up without being expected to be made of sugar and spice and all things nice.

Looking around at the women on the machines, I'm reminded of those laboratory rats trained to press certain buttons repeatedly in order to release little tablets of food. The big woman scores a win, the machine fires coins into the feeding tray and she hurriedly grabs her prize in her vast pink hands and barges out of the hall – perhaps to pay her electricity bill before she's cut off, perhaps to buy a present for her grandchildren, perhaps to buy a couple of bottles of rum.

Next to the squalor and degradation of slot-machine gambling, bingo is almost stylish. Almost. Once upon a time it must have appeared terribly modern. If cinema replaced God in the Thirties, then in the Fifties and Sixties bingo replaced cinema. A shiny new consumerist religion for the proles, with flashing lights and light-entertainment touches, bingo was a New Improved Christianity, one that offered rewards here and now rather than in the hereafter. It's as if capitalism had deemed that the church was ripe for asset-stripping and decided on a takeover. The parallels with Christianity are too close to be ignored: tacky production values, bad interior decorating, an overwhelmingly female congregation and an underwhelmingly male minister. Even the number boards are reminiscent of the hymn and psalm boards in church. Some bingo-goers go so far as to sing warm-up 'hymns', with lyrics such as 'Legs eleven, I'm in heaven . . .'

The cinema replaced the church's consolation with aspiration. The cinema was where you planned big plans, dreamed big dreams, where you learnt to smoke like Bette Davis, where you had your first kiss and where romance blossomed. Bingo, on the other hand, recognised the way aspirations have a habit of collapsing into desperation, the bitter shortcomings of romance and the cruel tricks it plays on women: 'the dream has gone but the baby is real'.

So it's entirely appropriate that many of these women could be playing bingo together in the very cinema where their old man proposed to them. Bingo is rather low-key, rather naff, rather modest in its pretentions because its audience has learned to be suspicious of big gestures. Flattery turned too easily into drudgery. Bingo doesn't promise you the world – just enough to buy a new washing machine.

'It's mine! I won it! Give it to me!' one wiry, blue-rinsed woman in her sixties is yelling at an even wirier, silver-haired (with a hint of peach) woman seated next to her. One of the men in bow ties and striped shirts has just delivered them a discreet sealed envelope that prizewinnings are put in. Usually the women here affect a disinterestedness in the contents of the envelope, as if actual vulgar cash were not the point of all this. But, heads shaking and necks flapping furiously, these women are conducting a no-holds-barred tug-of-war over the envelope, like a couple of starving turkeys over a worm.

'We agreed we'd share the winnings! That's what we agreed! Half of it's mine! Fair's fair!' the slightly less wiry woman gabbles loudly, pulling determinedly at the envelope. It looks like someone reneged on an agreement. Apparently it happens quite often. Lifelong pals can fall out over bingo winnings. Bingo offers a sense of community, a heart in a heartless world, but it can disappear the moment you call 'house'. Mrs Blue-Rinse's name will be mud for weeks. She'll be sent to Coventry, but she'll have her

42

winnings to keep her warm, and later there'll be some other scandal for everyone to gossip about and her crime will be forgotten. One of the bow ties rushes over to smooth things out and the angry voices subside. Perhaps arbitration will succeed.

If bingo is a kind of religion it's a very profane one and is not at all sentimental. The god they they're praying to is not the God of Heaven but of this world. Mammon, in Top Rank land, is Lord. Bingo has a kind of pagan ruthlessness to it. It's a type of numerology, in which apparently random figures slowly take on meaning in the sheets which the punters have been dealt. Numbers measure out the achievements of women at this age and make up most of their conversations – not just the years they've survived, but also the children, grandchildren, weddings, anniversaries, husbands, gallstones and hip replacements. These women have known a life of back-breaking, disfiguring work, some of it paid, most of it not – childbirth, child rearing, husband-nursing, housekeeping – knowing all the time that other people held the numbers that mattered – the vital statistics, the postal districts, the incomes, the social classifications.

Stuart begins to climb into his pulpit again and I hurry back to Joyce and her pals. Before he starts reeling off the numbers once more, I ask them if there's a story or tradition attached to the trolls, the plastic creatures with long, brightly coloured hair that they keep stroking for luck. 'Oh, we won them in that crane-grabber game at the back of the hall,' Joyce tells me.

'Fiiive and threee – fifftee-threee . . .' Stuart has started up again and I've given up trying. Joyce keeps glancing over at me encouragingly, but I just can't cut it as a bingo player. I wonder instead about how a boy like Stuart gets his 'calling' to read out interminable lists of numbers in that irritating fashion to an audience of old women. Is it nature or nurture? Was he born a bingo caller or did his mother make him one?

Whatever the origins of Stuart's vocation he clearly intended it to be a stepping stone to something bigger. He has already told us several times that this is his last afternoon as a caller. Next week Stuart is appearing on *Stars in Their Eyes* as Neil Diamond. And could we please stay on after the last afternoon session to see him perform a few farewell 'numbers'? How touching. How poignant. How little Stuart understands his audience.

'All right, all right, just get on with the bingo,' grumble several of the women near me. Stuart is acting out a one-sided love affair with the old ladies here. He thinks of them as fond, sentimental grannies who just love him to bits and will be devastated by his leaving. Some hope.

Finally Stuart's last session comes to a close and he announces that he just needs five minutes 'to change into my Shirley Bassey outfit' before dashing into the men's loo. (The Shirley Bassey reference was just a joke, I hope.)

But Stuart doesn't change into anything. Some lovely old dear has stolen his stage clothes. 'If anyone has come across a plastic bag with a silver suit in it,' pleads another caller on the PA, 'could they please return it to Stuart, as it was made specially for him and is rather expensive, as you might expect.' Undaunted by this act of heartless sabotage, Stuart goes ahead with his performance. His first number is Neil Diamond's 'Hello, My Friends', delivered with that sincere, working-men's club cabaret vibrato. I'm quite moved. So are most of the old gals. They've left.

Being a sentimental young fool, I stay on and am rewarded for my faith with a 'really smashing' rendition of 'Could It Be Magic' – one part Neil Diamond, one part Take That and two parts bingo (which, of course, amounts to the same thing as Barry Manilow). As Stuart belts out the 'number', snapping his fingers and shuffling his feet, I'm reminded not for the first time of Gary Barlow and all those boys who have their mother's taste in music. Before bingo, didn't they become priests?

November 1994

SHOP TILL YOU DROP

DO YOU REMEMBER the future? Do you remember when we had one and we couldn't wait for it to be delivered? Do you remember how much brighter, smarter, how much more convenient, how much more spacious and *gracious* it was going to be? I remember the future, and now, as a visitor to Brent Cross Shopping Centre, I'm part of it!

And what a future it was. When Brent Cross Shopping Centre opened in 1976, it was the first American-style shopping mall in Britain and it quickly became the template for dozens of others, from Manchester's Arndale to Shef-field's Meadowhall. It possessed all the key ingredients of that now tweely nostalgic faith in 'the future' and 'progress' that have made shopping centres *the* architectural achieve-ment of the late twentieth century: giganticism (one million square feet under one roof! More shops than the centre of Oxford!) planning (seventeen years in the making!) and grandiosity (Italian marble everywhere and floodlit, domed ceilings!). Verily, this was a building which just begged for those dreadful 'cathedral of shopping' comparisons.

But what really tells you that this is – or was – 'the future' is that every low-budget science fiction film of the Seventies, from *Planet of the Apes* to *Buck Rogers*, always portrayed shopping centres just like this one as the City of the Future. People in togas swanning around some shopping mall with their noses in the air and nothing very much to do was everyone's vision of Utopia. It was, quite rightly, taken for granted that the earthly paradise that the wondrousness of technology and the ruthlessness of capitalism would deliver us would be the leisure to go shopping endlessly without ever having to worry about getting our hair wet.

But this vision of the future never included plastic bags. Everyone is clutching them today at Brent Cross as they mill past me on the walkways. With logos like 'Next', 'Ravel', 'Evans' and 'Feet First' everywhere, the future looks decidedly naff. In fact, none of the vulgar realities of shopping were ever represented in those sci-fi utopias: the waiting, the jostling, the 'accidental' walking into people who fail to move out of your way quickly enough (or is that just me?) Only the gracious soul of shopping was ever portrayed. Utopia never had to contend with special coaches from Slough.

Nevertheless I'm thrilling to the sheer *unnaturalness* of it all. As I stand next to a water fountain which smells of bleach, surrounded by plastic plants, breathing in conditioned air, surveying the gleaming, polished metal and marble of the super-clean malls and walkways, I am gratified by my inability to see a window or natural light anywhere. I could be shopping on a dead planet spinning round a dying star in some far-flung corner of the galaxy. And you can see how, nineteen years ago, Brent Cross must have made its first visitors feel terribly important. What could be a more eloquent testament to the sheer *smartness* of mankind than his ability to do away with the world as God created it and replace it with a shopping centre? As the information booklet tells you, Brent Cross Shopping Centre makes all-weather shopping possible all year round. Snowstorms might rage outside, heatwaves might bake the outer walls but we can still buy kiwi fruit from Marks and Sparks or a new pair of Saturday Night pumps from Dorothy Perkins without having to contend with so much as a draught or a moist upper lip. In Brent Cross there are no seasons, except as excuses for new fashion lines.

The unnaturalness of the place is also advertised in the uncanny cleanliness of it all. And this is how it should be.

After all, cleanliness is next to godliness. The banishment of dirt from the shopping centre is the banishment of disorder, decay, *death*. Consumerism and a throwaway culture are hardly worth the bother if they don't help to kid us that we are immortal. Tomorrow is always today in the white-hot future of consumerism, and yesterday doesn't even exist. Everything must be bright and new; everything that is dull and old must be flushed away. Likewise, the shopping centre's heavenly hygiene, its intolerance of matter in the wrong place, is about the repudiation of the earthly pollution (sin?) that mass consumerism causes. Thus a trip to the pristine loos at Brent Cross is a religious experience (although I must admit that I always thought that the way you knew for sure you were in Hell was when the loo walls have no graffiti or rude drawings on them).

The message of the shopping centre is that here money can buy you something far more valuable than happiness – it buys you *gracious living*. In exchange for mere money, the shopping centre provides you with a life no longer buffeted by mortal concerns such as the spite of Fate and the trickery of Nature, but instead a lifestyle, one created by the commodities which you *choose* to buy. The shopping centre says: outside everything is chaos, anarchy, something you can never control; in here it is harmony, stillness, grace; change comes only when you, the consumer, decide to pay for it, in the form of a new outfit or make-up. Hence the calming fizz of the fountains, hence the soothing sweet-nothing murmur of the Muzak, and hence a man with his eyes closed playing a Mantovani-esque medley of 'Chariots of Fire' and 'Love Story' on a baby grand.

Hence also nothing useful is sold in Shop City. The whole point of these places is to celebrate the liberation of the human race from such mundanities as utility, graft and thrift, and display instead our indulgence, our frivolity, our idleness. A Minnie Mouse toothbrush holder from the Disney Shop or seaweed-and-pomegranate shampoo from the Body Shop are the crowning achievements of Western culture; if we ever do make contact with an alien civilisation these will be the first gifts we proudly exchange.

The only teeny-weeny flaw in the paean to the sophistication and resourcefulness of the human race that is Brent Cross, is the people. Blocking the smoothly purring escalators with their lumpy bodies and littering the gleaming, sweeping walkways with their plain surburban features and dowdy clothes, they are an eyesore. Hell, to paraphrase Jean-Paul Sartre, is other shoppers.

Unfortunately you can't do without them. Other shoppers are an integral part of the Shop City experience, which is, after all, designed to produce a 'shopping ambience', as the planners of these places like to euphemistically call their attempts at fucking with your head to make you shop yourself silly. Combined with the low lighting in the malls and on the walkways, the sadness of the other shoppers is probably the best weapon in the armoury of the planners. The whey-faced drabness of the other shoppers is dramatically contrasted with the brilliantly lit shops stuffed with their 'exciting' goods. The psychology is very simple: you look around you, you don't like what you see, you don't want to be like these grey people, so you rush headlong into the halogen-illuminated boutiques for a make-over. Of course, this psychology relies on the safe assumption that you will never realise that the saddo people you are surrounded by have been doing the exact same thing for years.

Once inside one of these boutiques you find that life really is a party – or at least spending money is. The lights, the smiles, the pounding dance tracks, the inviting layout of the shop and the piles and piles of goodies just waiting for you are positively heart-warming. To refuse to put out would be a real downer. These shops have gone to great expense and trouble to seduce you; and after all, surrender is so pleasurable. If truth be told, shopping is more like sex than sex these days. Who now admits to post-coital guilt and who *doesn't* admit to post-Visa anxiety?

Alas, however successful the shopping centre has been at

superseding sex it has yet to manage to bring a halt to reproduction. Brent Cross is full of the evidence that its ungrateful clientele have not abandoned Nature altogether and are still breeding as prolifically as those creatures called rabbits used to before they became extinct. Prams and double pushchairs trundle in formation up and down the malls. Sprogs run hither and hither, hyperactive on McDonald's milkshakes and crisps. Mothercare does a roaring trade in Pampers and Care-Bear bibs.

And yet Shop City is not altogether beaten. One of the little offenders has somehow become detached from his parents' family convoy. A security guard holds his hand while talking into his radio. The toddler is dressed in new, tiny white trainers and a matching blue sweatshirt and trackpants. He is chewing on a discarded balloon, his hands and mouth obscenely filthy. His very existence is an affront to the future. The simple but obvious pleasure – judging by the glazed look to his eyes – he gains from chewing on a worthless discarded balloon pricks the whole bubble of consumer capitalism. His grubby hands and mouth contaminate irreparably the purity of the shopping centre: somewhere and somehow this boy has found – gag me with a spoon – dirt.

Do parents often lose their kids? I ask the guard. 'Oh yes, very often,' he says shaking his head sadly. 'They can be very careless. I think they expect that the kids won't be able to go very far and that anyway we'll find them and bring them back.' Maybe they don't want them back. 'Sometimes you wonder,' he replies smiling, thinking that I'm joking.

But I can sympathise with these forgetful parents. This is a throwaway culture, after all. Yes, kids do mean that you can buy more things – cute, tiny white trainers and darling little sweatshirts, for instance – and, even better, you'll have to replace them long before they've worn out ('because the little blighters really shoot up'), but that game soon becomes dull and you're left with a grubby boy chewing on a balloon. Hardly gracious living.

49

Some parents seem to be trying other methods of disposing of their kids. Another security guard is standing at the foot of the escalators, watching the shoppers ride up and down. 'We have to stand here in case there are any accidents,' he says in a weary voice. 'People do some stupid things, you know, like letting their kids sit on the escalator. You'd think they'd know that's dangerous.' Yes, you would, wouldn't you.

I decide it's time to leave Brent Cross, Britain's Premier Shopping Centre and go back to the present and leave 'the future' behind. It seems that the future wasn't what it was cracked up to be after all. It seems that the future wasn't actually brighter, smarter or more gracious. It seems, actually, that the future turned out to be a bit dim. 'The people here can drive you mad sometimes,' confides the guard to me just before I go. 'They can be so dumb. They ask you the stupidest things. They ask you stuff like, "Where's Marks and Spencers?" and it's right next to them. Or they ask, "What's in Marks and Spencers?" and you want to tell them to go and look for themselves. Honestly, sometimes I think people leave their brains at home.'

January 1995

BOXED INTO A CORNER

SOFT FOCUS YELLOW-ORANGE filters, big smiles, optimistic music, lop-sided camera angles, cute babies, maniacally happy couples: people *really enjoying* life. What's being sold here? A financial institution? A political party? McDonald's? Prozac? No, it's the titles for *Good Morning with Anne and Nick*.

And look! They live ordinary, consuming lives like you and me! There's Nick driving away from the supermarket, leaving Anne to wheel her shopping trolley into the fray. Now nice Nick's at the vet, peering into some mutt's mouth, while lovely Anne visits a garden-centre. In fact, Anne and Nick are more like you than you are – they make a better job of it, they don't stagger through the day looking like shit and getting nothing done. *They* have a busy schedule, lots of appointments with interesting people, know exactly what they want and, most of all, have a professional wardrobe and make-up department at their disposal. So why not let them live your life for you? Presentable, affable, edible Anne and Nick manage, like the ads they've sprung from, to make life run as smoothly as you would if you could only be arsed.

'Good morning!' trills Anne, bubbly in the Asti Spumante sense of the word, at the end of the credit sequence, followed by Nick telling us the time and date. The logo fades to reveal the ideal couple, immaculately turned out, sitting pertly forward, backs straight, on a colourful sofa in a tastefully-but-not-too-tastefully decorated living room, mugs of coffee

51

steaming on the low table in front of them. And everything is so happily matched! Sofa with wallpaper, carpet with curtains, Anne with Nick – they appear the same gnomic size, have the same faces. What bliss! In Barratt show-home land every morning is a Good Morning!

Welcome to the world of daytime TV, or DTV to use its psychiatric abbreviation. As anyone with any gumption knows, DTV is breakfast TV for losers. It's a way of fast-forwarding the day for terminally passive people whose lives are already over or never began. DTV is for housewives, the shift-worker, the shiftless, the part-timer, the temp, the pensioner, the 'self-employed', the unemployed, the unemployable. In other words, DTV is the future. Sneer at the frivolity of DTV if you like, and think of its audience as victims, but DTV is the medium for the meek who are inheriting the Earth.

Not that there's anything meek about Anne Diamond. Her masquerade of femininity fools no one. She may make girly cooing noises and appear pleased as punch to have 'hubby' around the house to handle that manly technical stuff like the date and time. But Anne is bright-eyed in a slightly feral way – more ferocious ferret than chirpy chipmunk – and seems to know something that she's not letting on. But we know what it is anyway: Nick has no balls.

After his masterful rendition of the date and time, the first thing Nick says this morning is, 'And we'd like to say a special hello to Andy Bryant in Sussex, because at the moment he's having a vasectomy with no anaesthetic – just hypnosis!' Nick affects an 'Ouch!' expression, trying to convince us that he has something to fear from such an operation. Anne just grins indulgently. In the world of DTV all men were neutered long ago.

Hidden among the usual features on flower arranging, horoscopes and cooking, is a shocking piece about four wives of England cricketers, dissatisfied with their husband's underwear. The women display these unfortunate men's Mickey Mouse boxers, lipstick-kiss-printed briefs and

52

baggy, off-white Y-fronts like trophies, complaining that they are passion killers.

This sad parade of men's undergarments testifies to the inadequacy of men in the private world and the new-found power of women to unman them in the public world of DTV. As if to rub salt into the wound, a fashion show follows, with four hunky male models in designer underwear – for the wives' 'inspiration'. Suddenly the TV screen is filled with looming and alarmingly bulky, cotton-clad *membrum viriles*, helpfully lit from above in case you wanted to know the model's religion. Flushed and wide-eyed, the wives are clearly 'inspired', but Anne gives the game away. 'Are you sure it's the underwear and not the models that you're impressed by?' No one is left in any doubt that it isn't the naff underpants that DTV women would like to change but their underwhelming husbands.

Nick, as so often happens to men on DTV, is left looking spare. 'It's amazing,' he comments, resorting to the jokey strategy he usually employs to hide his embarrassment, 'how popular dressing on the left is these days.' A little later he chips in with, 'I bought a pair of silk boxers a few months back; they changed my life.' The women laugh politely and carry on with their chatter. Poor Nick. Surrounded by the evidence of the humiliation of the male sex, he is reduced to making camp, frivolous remarks that apologise for his existence. Like society walkers, men in DTV are capons (but you have to have one around, for appearances' sake).

Over on 'the commercial channel', Judy and Richard's *This Morning* programme fails to grip in the visceral way that Anne and Nick do. Judy is quietly in control, but there is too much of a self-conscious attempt to present her, in her dark twinset, and Richard, in his navy suit, as professional partners. In fact, the whole programme is too much the Yuppies Who Care show. The view of Liverpool's redeveloped Victoria Dock through the studio window is sooo Eighties; the fake, heterosexual suburbanism of Anne and Nick, their parody of gender roles, the obvious dislike they harbour for one another beneath their grinning orange faces is so much more twisted, so much more Nineties . . .

DTV is where feminism's victory is total. DTV is victim TV – but victims who have got organised. In making public the private world of the home and 'feelings' – the inside outside – DTV extends the bounds of 'the feminine' into the world, engulfing it in warm fluffiness until 'the feminine' *becomes* the world and there is no inside/outside any more. Nowhere is this clearer than in the talk show, the arena in which private issues that expose men to attack – like child abuse, rape, wife battering and women-who-love-too much – are made as public as possible. The really cunning part of this strategy for feminine hegemony by talk show is in persuading the men to hold the microphone while the women grass on them. Both BBC's *Kilroy* and ITV's *The Time . . . The Place . . .* are presented by men.

Ah, but what men. What nurturing, sympathetic, empathetic, I-feel-your-pain men. Robert Kilroy-Silk, the acme of the male talk show presenter, is not like other men. In addition to being possibly the vainest man alive, he is capable of springing with perfect balance and ease from one end of the banked studio audience to the other, like a mountain goat grazing on suffering, without making his forehead shine. Asking women how they felt when their husband beat them up/cheated on them/gave them crabs, he holds his immaculate chin with his manicured fingertips and tilts his groomed head to one side in a masterful display of absorption which almost manages to hide his frequent glances at himself on the monitor. This is also a man who is unafraid to touch other men. Men who venture to share their childhood angst at an emotionally distant father or their inability to achieve erections can be sure of a reward in the form of a consoling, I'm-here-for-you clutch of their hand from Robert.

There is something else about Robert which is salient: he has that Adam Faith pop star look to him. (Of course, he was never a pop star – he merely spent years in the House of Commons thinking he was.) Over on ITV, *The Time . . . The*

Place presenter John Stapleton has a similar Sixties has-been-and-wasn't-that-big-anyway look to him, with his fake tan and hair straight out of a Cossack advert. DTV is a child of the Sixties, not just the Sixties of feminism but the Sixties of talking it out, of sharing feelings, of egalitarianism – putting the audience in the picture. DTV is the medium which elected to the position of most powerful man in the world, that other Sixties, female-dominated male, Bill Clinton (more of a born talk show host than Robert, and more sincere).

The social equality of DTV is easy to scoff at but it is quite genuine, at least in its earnestness. DTV presenters have to be 'classless' – hence the emphasis on chummy first names and the use of presenters who speak well but are not well-spoken (Robert's hint of Merseyside; Nick's soupçon of Midlands). On DTV the watchword is inclusiveness. Elitism is the enemy; the aspiration to live like Anne and Nick is supposed to be open to all. Media-crity demands that no one be judged and no one be excluded. Hence the regular items on wine-tasting and haute cuisine are treated in a jocular fashion: a kind of tourism of bourgeoisdom. Hence the competitions are non-competitions. E.g. *Quizcall* on Anne and Nick: 'What is the famous river which flows through India? Is it a) the Nile, b) the Ganges, or c) the Amazon?' Media-crity is so democratic that everyone can win.

And everyone can be famous. The confessional talk show offers the obscene pleasure of therapeutic fame, as people share dark secrets with you, an unseen stranger, that they cannot tell their partners or family. Through it, DTV presents the viewer with a promiscuity of the emotions: listen to their harrowing life stories, witness their courage in facing up to their eating disorder/kleptomania/passion for rough sex, weep for them and bond with them and change channels. By turning the most banal human weaknesses into *causes célèbres*, DTV makes the weak celebrities and all its viewers stars as their private, pathetic, humdrum desperation becomes not only meaningful but a point of identification and validation in a victim culture.

DTV does not make the real unreal, cheapening human

experience, as unhip critics would have it. (What do they know, anyway? They're nine-to-fivers.) Rather, through the values of showbiz, DTV makes the real 'hyper-real', larger than life – more significant than life, which is rather dowdy and, frankly, unconvincing. But there's one terrible snag in all this. In order to carry this off, you have to be American. We Brits don't have the bleached teeth, big hair and professional make-up skills that the American public is guaranteed in its Constitution. We still don't really believe that we deserve to be stars too. Our birthright, in addition to bad teeth and pale waxy skin which looks, under studio lights, like a turkey defrosting, is still the sullen, feudal legacy of deference which causes eyes to roll downwards and mouths to clam up as the camera and microphone approaches. The 'classlessness' to which British DTV pretends is a sham.

And so *The Chrystal Rose Show* is where British DTV goes horribly, horribly wrong. Foolishly inviting comparisons with the fabulous *Oprah Winfrey Show* by slavishly copying its format and employing a black female presenter, the programme just reveals that the British don't believe in themselves. Today Chrystal is asking 'Does London still have what it takes?' During the intro, not one but all three Covent Garden jugglers behind her manage to drop their skittles, thus answering her question. In the audience are the chief witnesses for London's defence – from the American franchises Planet Hollywood and Alien War. The Planet Hollywood reps are dressed in Hawaiian shirts, baseball caps and shorts kindly revealing their translucent, hairy legs. In an attempt at razzmatazz, the Alien War rep has come dressed as a gung-ho US Marine from *Aliens*. He's skinny, shaking, and mumbling 'Yo!' a lot in an American accent that makes Tony Blackburn sound like he grew up in Brooklyn.

The only hope for us is in the DTV world ahead is to turn being British into a claim for victim status. Or we could just watch Anne and Nick.

July 1994

HEY, BIG SPENDERS

I'M LOOKING FOR glamour, I'm looking for glitz. I'm looking for Party People whose faces feature regularly in *Hello!* I'm looking for really, really famous rock stars like Rod Stewart and George Michael and megastar footballers like Paul Gascoigne. I'm looking for High Rollers and Big Spenders. I'm looking for the Good Life and the High Life in the fast lane. I'm spending an evening at Stringfellows.

It's already past midnight and I'm beginning to wonder if I've come to the right place. No sign of Rod or Gazza anywhere. And the crowd here is not exactly glamorous. This could be Cinderella's and Rockafella's, Anytown. Faceless Men in Suits, mostly poorly tailored (the kind you see hanging up in the back of Ford Sierras tailgating in the outside lane on the M6), are dancing with women with blonde manes down to the middle of their backs and legs up to their armpits, wearing black skirts and white stilettos. There's lots of grinding, 'sexy' dancing – heads back, mouths open – and people seem keen to signal to anyone watching that they're having a whale of a time, but no one can hide the fact that this is not Bacardi Time. This is Day Trip From Crawley Time.

Yes, the provinces have taken over. But perhaps that's only appropriate, for wasn't Peter Stringfellow, the night-club impresario behind this and a string of nightclub-restaurants, a self-made man from the North, the archetype of Eighties aspirations? Once upon a time, people came to

57

Stringfellows to let the world know they had arrived. Now, judging by the clientele, absolutely anyone can come along and make the same announcement – but no one's listening any more. The flash Eighties' philosophy that expensive tastelessness was everyone's democratic right has obviously been kept alive at Stringfellows long after it had its credit rating revoked everywhere else, and has mutated into something even more alarming: *nouveau riche* values without the *riche*.

But it isn't only the aspirations that are dated. There's more chrome and black here than on a Fifties hearse and the dance floor itself, with its flashing lights underneath, is something straight out of *American Gigolo*.

So who spends the real dosh over the bar, where a magnum of champers costs £400? Clearly not these semi-detached *Hello!* wannabees making whoopee. 'The ones with the money to burn are tourists and Arabs,' confides a table waitress dressed in a pale pink frock composed of tights and a frilly chiffon shirt under her arms, making her look as if she is standing in a large frothy strawberry milkshake. Do they tip well? 'Yes – the Arabs and the Americans, at any rate.'

Devastatingly pretty, this unemployed architecture graduate decided to pay off her overdraft by putting her looks to profitable use without putting out. 'The invitations to "dinner" and the blatant invitations to bed get you down, but I just ignore them and take the tips and run,' she says.

And why not? Money is still what makes Stringfellows go round, even if the people who want to be seen spending it are now grossly outnumbered by those who hope it will rub off on them – and I mean 'rub off' literally. 'There are a lot of girls who come here looking for sugar daddies,' admits my waitress. Do they find them? 'Oh yes, they find them,' she assures me.

I think I spot two of those young women on the hunt for men to buy them candy. Blondes in flannels and blazers, they are pretending not to notice the rapt gaze of a short, fat, bald Asian-looking man in an expensive suit. But in a carefree, 'oh I didn't see you there, but yes you can buy me a bottle of champagne' kind of way rather than an 'eat shit, fishface' fashion. I interrupt this timeless mating ritual to ask the suspect sugar daddy why he comes here. 'To enjoy myself!' he beams. It turns out that he's a lawyer and before I can ask if he's the generous type, the architect table waitress delivers his drink and he thrusts a serious note into her hands, clutching them and leering into her face. He whispers something in her ear; she gives a brief smile – so tired – and a quick shake of the head. Another invitation? I wonder whether it was 'dinner' or less indirect.

Back to the dance floor. More suits have arrived. One cheap dark blue affair with light blue shirt and red tie is dancing with a blonde frizz in hot pants about two decades younger than him. With his nasty suit, no neck, *Daily Mail* issue smug suet-face and mousy non-haircut he could be just another sales rep, or he could be a Tory MP (now that, post-Thatcher, they are one and the same). His porcine frame bounces heavily around the dance floor as he makes disco gestures with his short chop-like arms, padded shoulders of his jacket riding up. As his partner encourages his irony-free antics with a smile that seems to my cynical eye a tad frozen, I can't help but wonder if all heterosexual relations come down to the same thing, and the clever girls make sure that they're paid by the hour, in cash, in advance.

No wonder a generation of straight kids have run screaming from the High Street disco into the arms of rave and ecstasy, leaving behind them the grotesque world where one sex has no body and the other has nothing but a body, where one sex stands and letches while the other dances around their handbags, for a night out where both sexes are allowed bodies and the sweaty desires which go with them. Forget phallocentrism. In Smart Shoes Only Land the sexual difference which calls the shots, the bulge in the pants which signifies power, is made of calf-skin and is full of plastic.

Amid the sea of suits, five very drunk men in brightly coloured pullovers and slacks are huddled together. Are they golfers? They turn out to be officers from HMS *Ark Royal*.

Why do they come to jet-setting Stringfellows? 'Because ish open after the pubs shut an' they let ush in free,' confides one of the more sober members of the party into my ear.

I notice a fortyish man, probably quite good-looking the last time there was a Labour Government, in a checked sports jacket and sensible tie standing by himself quite close by. It's the same man I noticed standing next to me at the bar when I arrived. My suspicions were aroused then but quickly dismissed – after all, what homo in his right mind would go looking for men here? He's studiously looking the other way but his body line and glances out of the corner of his eye tell me that my first suspicions were correct. I toy with the idea of flirting with him, but decide it would be too dreary to bear. Also, I'm confused: I can't quite decide whether getting cruised by another man in Stringfellows is a compliment or not. I move on.

Two very attractive girls seated coquettishly on one of the two-tone, conch-shaped sofas littered about the place are on a break from Edinburgh. They're not impressed. 'I thought it was going to be much more classy,' says one of them. 'In fact, it's crap. We work in a nightclub in Edinburgh and it's better than this place.' Their evening did not get off to an auspicious start: 'When we arrived we went into the ladies and the woman in there said, "Watch your handbags, there's a funny crowd in tonight." ' Definitely not the sort of thing that girls looking for generous gentlemen like to hear.

The doorman of twelve years' service is only too well aware of the slide in standards. 'To be honest I think that we're now going for volume instead of quality. Gone are the days when you'd find Rod Stewart down here.' Apparently the footballers still make the pilgrimage; I've just been unlucky tonight. 'We often get Arsenal down 'ere. They can cause a bit of trouble – high spirits, y'know.' But footballers horsing around aside, the doorman recognises that Stringfellows is probably clinging on to a bygone era: 'Now that Xenon's has closed we're probably the last place of this kind left.' As if on cue, a City executive type with sick down the front of his double-breasted suit staggers past us and into the street.

Outside the club, sleeping in an adjoining doorway, are three homeless young people wrapped in sleeping bags and blankets against the bitterly cold February night. One of them, a Glaswegian with a ropy scar across his neck, from a knife-wound that must have been big enough to decapitate him, has been homeless for three years since he lost his job at the beginning of the recession. Do the patrons give you any money? 'Some do,' he says, 'and they can be very kind. But most of them ignore us.'

In another doorway the inebriated exec is lying moaning. The people trying to sleep there move away. I suddenly realise what is intriguing about him: he looks like a yuppie – he is, after all, wearing the classic signifier of yuppiedom, the double-breasted suit – but he can't be. What yuppie in the Nineties would be seen wearing such a cliché? He is definitely another sales rep.

I ask the Scot with the alarming scar, if he won the pools would he go to Stringfellows and buy £400 bottles of champagne? 'Noo way,' he insists, shaking his head. 'After living on the streets for so long I've learnt not to waste money; I wouldnae blow it on a club like that. I really don't understand why people go in there.' The moral of the tale: good taste is to be found sleeping rough in the doorways outside Stringfellows rather than within its mirrored walls.

It is a truism that every decade is doomed to be seen as the epitome of bad taste by its successor. But the Eighties really was – or at least the version of it represented by Stringfellows. What could be more tasteless than petit bourgeois values plus conspicuous consumption? Ironically, in the Nineties, Stringfellows has become a part of that 'classic' Eighties phenomenon – the 'heritage' industry. Those who missed out on the loadsamoney Eighties can come and re-enact them with themselves in the role of Rod Stewart or George Michael.

But as with all heritage industries, what is most depressing about the place is not what it says about the era it purports to represent but about the present day. Stringfellows, a temple to conspicuous consumption where the only people left consuming in a remotely conspicuous or religious way are foreigners, is all that is left of Britain in the Eighties – the failed, tired glamour of a decade which turned out to have none in the first place. The tourists that come here are actually making a shrewd economic choice: just one evening in Stringfellows splashing money about and they impress the natives, get to feast their eyes on bosomy blonde unemployed graduates *and* see more of the real Britain in one night than they would in a month of visits to Buck House and St Paul's.

Party Person is on his feet again, whey-faced and tottering dangerously. He manages somehow to flag down a cab without getting run over. The cabbie, desperate for a fare or unnaturally merciful for his kind, lets the High Flyer topple into the back and whisks him off, back to the Nineties and a terrible hangover.

June 1994

SOLDIERING ON

THE MUSICAL DRIVE of the King's Troop Royal Horse Artillery isn't what it used to be. Of course, like every other display at this year's Royal Tournament, it's exactly the same as it always has been. But it isn't what it used to be for me. As a kid in the Seventies I'd never fail to be stirred by the thunder and clatter of the 'thirteen-pounder guns and carriages that actually saw service in World War One, each weighing more than a ton' (as the announcer would inform us year after year), as they were dragged around the sawdust of the Earls Court arena in perfect formation by soldiers astride cantering black horses, in precisely the same routine as the year before.

Ah, the tradition! The splendour! The clockwork precision of it all! Yes, yes, perhaps it *was* something to do with the dashing black and gold tunics and the tight, amply-but-firmly-filled pants, complete with saucy red stripe from hip to ankle, which rose and fell in the saddle in breathless synchronisation. Whatever. The fact remains that twenty years on, their charm seems to have faded and their vigour appears somewhat dissipated.

But then, Earls Court Exhibition Centre – home of the dusty *Daily Mail* Ideal Home Exhibition as well as tonight's musty Royal Tournament – is a temple to all things British and faded. This evening, Earls Court is not so much a home to defenders of the realm as a retirement home – a curious, twilight, end-of-Empire place filled with grandparents from

63

the Home Counties looking after their grandchildren while their own children go raving in Ibiza. It's where granny can say to her grandkids, look, this is how neat and tidy and well-ordered the world used to be, before your blasted parents went and spoilt it all.

The sad advertising around the arena – for the *Sunday Express* and Wall's Ice Cream – is from a Fifties Britain longing for Imperial certainties, a refusal to face up to post-war upheavals. The Royal Tournament is a Britain before rock 'n' roll, before sex, before consumerism: a Britain where 'fun' was spending two weeks at a military camp called Butlins.

Most of all, this is the Britain which ran an Empire (not the one that built one). A Britain which prided itself on its organisation – the point of which was to make everything predictable and nothing unexpected. This is a Britain which thought that the acme of show business was *formation* – drilled, mass, synchronised everything. A Britain choreographed by Busby Berkeley but without the camp.

So, gasp! as you witness the Metropolitan Police Activity Ride, in which mounted policemen in glamorous and fetching standard issue blue serge engage in such hair-raising activities as formation jumping over fences two feet high while *simultaneously taking off their jackets* to a Seventies-style medley of 'classic' military music (with a disco hand-clap)! Swoon! as you watch the Army Motorcycle Dispatch Riders Display Team surprise everyone by making a never-seen-before *human pyramid*!

All of which might be quite enjoyable in a limp, Blue Peter-ish kind of way, if it wasn't for the fact that the Royal Tournament *thinks* it knows what camp is. Thus we have the Royal Engineers performing a 'ballet' with JCBs, complete with flashing lights, balloons and sparklers, to the strains of *The Blue Danube*. 'Camp' for the military is a way of telling us not to be completely taken in by appearances and pointing out how sensitive, how light-hearted, how human a war-machine can be underneath its ruthless, deadly badly tailored exterior.

This attitude also explains the fact that there are more animals in this show than *That's Life*. This is partly the Royal Tournament demonstrating that it knows its audience (grannies and kiddies), but it is also part of the very ethos of the RT itself. If there's one thing that the British love more than organisation, it's animals – because animals are allowed the individualism, personality and affection that are ruthlessly drilled out of humans. Thus, in addition to the various mounted displays, we have a presentation called 'Animals Who Have Served'. A parade of creatures, everything from reindeer to elephants, who have selflessly helped man in his military compaigns over the centuries are led around the arena to a chorus of 'ahhhs'. The sentimental is thus brought together with the regimental.

The announcer, whose voice is so fruity and his tone so supercilious that he is clearly trying to convince us that he is in fact Harry Enfield, informs us sincerely that 'soldiers love animals' – unwittingly reminding us of other ways in which animals have 'served'.

One of the perennial favourite animal acts at the RT is the RAF Police Dog Display Team. Here the animals exemplify the qualities which we in RT Britain are supposed to cherish in humans: obedience, loyalty and self-sacrifice. Most of all they represent courage, as they jump through flaming hoops and chase fiendish foreign saboteurs dangerously firing blanks in the air and waving their padded arms.

The more-human-than-human role of the dogs is amplified by the way they are forced to do dumb human things, like climbing ladders. This is why the favourite image of the RAF Police Dogs is a dog balanced gingerly on a ladder designed for two feet and two hands, gazing down anxiously but trustingly at its handler who in turn looks up with encouragement. The exchanged looks of love and the symbolic reversal of positions – handler beneath dog – fit snugly with the sensibilities of a nation which wills more money to the RSPCA than to the NSPCC.

It is hardly surprising then, that one of the RT's other classic acts – the Field Gun Competition – sees men taking the place of horses as they drag Boer War field guns from one end of the arena to the other. The Navy is very proud of its Field Gun Competition – so proud that it spends large amounts of our money on it every year, effectively making the teams train full time. Why? Well, because it's 'traditional' of course (it commemorates the relief of Ladysmith). But I suspect the real reason has something more to do with the hysterical butchness of it all.

All those strapping, steak-fed young men are, I am reliably informed, so dedicated that they are prepared to give up their girlfriends and even beer to live, sleep and eat Field Gun Competitions with their comrades. The fact that they get fit enough to haul heavy bits of steel over walls at high speed – apparently unafraid of the mashed fingers, faces and scuffed nail-polish that might result – is a wonderful advertisement for the active virility of the Navy. Such a good advert that you might even forget for a moment that in today's high-tech Navy, like much of the military, pressing buttons while sitting on your bottom is probably the most manly form of activity you'll ever find yourself engaged in. The Field Gun Competition is so important to the Navy because without it we might think them a bunch of glorified floating typists.

But the Field Gun Competition also represents another contradiction of Tournament Britain. While it is sold by the Navy as a spectator sport – encouraging us to support individual teams – it fails because, in the end, this is the Navy and no one is allowed to 'win' anything. Instead, awards are *allocated*. So I cheer on my chosen team, sweating and grunting with them as they heave-ho, admiring their precision teamwork and thick forearms. And they assemble and fire their gun first!

But how naïve I was to think that because they finished first they'd won. Penalty points have to be deducted for infringements too petty and arcane to explain. The 'proper' result is announced some twenty minutes later: my team loses. This is the unchanging moral of military life: no matter how well you do, there's always some bastard with a clipboard and more gold braid who decides.

However, some things do change. Even here at Earls Court, there are signs of a grudging acceptance of new realities. For a start, there's the commercial sponsorship of each display – something that would have been seen as something of a national humiliation not so long ago. The Field Gun Contest is sponsored by Wall's Ice Cream. At the end of the 'Animals Who Have Served' display, all the animals are led into an 'Ark' (really the exit with some cardboard added), followed by two Maverick pick-up trucks as the announcer intones *sans* irony, 'And the Mavericks, sponsors of this display, went into the Ark two by two.'

Then there's the strange emphasis on 'cooperation with our European and North American partners'. Most worrying of all, in the final ceremony a giant United Nations symbol inflates above the arena while the announcer tells us that in an uncertain world 'our hopes now lie with the United Nations'. Excuse me? Did the UN defeat Hitler? Did the UN win back the Falklands? No! It was the Metropolitan Police Activity Ride!

The unhappy truth is that Royal Tournament Britain has finally woken up to the fact that World War Two is over and so is Great Britain. Like Russians fed a consoling diet of sugary lies about economic and social achievements, the RT British are emerging into a world of harsh and humiliating truths about their country's crapness.

As evidence of this, every other display is now introduced with an announcement that 'due to the recent defence reorganisation' (note that even in defeat the British are organised), this will be the last time we'll see this team of formation potato-peelers or that team of synchronised stone-painters. The audience is clearly unsettled by this unwelcome reminder of how unsustainable Britannia's lifestyle has become.

Finally, there's nearly a riot when it's announced that 'sadly, this is the last time we will see the RAF Police Dog Display Team, as the RAF Police Dogs Unit has been axed'. Hisses and boos reverberate around Earls Court. Grannies

67

and kiddies are united in their outrage. The bounders! The socialists! (Never mind that it's a Tory government.) This is taking things too far!

How could they be so cold-hearted? After all these years of devoted, loyal service climbing ladders, licking hands, rolling over and playing dead – are these doggies just going to be thrown on the scrap heap? And who, it must be answered, is going to guard us from those foreign saboteurs with padded arms who have always been so jealous of our superb Royal Air Force and its sparkingly up-to-date Spitfires?

But even if the Royal Tournament represents only a Fifties nostalgia for Twenties Britain, there is still something from that era worth feeling nostalgic about – the famous friendliness of the British squaddie and matelot. This is something best exemplified by the experience of Fred Barnes, a music-hall singer between the wars, who was arrested in Hyde Park for 'friendliness' with a sailor. Judged a threat to the morals of servicemen, he was banned from attending the greatest opportunity to meet them that London afforded – the Royal Tournament.

Not that this stopped Fred, and a near-riot erupted each time he was spotted inside Earls Court as the MPs chased him around the auditorium. However, scores of young sailors ran to find him first and hide him. As one witness quoted in Richard Davenport-Hines' 'Sex Death and Punishment' put it: 'Surely the laughing young sailors also had sympathy for a hunted thing: and perhaps amused admiration for one who, confronted with this frightening restriction imposed by the combined authority of the War Office, the Air Ministry and the Admiralty, should remain undeterred.'

Now there's a tradition to replace the Field Gun Competition! The Fred Barnes Memorial Race: The Empire vs The Queen and Her Admirers, sponsored by Amyl Nitrate.

October 1994

68

A LITTLE BIT OF GIVE AND TAKE

IN GREEK MYTHOLOGY Maenads were 'frenzied women', worshippers of Bacchus who were apt to 'rend to pieces' unfortunate men who passed their way. They were known by their unearthly shrieking howl and wail – often the last thing a man might hear. Tonight the ancient noise floods the auditorium and makes my knees knock. Tonight a cyclone of screaming, whistling, whirling teen-girl frenzy is surging around me and quite unmanning me. Tonight Take That play Wembley Arena.

The entrance of the 'lads' is still some time away, but that doesn't stop the girls exercising their vocal cords and advertising their appetite. They are hungry for masculine meat. Their banners proclaim their ravenous intentions: GIVE US A SNOG, ROB, and A QUICKIE IN THE DARKIE, MARKIE. They want it now and they will not wait. I sink even lower into my seat. But I flatter myself – these girls aren't interested in stringy old steak like mine; they want prime, pumped, waxed, tanned, moisturised boy-flesh.

Nevertheless I can't help looking around for another male to cling to. I spot a 50-year-old steward guarding one of the exit doors. 'I'm too seasoned to be scared,' he says. (I think he means 'experienced' rather than 'flavoured'.) 'I've seen it all before with The Beatles. Now *that* was real hysteria. You had to stretcher out hundreds of fainting girls in those days. We hardly get any now.'

But isn't that just it? Isn't that exactly why we should be

scared? I mean, these girls are ball-busters, they're *in control*. They know what they want and they're gonna stop at nothing to get it: it's the men who are fainting now. 'Well, their banners can be a bit explicit,' admits the steward. 'Some of them are too obscene to allow into the building and we have to confiscate them.' What sort of things do they say? He flushes red. 'I can't tell you that,' he says hurriedly. 'You'll have to use your imagination.'

Unfortunately my imagination is already working over-time. From my lofty vantage point the arena looks like the inside of the wrecked spaceship in *Alien*. Those rows of teeny-boppers look just like the cute pods in the vast cargo bay that John Hurt got a little too close to. Lurking within each one of those diminutive schoolgirls is a ruthless appetite to consume the world just waiting to burst out. These girls – with their flashing red plastic horns (symbol of the '94 tour), TT scarves, key-rings and slurpees – know that the teeny-bopper juggernaut of *Smash Hits*, *Home and Away*, *Live and Kicking* and boy bands is just a taste of things to come.

The multi-million pound Take That roadshow, bringing joy to thousands of girls, is the shape of the future economy of the Western world. Making these girls happy will become the economic imperative of the twenty-first century. They are the consumer queens of tomorrow and capitalism will organise men, material and technology to pleasure them as long as they have cash to spend. These are girls who are becoming women in a world whose only use for men who don't sing, dance and flash their pert buns is lifting the amps on and off the stage.

Lucy, Jane, Trish and Caroline are demure sixteen-year-olds who have travelled from Swindon to see their heroes. They are chaperoned by Samantha, Lucy's mum. 'I can't wait to see them get their kit off – *phwooaaarrr*!' shouts Lucy into my ear. 'What I wouldn't do to them if I could get my hands on them!' What about the other boy bands? What's so special about TT? 'They're just the best,' yells Trish. 'They really know how to make you feel good; they really try. Plus none of the others have got their sex appeal.

They can dance, wiggle their bums and sing – plus they're very shaggable.'

Who's your favourite? 'Howard!' 'Robbie!' 'Mark!' 'Jason!' they all scream at once. 'Mark's brill 'cos 'e's so short an' sweet an' lovely an' 'e looks like you could do anything you like to 'im.' 'Howard's brill 'cos 'e's gorgeous, 'cos 'e's got pecs and 'cos 'e's got a big package – 'e's really, really well-endowed!' How do you know? 'You can't miss it when 'e comes on stage!' they hoot. 'It just about pokes your eye out,' adds Lucy's mum helpfully. Pardon me, but didn't the *Sun* tell me that mums were shocked by the saucy new TT show? 'I am shocked,' admits Samantha. 'I expected them to get their kit off.' And what does your husband think about all this? 'Oh, he's quite into it. He does TT numbers in a thong after the pub on a Sunday.'

But the key question has to be, what do TT have that Swindon boys don't? 'Money,' shouts one lass. 'Talent,' another. But mum speaks for them all when she says. 'All the good-looking boys round our way are married or gay.'

At last the boys make their entrance and the crowd ululates, trills and whoops, rising to a maelstrom of sound matched only by natural disasters or a squadron of Concordes taking off. The boys rise up from beneath the stage on a platform, clad in tech-noir army uniform – boots, grey uniforms and silver helmets – singing 'We're gonna make you feel so good.' Toy soldiers played by toy boys. Perfect. A salvo of cuddly toys lands on stage, beginning a bombardment that lasts all night. (I can't decide whether this is a sign of the girls' initiation into womanhood, a putting away of childish things or merely an exchange of one sexless comforter for another.)

Like the troopers they are, the munchkins from Manchester skip, jump and shuffle their way through their impressive back catalogue. The air is heavy with sweat, oestrogen and Lily of the Valley. Girls are ignoring exhortations not to stand on their seats, bopping their backsides off with a determination and energy which makes you wonder how much TT have to do with it. Yes, the boys are nice little movers, they do have some very catchy numbers and they promise to 'make you feel so good', but it looks like these girls are the sort to take care of their own orgasm, thank you very much.

Half-way through the show the boys leave the stage for a costume change. A giant metal walkway covered in flashing lights descends. The boys re-enter in powder-blue Sgt Pepper suits, climbing some steps on to a walkway which connects them, over the heads of the girls, with a circular construction dangling over the middle of the arena. It looks like a cross between a bandstand and a space ship. Once there, they begin their Beatles medley, performing first to the back of the arena and then 'in the round' to the whole audience.

This is a master-stroke of staging which emphasises three essential myths of TT all at once. TT are the rightful heirs of the Beatles; TT are such thoughtful boys, so eager to please that they manage to find a way of reaching *all* their fans; and TT prove how unthreatening ('masculine') technology is – in the service of making you 'feel so good'.

But this vision of the boys dancing, prancing and singing above the heads of their frantic fans says something else too. It says how TT are so near yet so far, so personable yet so untouchable, so intimate yet so distant. Just like the 'masculinity' which TT proffer, there is never any chance of consummation. What TT give with one hand (we are talented, good-looking, gentle boys who exist only to give girls pleasure), they take away with the other (and we might be gay). Which is fine by the girls, as the TT circus is all about tease – the untouched in pursuit of the untouchable.

The salute to the Beatles also shows the boys' determination never to disappoint their audience and grow up. They won't make the mistakes the Beatles made – they won't desert pop for rock, they won't take drugs, they won't get political and expect to be taken seriously, they won't get married (OK, so Gary might run off with Elton John). TT are the Beatles as your gran would like to remember them – all McCartneys and no Lennons.

Time is the greatest threat to passion and to boyhood. So

the next number, 'Babe', underlines the boys' postmodern mastery of it. A projection screen shows black-and-white film of VE Day celebrations and returning troops. Little Markie steps out of the screen (through an ingenious slit) in an RAF greatcoat with a kit-bag slung over his shoulder, singing 'Babe, I'm back again'. Doesn't it just make you want to hug him till his little ribs crack and puncture his lungs? The message is clear: TT were always here, are always here, will always be here to 'make you feel so good'.

Sentimentality dealt with, the boys turn their attentions to 'sex' in the second half of the show, changing into black net shirts and hot-pants – well, everyone except Gary, who's still wearing trousers. What's the matter with his legs? Are they just fat or do they betray signs of – God forbid! – secondary sexual characteristics, i.e. hair? Can't he shave them like Howard? Alas, Gary's shyness about showing a bit of leg spoilts the effect of the black net shirts. They look less 'sexy' more a carefully contrived compromise which allows you to glimpse Gary's flesh but breaks up the lines enough to prevent you deciding whether he really is a pudding or not.

That the lyric they're singing is 'Give good feeling to me' is not without significance. Now that 'sex' has replaced romance, the boys sing a passive version of their initial promise to 'make you feel good'. The girls do their best to satisfy the boys. They gasp like a steam piston as TT offer themselves to them. They roar like Niagara when TT throw themselves down on the stage. They thunder their feet like buffalo as the boys slowly crawl to its edge, and wail like a missile attack when TT stand up and thrust their hips at the crowd. Howard takes off his shirt and the screaming melts my ear-plugs.

As an encore, the boys perform 'Pray' in white smocks, looking very angelic with their hands pressed together and heads bowed. But after the song finishes they are dragged into 'Hell' by little devils. Then out of the pit comes Lulu in red, followed by the boys who have now been Satanised, wearing red horns – and very little else – for 'Relight My Fire'. Howard is wearing a black leather jock-strap and a pair of red chaps with his bum poking out the back, which he sticks out at the audience and slaps repeatedly. Gary, meanwhile, is clad in blazer and flannels. Thus TT negotiate all the key dilemmas of girl teendom: virtue and sin, love and sex, rough trade or boys in blazers.

The grins on the faces of the TT 'lads' tell us that they are the only people here tonight enjoying themselves more than the fans. 'Ree-light my fi-yer/Your love is my only dee-zyer/I *need* your love/I *need* your love,' they croon sincerely to Lulu, cavorting around her. It's only fitting that the nearest thing to heterosexuality which these future mothers of our nation have witnessed all evening is pretty boys in bondage gear singing a gay disco classic to *Lulu*.

So what do the Swindon mob make of the rumours that TT are gay? 'That's just bollocks,' they all agree. 'People are just jealous of their success and want to bring them down,' says Caroline. And, hypothetically speaking of course, if they were gay, would it stop you chasing them? 'No,' she says, unphased. 'I'm into gay men.'

December 1994

THE NOBLE ART

'I COME 'ERE for the blood!' A small but tubby man shouts at me, nearly falling over. He's thirtyish and has a building-site haircut and face. He's very drunk. 'I've come all the way from the Isle of Wight tonight!' he says, adding ' . . . for the blood!' Don't they have blood on the Isle of Wight? 'Yeah. They've got plenty. But they want to hang on to it down there. They've got no sense of sport.'

It's a Friday night at the National Sports Centre, Crystal Palace. Tonight's bloody entertainment is the British Light-weight Boxing Championship. The crowd here are all keen sportsmen, but not all the punters have come here for blood. For some of them, boxing is about something more inspiring.

'It's all about discipline,' a short, well-scrubbed and rather mild-mannered man in his late thirties tells me. 'It gives you self-confidence and determination. Everyone needs to have a goal in life. And it teaches you how to look after yourself – you've got no team-mates to rely on in the ring.' So it's one man against the world? 'It's one man against another man, doing the best he can.'

Boxing is a godsend for short-arses, momma's boys, pretty boys, outsiders and those who didn't make the football team. As every schoolboy knows, when you are being bullied there are a limited number of options: run faster and sooner; give them your dinner money; beg for mercy and offer to be their slave; become a comedian; learn

75

to enjoy it; or take up boxing. The boxing option, of course, also contains an element of 'learning to enjoy it' – making the taking of punishment, as well as the giving of it, a way of life. As the victims of Operation Spanner discovered, you can be sent to prison for doing in the privacy of your own bedroom what is regularly done in a boxing ring in front of an audience of thousands.

But the sadomasochist's offence is not assault, mutilation or torture – all of which boxing celebrates – but in not having a sense of 'sport'. His crime is in agreeing beforehand with his opponent (rather than with a manager) who will be the 'victim', and in failing to turn the ensuing spectacle into a multi-million pound business.

The first of the warm-up fights tonight is between a black boy and white boy, both in their mid-twenties. The white boy is wearing a very flash pair of red and white satin shorts. He has a blond flat-top and a slightly too tasteful range of tattoos. He is short and naturally scrawny in a way that even the beefing-up of his training can't quite disguise. In fact, he represents the classic physiognomic type you find in gay bars: he has that slight vulnerable look of determination on his face you find there – that sense of knowing everyone's watching you and it's a case of kill or be killed.

His opponent, on the other hand, looks much more relaxed and confident. Perhaps it's the way his body absorbs the light, or perhaps his musculature is more convincing, but his physique appears more solid and tangible. He is getting the better of his opponent: his punches are finding their mark and soon the white boy has a cut beneath his eye, blood streaming down his face. The man from the Isle of Wight is getting his money's worth.

A bell sounds for the end of the first round and they return to their corners. The white boy's trainer – a large, soft man with no neck and a surprisingly gentle, matronly face – fusses over his boy, delicately dabbing a white towel to his injured eye. The boxer affects that truculent look required of boxers when they are being pampered in their corner, like a small boy whose mother is applying a sticking plaster to a scraped knee.

But the ministrations are in vain. A minute into the second round the referee stops the fight, examines the white boy's cut, shakes his head theatrically, and awards the fight to his opponent.

The next bout sees another fight between a black boy and a white boy, the latter again with short hair and tattoos, one bearing the legend 'I'm hard'. His trainer is ancient. When he puts the gumshield in his charge's mouth it looks as though he's lending him his false teeth. The black boxer, once again, looks in better shape: the white boy looks unfit, a bit too fond of chips and lager.

These boxers seem more powerful than the previous couple and the noise of their punches sounds like a baseball bat on a side of ham. The audience, strangely subdued during the first bout, is now beginning to be aroused.

'Caam orrn, Stevey! Jab 'im!' A man behind me shouts helpfully to the youth in the ring. 'Do the jab! Jab! Jab!' The vast majority of the audience, which is 90 per cent white, is cheering for the white boxer, yelling advice like the man behind me.

But one of the few black men here, a vast man – at least six five and with the largest jaw I've ever seen – is on his feet yelling to the black boy in a voice which makes my seat shake: 'Blast 'im! Gaworn, boy! Blast 'im!' His encouragement must have been heard because a few moments later the white boy is on the canvas, out for the count.

Suddenly, out of the wings, a medical team with a trolley laden with a stretcher and other equipment, rushes up the ring. (Never let it be said that the world of boxing doesn't take care of its pieces of meat.) But the boxer comes to and raises himself from the floor. The brain-damage squad wheel their trolley back to the wings with an air of dejection.

In the row in front of me is a proud dad with his three teenage sons enjoying the manly entertainment. The two on his left – ugly, big-boned and badly dressed – are clearly *his* sons. On his right sits a cute, fine-featured sixteen-year-old;

with his gelled hair, blue flannel shirt, 501s with wide black leather belt and lots of gold jewellery (this is south London), he is clearly his mother's son. While the other brothers slouch in their chairs, legs apart, pretty boy sits primly upright, legs pressed together. Perhaps he should take up boxing – I feel like 'bullying' him myself.

Finally, it's time for the big fight. The challenger, from Preston, enters in his shiny dressing gown to the blare of Simple Minds' 'Waterfront'. In his thirties, he too is blond and, looks as though he might have been pretty before taking up boxing. The champ, a black boy from Tooting, and at least a head taller than the challenger, enters to the heavy, reeling thump of rap music. The white crowd, for the first time all evening, is cheering the black boxer. He's a local boy – Tooting is just down the road. If you're local and you win, then white folks graciously overlook the fact that you're black.

The contest begins and the challenger, who looks a bit of a lost cause, is nevertheless showing a good deal of what those in the business like to call 'spunk' and keeps coming at the champ. Meanwhile, the referee – a man with a face which looks like a (late-period) Peter Sellers character and hair that either is a wig or should be – paces, bounces and skips around the sparring duo in a way which looks quite deranged. I wonder how the boxers manage to keep their hard, serious boxing faces on with this loon circling them.

Down by the ringside, looking remarkably bored, are the judges with their black ties and red noses. Their crumpled faces and cold, watery eyes take in the action impassively, awarding points in case the match is not decided by knockout. They may be the grandees of the boxing world, but they do not, it has to be said, provide the best advertisement for the sport. Why spend a lifetime in the school of hard knocks, training your heart out, when by middle age a regimen of ten pints a day would have produced much the same effect?

The crowd is really getting worked up now. 'Beat up 'is face, Ricky!' screams a voice that sounds as if it might be from the Isle of Wight. Charming. If boxing were a gay sport, then I suspect that the Marquess of Queensberry Rules would probably be modified to proscribe any blows above the neck, unless broken noses become fashionable.

In contrast to the previous matches, this fight runs to several rounds. Since it's a title fight, each combatant is nursed by three men. One standing behind him takes the gumshield out of his mouth and replaces it with a bottle of water; another standing outside the ring at his feet holds a bucket for him to spit into; while the trainer has the best job of all – smearing vaseline on the boy's face (apparently it helps prevent cuts) and whispering urgently in his ear.

Of course, these sweet nothings consist of manly tactical advice and morale-boosting pep-talking, along the lines of 'You've got 'im where you want 'im, my son, now work 'im over with the left . . .' But to me it seems as though the trainer, caressing the face of his boy, looking him in the eye, is saying 'I love you'.

Perhaps it wouldn't be surprising: the trainer-boxer relationship is probably the closest that two people could have who aren't mother and child. Which is appropriate, since a trainer's job is to 'rebirth' the young man with a chip on his shoulder or the world on his back and turn him into someone better adapted – into a winner.

Of course, this relationship is often called 'father-son' to legitimise the intimacy as a kind of idealised version of what father-son relationships are supposed to be. The trainer instructs the boxer in how to be a man and survive the world – to 'look after himself'. But the way he does this is by simplifying it for his charge. The world is a scary and complicated place for you and me, but not for a boxer. For him there's boxing, there's gym work, there's boxing, there's sparring, there's boxing, there's jogging and there's boxing.

'He knows my limits better than I do,' is the cliche of boxers about their trainers. It is the knowledge of lovers about their loved ones; in other words, I'm glad to have someone who does the knowing of me for me, so I don't have to do it myself.' And, of course, if you're any good then various powerful men – managers, promoters, mobsters – will decide that your body belongs to them. They'll pay you a good price for it, mind, and you won't have to look after yourself any more – everything will be taken care of. Until your brain turns to mush. Until then you will be their thoroughbred, their chattel, their . . . moll. Given this, it's a sad irony that so many boxers are black.

It's now the seventh round and the blond from Preston is groggy on his feet, bleeding profusely. Once again the crowd smells a kill. 'Finish 'im, Ricky! Murder 'im!' The plucky challenger still manages the odd punch, but he's going down. He tries to buy time by employing those strange boxing embraces, which, like the infantilism of the corners between rounds, I find more interesting than the boxing itself. The image of one exhausted and nearly defeated male clinging to another in a desperate bid to prevent his opponent from delivering the coup de grâce is strangely familiar to me.

Blows continue to rain down on the shortie from Preston; he looks like a drowning man. I can almost hear his brain cells expiring. Though the scene is ghastly and the crowd's bloodlust ghoulish, I do, just for a moment, glimpse something heroic, if not poetic, about boxing. As, blow by blow, this boxer loses the struggle and his grip on consciousness, I see the doomed attempt of one man to resist the cruel force of a world that wants him prone and bleeding on the canvas – a condition with which we can all identify.

July 1995

BLUE FOR YOU

'D'YER KNOW WHY women have noo brains? I'll tell yer. Because they doon't have a knob-end to keep 'em in!' No, it's not American queer theorist Judith Butler speaking, it's a fat bastard from the North-East in a flying helmet and a bizarre multi-coloured quilted suit that looks as if it's been used to line the basket of a cat with a particularly gippy tummy.

I'm in deepest, darkest Essex, surrounded by Essex boys in Top Man slacks ('No Denims') and Essex girls in little black dresses from Miss Selfridge. Roy Chubby Brown, the stand-up comedian who specialises in entertaining the proles with his blue ruminations on gender politics, is making one of his rare forays south of Scotch Corner. Tonight he's playing the swanky Circus Tavern on the Southend Road, a vast Berni Inn of a place, home to acts like Bobby Davro, Jim Davidson, Mike Reid and Nookie Bear. You can tell it's swanky because it's a sit-down affair with dinner included in your ticket: battered cod, moussaka, boeuf bourgignon – all with chips, of course.

My appetite, however, is more excited by the dishes with legs. It seems as if every single one of the lads here tonight has one of those big, round, hard bums that sticks out immediately beneath the waistband (how I approve of that 'No Denims' rule: trousers show off a boy's buns so much better). They also have that clear complexion that you can

81

only achieve working in the outdoors assembling scaffolding and laying roofs, eating Mum's home cooking, playing footah on Sundays and never being troubled by a single thought in your life. Except how awful it must be not to have a penis.

'I'd 'ate to be a woman wiv periods an' all that,' opines Chubby. ' 'aving to walk around wi' a tampax in yer wallet just in case. Ringin' up werk to say, "I won't be in today, pet, I'm flooded off me feet".' The boys roar and cheer this one even more than his earlier explanation for female stupidity (which was, let's face it, rather even-handed). This is what they came out for: to hear a man put women in their place with his tongue instead of his fists – after all, they can do that at home.

Mind you, the Essex girls seem to like Chubby too, even if their laughter does sound a little hollow, especially when he's poking fun at their 'minges'. Sitting next to me are Tina and Jasmine and they're having a fab time (as far as I can tell beneath their Boots suntans).

They're in their early thirties, but there's a bit of a mystery surrounding their occupation. 'Let's just say we make pictures, an' leave it at that,' says Tina in her dentist's receptionist voice. When I ask them why they came along tonight they misunderstand the question, thinking I asked them why they've come as a couple of girls alone rather than with their fellas (these things have to be explained in Essex): 'It's less embarrassing if we come wivout our 'usbands,' says Tina. 'No, I meant, why do you like Chubby?' I insist. 'Why would a woman pay £25 to hear a man insult them?' Silence.

Like most of the people I've asked tonight, they don't want to explain why they like Chubby. It's understandable really. You don't go to see an act like Chubby Brown's to explain anything; Chubby's fans are not, by definition, likely to be leading what you would call an examined life.

Tina gives up trying to answer my party-pooping questions, grabs my pad and pen and writes in big, round curly letters, the kind with little circles over the 'i's, 'You will enjoy yourself, *if* (underlined five times) you have a *good* sense of

82

HUMOUR.' Underneath this she draws a big smiley face, and, nestled in kisses, 'Love Tina + Jasmine (We love you).' In Essex no one can hear you scream.

Some obvious squaddies at the table next to mine are having a better time than Tina and Jasmine, or at least making a show of it. In fact they seem to have turned Chubby into a bizarre love-cult, memorising his jokes off by heart and breaking into chants of 'You fat bastard, you fat bastard' interspersed with 'Chubby – we love you' every time they get particularly excited. One of them leans over to nudge me, face shiny from laughing too hard and drinking too much lager, and shouts ' 'e's fackin' magick innee?' I nod and grin back at him as enthusiastically as I can manage, but it's sadly unconvincing and he instinctively realises his mistake turning hastily back to his chums.

A little later Chubby makes a joke about a woman he knew who used to live near an army camp who'd 'had more soldiers in 'er than a boiled egg'. The squaddies are driven into noisy ecstasies by this recognition (of their existence? of their desperation?) by their hero and hold up a Take That scarf (don't ask me what *that* means).

'Are you a socialist?' Tina askes me out of the blue. 'Er, no,' I stumble, 'not exactly . . .', completely flummoxed by this apparent stab at political discussion. Then it dawns on me. She's not striking up conversation. She's rumbled me as an outsider, like one of the pod people in *Invasion of the Body Snatchers* who realises that you haven't been absorbed, that you're not 'of the body'. I half expect her to point at me and emit that ghoulish, inhuman scream. Fortunately she is too interested in Chubby's *bons mots* on oral sex to do this.

But of course, she's right: I'm the alien and she and the others are the humans. In Essex, socialists are those strange, cold, intellectual people who read big newspapers, have books in their living rooms and go round spoiling good, ordinary decent people's fun by asking questions and being misanthropic. Socialists think they're better than you. Worst

83

of all, socialists don't have a sense of HUMOUR. Socialists, in other words, are MIDDLE-CLASS.

But if only those earnest social planners of the Forties and Fifties who cleared the East End slums could have guessed how it would turn out. With feverish zeal for a Better Tomorrow, they built New Towns in Kent and Essex, green New Jerusalems for the working classes to live in, where their children could grow up clean and strong, away from the filth and degradation of urban dwelling. Filled with altruistic concern for the future of the children of the disadvantaged, they provided them with free milk and nit nurses, only to see them grow up, vote for Thatcher The Milk Snatcher, stone-clad their council homes and pay £25 per head to wallow in the filth and degradation of Chubby Brown:

'My Dad told me to shag women over a cliff – that way you can be sure they're pushing back.'

This proletarian sense of HUMOUR, as Tina's adorable little note to me managed to intimate with its threatening underlining, is a compulsory ideology that you stray from at your peril, if you live in a place like Essex. Chubby's 'comedy' tells us that the world is divided into the fuckers and the fucked, the penised and the unpenised and – surprise, surprise – it's the fuckers who are on top. There is no appeal, no possibility of mitigating circumstances being taken into account – this law of desire is universal, ineluctable, inexorable, and it can't be repeated too often. There's consolation in this mantra for both sexes: 'working class' as a political identity has gone, all that is left is 'working classness', a certain no-nonsense, gritty view of the world that Chubby Brown exemplifies again and again.

But repetition is also the consoling heart of heterosexuality everywhere; it sows meaning where there is none. Sex may make us but it also undoes us; sex is a horrific natural disaster without end – but by endlessly 'saying' it, by repeating its laws and its crimes we hope we can master its horror – the men who say 'fuck' in every sentence and are

84

always telling dirty jokes are like little kids telling ghost stories in the dark to scare one another.

And boy, is there a lot of fear to master. ' "Eat me beaver!" this girl said to me,' shouts Chubby, before spitting impressively on the stage. ' "Eat yer beaver!" You don't know what the difference is between a beaver and a skunk.' For the straight lad, the female body both attracts and repels, its penetration is necessary for manhood and yet its biology is nightmarish. Moreover, without women, who would operate the washing machine?

Chubby knows that these Essex boys here tonight are in love not with women but with the image of themselves as men: phallic, thrusting, *on top*. 'Why do women go on about men's penises, for God's sake?' he complains. 'They all bloody fit!' (Loud virile cheers.) But it's Chubby and the lads who go on about men's penises. Their own size-queenery is projected on to women. This is another reason why the lads fear the female sex – women know the truth about the actual proportions of their manhood and it might get back to the lads that John's manhood is more cocktail stick than pork sword.

The legendary prowess of black men is another threat: 'How many times have we heard coloured men have bigger dicks?' asks Chubby. 'Fuck off: coloured women have tighter minges, that's all!' (Loudest cheers of the night.)

Curiously Chubby is disappointingly lenient with those men that threaten to let the side down: those batters for t' other side, the poofs. He begins promisingly enough: 'Someone died of AIDS – some star. Eeeee, I can't stand all of that fookin' poovery!' But he doesn't deliver. Instead he goes on to say, 'You've got a choice, haven't you? Minge or arse. I wouldn't mind sleeping with a bloke – after a good shag we could talk about the match.' I feel like demanding my money back. Not only is Chubby not nearly anti-gay enough, he's a bit of a shrewd cultural commentator. He's put his finger on the 'shocking' ambiguity of being a man's man, the way homosexuality, on paper, looks like the logical next step for men who like to be with the boys.

85

There is something, it must be said, a little bit 'gay' about Chubby – and not just the fact that he resembles and sounds like a northern drag queen at the Vauxhall Tavern. In the build-up to his entrance, slides flash on screen chanting his progress from a fat smiling baby to a big fat bastard. But in the intervening period, I can report, Chubby was quite a looker. Slides show a pretty schoolboy in the 1950s, a cute rating in the Navy in the 1960s and a dedicated follower of fashion, including glam and punk rock in the 1970s. Chubby was a bit of a narcissist. Ironically, and rather sadly, it was only after he lost his looks and his youth that he became the 'pop star' he clearly wanted to be all his life.

Chubby's been on stage for an hour now and all this talk of fucking is exhausting, not to say depressing. But as I make to leave, it occurs to me that Chubby really is Judith Butler. His incessant gabble about fucking, pricks and cunts and the exposition of the logic of coitus is actually an attempt to *deconstruct heterosexuality*, to over-expose it and reveal it as what Butler has described as an 'inevitable comedy' of 'normative positions that are impossible to embody'. No one – not even Essex girls and boys – can live up to these laws of desire.

'There are lots of lads here tonight having a good time. But one of them will spoil it. He won't get into a fight. What he'll say is: "I'm going home now, lads, and I'm gonna *hoy one up the fookin' back alley*, I'm gonna *snap the bitch in two*, I'm gonna *break her fookin' back*.' But excuse me lads. Girls have babies. Unless your prick's twelve pounds seven ounces – noo bloody chance!'

February 1995

CAMP FOR BEGINNERS

'THAT'S QUITE ENOUGH of *that*!' says Andi, the 'nice' black presenter of *Live and Kicking*, cutting short Kylie's striptease in her latest video. 'Oh, I wanted to see a bit more,' says the female presenter, clearly disappointed. 'Really, Emma, I'm shocked,' admonishes Andi, his knees and lips pressed firmly together, deliberately overdoing his Miss Prissy routine. 'And you a married woman as well!' Over on ITV, on their rival kids' vehicle *What's Up Doc?*, 2wo Third3 are being interviewed by a man in a blue wig and pantomime dame's frock: 'So tell me, boys, don't you have a Jimmy Somerville connection?'

Back in the dark days of Noel Edmond's *Swap Shop*, Saturday morning TV was that bit of telly before Dad pulled on his underpants and came down to watch *Grandstand* and demand lunch; a safe way of keeping the kids occupied while Mum and Dad tried for another. Nowadays it still gives Mum and Dad a chance to reproduce, but if they knew what was keeping their kids quiet today they might not bother. If children are the future then the future is as camp as Christmas.

And in case you'd forgotten how camp Christmas could be, Saturday morning TV will remind you. On *Live and Kicking* the seasonal jokes are coming thick and fast (oo-er). 'There's a man in a red frock outside who wants you to help him pull his sleigh,' says one of the in-house comics to another; in another sketch they're dressed as rock stars:

87

'Look, I just wanted your autograph, nothing else, OK!' a red-faced man shouts at one of them who is sheepishly clutching a sprig of mistletoe in his hand.

Over on *What's Up Doc?* two *very* nice men, sporting moustaches and raised little fingers, are showing their female presenter friend how to make pot-pourri. After this practical item, the cast of the show perform an irreverent version of *Cinderella* in which Prince Charming (alias Andy Crane) is fought over by the Ugly Sisters, one of whom, in the best panto tradition, is anatomically male: 'Forget her,' he advises the Prince, 'marry me – I've got a little something she hasn't!' (Knowing wink to camera.)

But, worried parents of our nation, please do not smash the telly and write outraged letters to your MP. Contrary to appearances, your children are not being taught how to be roaring homosexuals (just how to act like them). In fact they are receiving an education which will serve them far better in the world than anything they are likely to be taught at school. Saturday morning TV is inculcating a sensibility which will enable kids not only to survive but *thrive* in the shallow, media-manipulated, consumerist inanity that is modern life. *Live and Kicking* and *What's Up Doc?* are saving your kids from capsizing in the riptide capitalist currents that you and your parents bequeathed them. Saturday morning TV teaches your kids to love the life-saving styles of irony, parody and excess. And it gently sends up the outmoded mainstream sensibility of yesteryear: naff.

On *Live and Kicking*, Andi and Emma are going through the weekly ritual of reminding kids how sad and tasteless the square world of adults is. Usually they're holding up corporate calendars that kids have sent in. You know the type, a JCB calendar with a different model of excavator for every month. This week it's corporate Christmas cards. One marvellous card is from Ferrosan, a food supplement company – it features a pile of vitamin bottles with a bit of tinsel on the top. Andi and Emma don't do anything so crude as to actually laugh at these pathetic examples of grown-up sadness (the calendars are usually produced by the company

88

Mum or Dad is bound to by chains of adamantine mortgage repayments). Instead, camp enthusiasm is offered: 'Oh, that's very nice, very tasteful, isn't it, Emma?' 'Oh, yes, *very*,' replies Emma.

The raspberries blown at adult convention continue in the form of *Run the Risk*, a competition, like all Saturday morning kids' TV competitions, which is really an anti-competition. The emphasis is on spectacle, excitement, mess and, most of all, humiliation – never on winning. Contestants have to fill reservoirs on a revolving platform with gunge from buckets with holes in them. In case they look as if they're getting somewhere, one of the presenters will 'give them a hand' (basically knock them over and into the gunge). Another game involves throwing outsize cream cakes over a wall while some hapless kid tries to catch them on the other side. The result is, splendid and joyful total mayhem in which the details of who actually wins are lost. Which is, of course, the whole point.

The next item on *Live and Kicking* is a cartoon, *The X-Men*, which is a transparent yet sophisticated parable about queerness. The X-men are mutants, men and women whose abnormality makes them feared and hated outsiders and yet also gives them strange and wonderful powers beyond the ken of ordinary people, which they use for good. Unfortunately, some bolshie renegade mutants have decided that mutants and normal people cannot live together and have begun to use their special powers against society for separatist ends: 'Mutant liberation begins now!' proclaims the renegade leader. 'If we don't act to stop them soon, anti-mutant fever will sweep the country!' warns one of the good (reformist) mutants. And sure enough, the robotic Sentinels (the fascists) rebel against their human masters and try to take over the world. The horrified creator of the Sentinels is the classic right-wing liberal: 'My God! I thought I was protecting normal people from mutants and I created something much worse!'

Fortunately the good mutants defeat the Sentinels and the strip ends with the leader of the anti-mutant faction's recantation: 'We must be careful that when we control those mutants who use their dangerous powers for harm we do not harm those who use them for good.' (Yes, the moral of the tale is more Stonewall than OutRage, but, until?, the Sentinels were defeated by the reformist and revolutionary mutants working *together*.)

Next, the book review section. It's presented by an American woman with horn-rimmed glasses and drop earrings whose unreal proportions make her look as if she has stepped out of the earlier cartoon. A rainbow-coloured lamé jacket barely covering her earth-motherly vastness, she delivers her verdict in a slow, breathy, sultry, suggestive way that makes you want to check what they're putting in kids' books these days. When she says with a voice like warm baby oil that a book is 'just the best pop-up book I've seen and I vote it top of the . . . pop . . .-*ups*', you're not really sure whose mind is reading in things that it shouldn't.

The media savviness of the show continues with a regular feature, *Bergerac Big Nose*, in which clips from a Fifties TV series based on Cyrano de Bergerac are dubbed over in a *Whose Line Is It Anyway?* fashion. This week's highlight comes when Bergerac's chum climbs the ivy to Roxanne's balcony: 'I feel like a Gladiator,' he says, 'So do I,' replies Bergerac, 'but where can we get one at this time of night?'

After more silliness and mayhem in the studio comes *Electric Circus*, a review of TV shows and video games presented by another American, John Barrowman. He has creepy good looks and that American show-business habit of smiling continuously while he is talking so as to show off the expensive dentistry his mom paid for but which only makes me think that he was born sadly deficient in lip tissue. This, combined with the fact that he has a Valley Girl accent and that West Coast habit of gushing about how fabulous absolutely everything is makes it impossible, try as you might, to take your eyes off him – like some suntanned motorway accident. As for camp, well, in this week's instalment he goes shopping with a character from *Neighbours* ('nuff said).

Both presenters are bizarre caricatures of American media types that are meant to be enjoyed *ironically*. In fact, anything to do with the media is given neon quotation marks and bold type by Saturday morning TV. This is as it should be: an awareness of the gap between surface and content is the best skill kids can be given when it comes to dealing with the truly phenomenal coercive power of the media in general and advertising in particular.

As further evidence of this, over on the commercial channel (where the hard-sell ads for endless toy-junk comes every ten minutes or so) they're showing a cartoon called *Pinky and Brain* ('One of them's a genius; the other one's insane!') about two lab mice. The dim one, Pinky, has an Australian accent; the bright one sounds not unlike Orson Welles. 'What are we going to do tonight, Brain?' quavers Pinky. Replies Brain: 'The same thing we do every evening, Pinky: *try to take over the world*!'

Brain's plan tonight is to brainwash the world into accepting his dictatorship via a subliminal message. He quickly realises that the easiest way to reach as wide (and undiscerning) an audience as possible for his message is to become a country and western singer. To guarantee his success he cultivates 'working-class values' – playing on pity and pretending to be very stupid: 'I am a lab mouse, I escaped from my cage/ Never had no job, never earned my degree/ But you will respect me – yes! – when my plan is unfurled/ You will call me your leader – I'll be King of the World!' The audience, of course, loves him and sings along blithely like the happy idiots they are. This kids' cartoon is the most scathingly accurate satire of media manipulation you could hope to find on TV. But then, Saturday morning TV is by far the best TV on the air.

Next up, a sketch involving a couple of puppet wolves that keep popping up on the show. They're singing outside a shopping centre, hoping to get some food. 'Oh look, there are some strappin' lads – I don't suppose you could spare us a bit of your bodies?' The boys look bemused and walk off (in fact they're Boyzone, a boy band that later perform their song *Love Me for a Reason*, complete with hand gestures that Shirley Bassey would be proud of). 'That's right. Have them all to yourselves,' spit the wolves disgustedly. But then a lovely old granny stops and fishes something out of her handbag. It's a human hand. The wolves yelp, 'Thanks! You've renewed our faith in human nature!'

The wolves have an uncouth habit of devouring people; they have a special spot in the show every week, 'Thrown to the Wolves', in which they eat a celebrity guest. This week a fresh faced boy from kids' soap opera *Byker Grove* wakes them up to demand their services: ' 'Scuse me, but you're supposed to eat us.' 'Don't flatter yourself!' comes the grumpy riposte.

No doubt Saturday morning TV is enjoyed by thousands of gays as well as kids. But watch out, boys – the future is not as rosy as you might think. Once upon a time heteros had babies and homos had camp. But no longer. The days of speaking of camp as the 'gay sensibility' are over forever. *Live and Kicking* and *What's Up Doc?* indicate that the next generation of breeders will be better at it than the pervs; they'll make Kenneth Williams look like Noel Edmonds.

March 1995

PERVERSE GEAR

WHEN I WAS just a little nipper, with just a little nipper's pee-pee, I used to like nothing better than to sit in my dad's parked car, playing with the lights and the electric windows, imagining myself, older, stronger, bigger – imagining myself a *man*.

Boys work out very quickly that Dad's car is the measure of his masculinity. Mum has her dresses, mysterious underwear and make-up. Dad just has his car. And it takes him away from home (where Mum is queen) into the world of men, where the one with the best 'specifications' is king. School playgrounds everywhere are alive to the sounds of little boys arguing about whose dad has the fastest, most expensivest, biggest car. And although boys grow into men and their acorns are supposed to grow into great oaks, men never quite lose the dream of having a better, bigger one than Dad or nature intended.

Here at the London Motor Show, men of all ages are queuing up to sit in parked cars and play with the lights and the electric windows. Unsurprisingly, the queues are not forming at the Fiat stand but at Mercedes and BMW. One of the longest queues here is for a Mercedes SL600 coupé.

And no wonder! What lines! What looks! What specifications! V12, 48-valve, 394 HP, ADS, ASC, dual airbags, alloy wheels (eight hole), automatic climate control (are you hard yet?) automatic transmission, electronic operated soft-top with automatic roll-bar (you're gagging for it), electrically adjustable heated front seats with memory, leather upholstery, metallic paint (you like that, dontcha!), memory for steering column and mirrors, MB security system, side-bags, RDS radio. And what a price! 60,000 Big Ones. (Yeah, choke on that price!) Needless to say, if this car were a dildo it would have Jeff Stryker's name on the box.

I decide to ask one of the lads queuing patiently to sit in on the Mercedes why they like fast cars and big engines. 'Because they've got more bloody poke, y'know what I mean?' says one unblushing young man in white jeans, knitted shirt and straight fringe haircut. (That's the marvellous thing about the working classes – they don't need to read Freud because they never repressed anything in the first place.) But, I quibble, I thought that cars were supposed to be feminine; aren't they called 'she'? 'Well, yeah, I suppose so. But', he laughs, 'I wouldn't be seen dead driving around in my fuckin' missus, that's for sure!'

Aren't cars wonderful? So hard, so powerful, so fast, so sexy, so smart, so envied by other men! No wonder men love them more than their wives. The habit of calling cars 'she' is a bit of necessary macho subterfuge which no one really believes in – not even Jeremy Clarkson. Men like cars that ooze masculinity, or rather, ram it home. The men who long to possess an E-type Jag or an Aston Martin DB7 (0–60 in 4.5 seconds) do not, you can be sure, see in its streamlined, surging shape breasts and big hair. But whereas no man would dream of calling his percy 'she', cars have to be female because, unlike (straight) men's penises they are permitted to be in circulation with other men. Hence cars have to be dubbed 'she' to avoid giving the game away completely and provoking homosexual panic. Only your wife knows how many inches you have; the lads only know how many cylinders.

I ask a chap in his thirties wearing a Barbour jacket and estate-agent haircut waiting expectantly for his moment alone with the Mercedes why he likes fast cars so much. 'Well, they're just very attractive and well-engineered,' he says, eyeing me suspiciously. 'It's difficult to describe the appeal. Your pulse rises when you look at them. It's a gut thing, you know?' His voice rises just a little bit too much at the end of this question and I get the impression that he really meant 'It's a guy think, you know?' and I've brought my membership of the male sex into doubt by having to ask this question at all.

But I persist, asking him why he's queuing up to sit in a stationary car. 'Well, er, because I'll probably never own one and it is so well-engineered, so beautiful.' But it isn't going anywhere. How will you experience its beautiful engineering if it doesn't move? 'Well,' he says, looking a bit sheepish, 'there isn't much else to do here.'

And he's right. The irony of a motor show is that there isn't any actual motoring. All these stallions are bolted to the floor; these transports of delight aren't transporting anyone anywhere. But perhaps this is the whole point of a motor show – the cars, stripped of their practical pretence, become pure objects of desire and dreams that carry you away not on their V12 engines but on your frustrated ambitions.

One of the large security guards at the entrance to the Mercedes stand looks to me to be a very well-engineered object of desire also, from what I can make out under his high-gloss suit. I strike up a conversation with him. Do people ever misbehave when they sit in these cars? 'Oh, yes,' he says. 'People are always breaking things off.' Like what? 'Oh, handles and switches from the dashboard, that sort of thing.' Obviously they're overcome with passion, I suggest, archly. 'I suppose you could say that,' he says hurriedly, suddenly developing an interest in the other side of the hall.

Strolling around the rest of the show I find my attention wandering again from the automobile design to the buttock design on display here. The place is awash with the latest products from the lad assembly lines in the suburbs, examples of British social engineering at its best. The models just keep getting better and better. As I look around at the sporty, muscular little numbers cruising around the hall I feel a great knot of pride forming in my chest (or somewhere) – pride in the Great British Family Ltd for turning out such great chassis, the National Health Service's fine bodywork and Proctor and Gamble, of course, for keeping the paint-work blemish-free.

By one of the many bars here (what would a motor show be without bars for men to talk about cars in?) I overhear a 'discussion' between two men, pints and fags in hand. It's one of those conversations between straight men where neither one looks at the other but stares into the distance or into their pint (if they want to appear thoughtful), talking out of the side of their mouth (and over the other), taking care that even their shoulder lines don't face one another – in case someone should mistake this conversation for a mar-riage proposal. 'Well, yeah, I know that,' drones one of the blokish blokes, 'but you've got to remember that the MD500 has much better spec on acceleration and it's got twice as many valves, plus . . .' 'Yeah, yeah, I know that,' says the other, not listening, 'but the thing is, what really matters is the cornering and the FG300 has independently computer-controlled low-slung suspension that keeps that baby closer to the road than a nigger on a white woman . . .' I wander on.

On Sunday afternoons, all across the land, you can observe men washing, cleaning, vacuuming and polishing their cars with painstaking care – and yet the moment they cross the threshold they pretend they don't know how to hold a duster or switch on a vacuum cleaner. This girly attention to carpets, upholstery and windows that happen to be attached to a chassis is acceptable masculine behaviour because a car, having wheels and an engine, is something which goes and is thus not *domestic*, it is something that takes you away from Mum or wifey and her suffocating house-proudness plus you can shag girls in it. And yet, what puzzles women is not so much that their men have such a strange double standard when it comes to housework, but that men will hoover under their car seats yet don't bother to clean under their foreskin.

I'm struck by how little interest there appears to be at the show in looking under the bonnets of these cars. Boys may still be fascinated by brake horsepower and acceleration, but they seem less and less inclined to get their hands dirty and more and more inclined to fiddle with the fittings and the stereo. The rapidly accelerating complexity of car engine design has reduced most men to the level of the woman in that old favourite guy-joke about the woman who told the garage mechanic that her car still won't start, although she'd emptied all the ashtrays and washed the windows.

If truth be told, cars are no longer just strap-ons, but a kind of womb – a *man*-made womb of engineering technology, where 'comfort' is the watchword, and mysterious 'automatic' devices take care of you, take decisions for you, protecting you from the world and its hazards before you're even aware of them. Automatic climate control, automatic seat adjustment, automatic transmission, automatic suspension, automatic airbags, automatic roll-bar and – not far off – automatic navigation systems negotiate the tricky business of living for you. The masculine auto-womb gestates a new type of man who need never actually face the risky business of being born.

But the future is here already. According to the Vauxhall stand, anyway. Their new Vectra car is described as 'for the next millennium'. This point is driven home by a stage show involving a cast dressed in sub-Rocky Horror glam-rock outfits. The lead singer, Vectra, his face covered in orange pan-stick, cuts a very dashing futuristic figure, clad in a black lycra all-in-one with glittering shoulder pads and an alarmingly large sparkly silver codpiece (Vauxhall's marketing department are no fools). 'Hey guys,' he shouts out in a cringe-making 'mid-Atlantic' accent, 'let's make the world a safer place' and proceeds to extol the hi-tech safety features of the Vectra, before breaking into a shameless version of Gary Glitter's anthem: 'Do you wanna drive in my car? Come on, come on! Come on, come on! I'm the leader! I'm the leader of the brand I am . . . I just wanna take you for a ride, take you for a ride . . .' No thanks, dearie; I prefer my cars straight-acting.

A large crowd has gathered but for the most part they're

not getting carried away with enthusiasm; they don't appear to have realised how much fun Vauxhall cars are. Most of the men are just staring, in a slightly embarrassed way. I suspect they're looking at the singer's enormous silver codpiece and wondering what their lives would be like if they had one.

After wandering around the show for a couple of aimless hours I find myself back at the Mercedes stand, queuing up to sit in the SL600 coupé (like the estate agent said, what else is there to do?). I watch several men in front of me, young and old, sit in the driver's seat, whine it backwards and forwards by touching switches, adjust the electric mirrors; they're trying out £60,000 of car, seeing if it will fit – as if they were in the market for such an expensive accessory.

One by one they perform the same ritual. Hands on the steering wheel, eyes half-closed, sniffing the smell of luxury, success and wealth, each punter is imagining what it might be like to drive such a car, imagining it speeding him to a much better, faster, bigger, more comfortable and more expensive life than the one he's driving now (or being driven by). Imagining what it must be like to be a *man*.

January 1995

BEMUSEMENT PARK

IN AN AGE when the spectres of nationalism, ethnic strife and civil war have come back to rattle and clank their chains and generally keep us all awake at night in Europe, it's nice to know that there's somewhere just outside Paris where you can go to forget history.

Reached by Eurostar from London's Waterloo, travelling through the Eurotunnel, Disneyland Paris is where you can have 'Eurofun' – by pretending to be American. If America's tragedy is that she has no history, Europe's is that she has too much. Europe's Eurodream of a United States of Europe is a fantasy of forgetting her past, of starting afresh in a world where the only remaining allegiance worth fighting for is brand loyalty. 'Euro' Europe, like Disneyland, exists only in the imagination of the very innocent and the careful calculations of consumer capitalism.

Which is all fine and dandy, but I wish I hadn't chosen the Haunted House as my first port of call. Set atop a hill, the Haunted House is a big Gothic mansion straight out of *Scooby Doo*. This place is full of spirits, ghouls and spectres (and that's just the French schoolchildren). Ferried about in little cans which turn this way and that to save you (in typical American fashion) the wearisome trouble of turning your head, you are assailed by skeletons, yawning graves, plague carts, withered brides in tattered gowns and chilling tableaux straight out of Edgar Allen Poe. If I'd wanted this sort of thing I could have gone to Oxford Street.

99

In the American Disney parks, from which all the rides here have been copied exactly, this sort of thing is carefree, wholesome entertainment since these animatronix visions are not part of the 'American Dream': they represent to Americans the Old World nightmares their grandparents escaped from. Sitting here a few miles from Paris, with its legacy of plagues, terrors and revolutions, listening to these mechanical horrors moaning in French, the experience is rather less carefree.

Walking quickly away from the Haunted House, I head for the Rocky Mountain ride, a kind of roller-coaster mocked up as a Western steam train. Nothing is quainter to Americans than the idea of a train. To Europeans, the train is something that takes them to work and occasionally to war. It takes them to a bright future (like the TGVs which stop at the railway station outside the park) or to a dark past (like the cattle trucks rolling towards Auschwitz). But to Americans, the train is something that Robert Redford and Paul Newman robbed.

This, taken with the fact that it was the Americans who invented the mass-market individualism of the car, makes it curious that the whole Disneyland experience is actually like a train ride or a conveyor-belt: people are freight to be moved around and processed. Queues form at one end of the attraction and are disgorged (with added fun) at the other end as 'the product'. In fact, one of the curious contradictions of the Disney parks is that, despite representing the acme of Americana, they are socialistic in concept: everyone pays a tax to the 'state' at the gate after which all the rides are 'free'; there is no market distribution of pleasure in Disneyland, just Soviet-style queues. Despite everything we know to the contrary, it seems Walt was a red, after all.

In the queue for the Rocky Mountain ride there's a sign in front of me which reads: 'Wait time from this point 30 minutes'. Behind me are some French schoolgirls who are pushing, shoving, shouting and generally displaying that French inability to queue of which Walt would not have approved. I disapprove too, and am thinking highly non-Euro thoughts.

French schoolgirls must be the most irritating strain of humanity ever bred: they seem to think that the whole world exists purely for their entertainment (when obviously it exists for mine). 'Would you mind not pushing?' I ask, turning on my munchkin tormentors. I put the question in English as a pointed insult and to let them know that at least someone here knows how to queue. They stop their screeching and shoving momentarily to stare at me sullenly, and then carry on. To hide my embarrassment I strike up a conversation with the English teenagers in front of me. Why did they come to Disneyland Paris?

' 'Cos it's cheaper than going to Florida,' answers one boy in Nike, sucking on a bucket-sized coke. 'But we've been there as well,' he adds. What was it like?

'It was better.' Why? ' 'Cos it was more American.' Quite.

I *can* see far too much French countryside. The trees, the green grass, even the sky and the sunlight, are just too *pastoral*. In America, the Disney parks were created out of hostile nature, sheer acts of will rising out of the desert (Anaheim, California) or out of a swamp (Orlando, Florida). Here the dreams of Disneyland are defeated by the location. If London Bridge shipped to Texas lost its identity, Disneyland loses its meaning when put *into* a context. The French philosopher Jean Baudrillard suggested that Disneyland is necessary to convince Americans that the rest of America is real. Maybe Disneyland Paris is necessary to convince Europe that Europe is a Dream.

The Rocky Mountain ride proves disappointing, so I leave Frontierland and head instead for Discoveryland, the section of the park dedicated to the future, and probably a much better place to forget the past. Unfortunately, the French have decided to use Discoveryland to show how it was Jules Verne (a Frenchman, *naturellement*) who discovered the future. Everything seems to have a Jules Verne theme: Captain Nemo's submarine and the Space Mountain ride (both based on Verne's books). Even the Time Machine exhibit offers a 360° view of Verne travelling through time: the French won't let the fact that H. G Wells wrote *The Time Machine* spoil their party.

Admittedly, the French do have a first-rate engineering tradition. The splendid Eurostar and TGV which brought me here are sterling examples. It's just that the French shouldn't be allowed to operate the marvellous machines they build. This point is underlined by the hilarious Star Tours ride in which punters inadvertently become part of a *Star Wars* dogfight in a flight simulator piloted by a mad French robot who doesn't know left from right.

In the 3-D cinema, Verne is briefly eclipsed by Michael Jackson as Captain Eo in a sub-*Star Wars* pop promo which, with coloured glasses, looks truly three-dimensional. But even 3-D photography can't make Michael Jackson look real. However, Michael Jackson is *very* 'Euro'. With astute marketing he has overcome his past, erased his history (familial, racial and sexual) and reinvented himself. He's a hero for the Eurokids in the audience. It's time to leave Discoveryland.

In Fantasyland I resist the lure of the white-knuckle Dumbo carousel and head for It's a Small World. Here we float merrily in a little boat along man-made canals through rooms with tiny puppets representing the peoples of the world, in their igloos, grass huts, wigwams and semis, all with insanely smiley faces and singing, 'It's a small, small world after all' in joyous little voices. The door to the final room has 'Hollywood' written in sparkly stuff above it. The room itself is full of glitter and rhinestone. All the little people of the world are here, singing in one rousing, united, peaceful voice. This is the Eurodream. No history, no nationalism, no wars; just a nasty jingle, lots of identical smiley faces and some cheap glitter – look at the Eurovision Song Contest. Just one thing bothers me: why are they all singing in German?

September 1995

TIJUANA BRASS

I'M LOOKING AT America's youth with its pants down. It ain't pretty but I want a piece of the action. I'm on the prowl, you see, looking to 'recruit' – and this is probably the best place to do it because there isn't a boy here who hasn't drunk the equivalent of a bottle of industrial-strength muscle relaxant.

Tijuana may mean little more than cheery Herb Alpert instrumentals to you, but to kids in the Californian border city and naval base of San Diego, Tijuana spells 'Party on, dude'. The reason for this is very simple: the minimum age for imbibing intoxicating liquor in California is twenty-one; in Mexico it is eighteen. This, and the fact that Tijuana is only a half-hour drive south, explains why hordes of American teenagers regularly leave leafy suburbs, green campuses and neatly ordered barracks to party and puke on the pavements of their Third World neighbour.

Tijuana must be difficult for the American mind to comprehend. Perhaps this is another reason why they drink so much here. Apart from the sheer disorganisation of everything, from street signs to sanitation (particularly shocking after the fastidiousness of well-heeled California), there is the poverty which litters the streets. Four-year-olds sit on the pavement, among the refuse and the dead cats, with their dirty palms outstretched. Many of the beggars have travelled from the rural interior of Mexico to try to cadge some dollars.

'TJ', as the kids call it, may be richer for its proximity to the United States than other parts of Mexico. But the image of a town unhooking its bra straps to cater for the apparently limitless hedonism of Yankee youth while its own children sell chewing gum and sleep in its doorways, is not an altogether attractive one.

The main drag for the brattish Yankee invaders is called, with sad Latin American irony, Plaza de la Revolución. Tonight the square is full of rampaging youths eager to combine the incompatible activities of getting legless and getting their legs over (though not, I hope, incompatible with someone like me getting their leg over them). Tonight is also a military payday. Their back pockets bulging, hundreds of 'squids' and 'jarheads' (sailors and marines) zigzag their way up and down the streets, deliberately walking into their sworn enemies, college boys.

I came here with the intention of preying upon America's clean-limbed youth while they prey on Mexico. In the sexual food chain I intend to be at the top. But who to choose? Jarheads, squids or college boys? It only takes a minute to eliminate the college boys (too smug) and the squids (too geeky) and thus plump for the jarheads. Lucky boys.

There's a certain irresistible poetic justice in the idea of seducing a US marine, historically the means of projecting US power in Latin America. But, even more persuasively, marines have a number of classical features which attract them to the homosexual predator. They are fit, they have short hair, they always suffer from a shortage of women and, best of all, they drink far too much. As a popular American gay joke has it – Q: What's the difference between a straight marine and a 'bisexual' marine? A: A six-pack of beer.

All in all, it's really very thoughtful of the US government to go to the trouble of giving teenage Midwestern boys a decent haircut, making them exercise, depriving them of female company and then sending them to southern California – Fagville USA – where they can bring a little joy into the lives of lonely homosexuals.

The big drawback is that marines, like nuns, always travel in threes. But that didn't stop me chatting up Troy, a recruiting poster picture come to life, in some bar where he was whooping it up with his two buddies. 'Hey dude, that accent's really cool!' he exclaimed, grinning his blond grin and slapping my back with his wide farmboy hands. 'I bet the chicks really go for that!' And so our romance began.

As the beers and tequila flow, so does Troy's life story. It turns out that, like many military boys, he turned to the US Armed Forces to save him from America. Back in his two-horse town in west Texas, he used to while away the hours mainlining crystal-meth. 'Man, I woulda been dead by now if it wasn't for the Corps,' he tells me. 'They gave me something to live for, y'know?'

His chaperones, Dusty and Jim, smaller and plainer than Troy, are boyhood buddies who joined up with him. There's something very touching about their friendship. 'He was my protector at school,' confides Jim later. A stutterer, life must have been hard at school and I get the impression that Troy is still his protector in the Corps. Nevertheless, their lifelong attachment to one another must end tonight, at least long enough for me to jump on Troy.

We move increasingly unsteadily from bar to bar, hassling the college boys along the way. Asked to explain this tribal animosity, Troy just shrugs. 'They're pussies,' he says, adding. 'It's traditional. I guess.' But I suspect that the hatred stems from the vague intimation that college boys are going to live the American Dream, while boys like Troy are destined only ever to defend it or be its victims.

The dark-eyed, long-lashed señoritas who would like a share in the Dream are everywhere, eyeing up their future green cards. But tonight I can afford a sense of solidarity with them; they know that the boys with the short hair who drink their fortnight's pay in two days are not the boys to dream with. Instead they do their best to attract one of the boys spending Pop's money like there was no such thing as an angry long-distance telephone call. Another reason jarheads hate college boys.

The evening wears on. Trays of sweet-tasting *cerveza* come and go, as do the neon names of bars and discos. And visits to the john – the only place I seem to have a chance of getting Troy away from his buddies. At last, I find myself answering the call of nature at the same time as him. Standing next to me, Troy has his hands on his hips (I should have known he'd be one of those 'Look, no hands!' pissers). I'm resisting the urge to cop a look at his joint when I catch *him* checking *me* out. 'Hey, Mark,' he says, half in jest, half in wonder, 'so it's true you English guys ain't cut!'

Now, you might be forgiven for thinking that here is a green light for me, that this studly young marine's expression of interest in the status of my penis might somehow be turned to my advantage. Shamefully, I lose my nerve for tackiness (for example, saying something like 'oh yeah, and look how easy it makes jacking off . . .') All I can manage is to mumble 'Er, yes', pull in my pecker and run out of the men's room.

Foreskins have never been a major fetish for me, but if you're English and you want to cruise jarheads then you'd better have your rap ready. Despite being programmed at an early age to revile these rather comical flaps of skin as unhygienic and therefore un-American, American men cannot help but experience a dim sense of mutilation and loss when gazing on the untampered-with variety. They think: so it's dirty, but that's what they said about sex, and look how much fun that turned out to be.

It's also an accessory which they can never have. Now that's what you call a Unique Selling Point. Most of all, the foreskin is a symbol of the Old World and its chaotic messiness. In America roads run straight, air is conditioned, teeth are bleached and foreskins are sliced – God is in his heaven and cinnamon is in apple pie. Americans have everything except smegma, and what Americans don't have, they want very badly.

Meanwhile, back at the bar. Troy attempts to recoup some of his virility by suggesting we 'go and cruise some pussy'. I wonder if the moment has come to tell him that 'I don't go for pussy' but decide that this confession would put the dampers on any chance of persuading him to take a closer look at my foreskin. With boys like Troy, any genital friction with members of the same sex always has to be prefaced with the timeless line, 'I'm no fag, understand? I really dig chicks but . . .' Which is fine by me. So I 'cruise some chicks' with him for a couple of hours, to buy some time and to make him feel better.

Much later, Troy and I have passed the point at which drunkenness excuses a couple of regular guys who want to get into each other's pants from the duty of pretending to look for women. It also happens to be the same point at which physical expressions of affection cease to be suspect – on the contrary, they become almost compulsory. Troy acknowledges this in the traditional way: 'Hey, man – I'm totally fucked up.'

Now he puts his arm around me and begins to recite sketches from Monty Python. I'm happy because I know this is his way of showing me he loves me. To American youth, Britain means Depeche Mode, Boy George, James Bond and Monty Python. Monthy Python, with its anarchic Old World surrealism, is the kind of comedy that American kids were denied until Beavis and Butthead and Ren and Stimpy brought them the smegma they craved.

Nevertheless, despite scenting victory, I decide to wimp out. I'm too pussy for this. It's 3 a.m. in Tijuana and I'm arm in arm with a drunken nineteen-year-old US marine with the face of an angel and the butt of Beelzebub, who's reciting Monty Python in a Texan accent you could marinate a T-bone with. We met just a few hours ago. Now we're the bestest buddies that there ever was. I can't bring myself to spoil it.

The heat, the beer, the game-playing, and now a Texan marine nudging me and asking 'Is your wife a goer? Know wot I mean?' proves a little too much. I abdicate my self-appointed position as avenger of Latin America and abandon my fiendish plans to ravish the virtue of the United

States Marine Corps. Instead I offer the boys a lift back Stateside.

At the border, as we queue to re-enter the neatly ordered New World, a skinny, ragtag band of Mexican kids – none looking older than ten – wash our windscreen in a determined last-ditch effort to prevent Yankee dollars escaping back over the border. Troy, the simple Texan, is moved enough by this scene of regional deprivation to offer a few dollars (all that is left of his pay packet), only to have them snatched out of his hand. By way of thanks, he receives loud demands for more.

Truly this evening has blurred the lines between who is the prey and the preyed upon, the fucker and the fucked, more than I care for.

August 1994

HOME TRUTHS

'AT 12.30 Mary Scott-Morgan will demonstrate vegetarian cuisine . . .' announces the mother of all mothers' telephone voice. The woman on the public address system at Earls Court is trying just a smidgen too hard to be posh. She's stretching her vowels so much they sound as if they might at any moment snap like non-M&S knicker elastic when too much is asked of it '. . . and at 13.30 Eina Sewing Machines demonstrating laundry tips . . .'

It could only be the *Daily Mail* Ideal Home Exhibition, that redoubtable British institution which so generously offers the British public a glimpse of a better world – a private Utopia where cooking is 'cuisine' and the bathroom towels always match the bathmat. A university of self-improvement, the Ideal Home Exhibition will show you, poor untutored peasant that you are, how to *live*. Laundry tips, nail care, fabrics and furnishings, spice racks, hair removal, labour-saving gadgets, foot spas, damp-proof coursing, fitted kitchens draught excluders – here are the solutions to all the social problems of a home-owning democracy. The outside world may be getting uglier, but our homes just become better insulated with each year's Exhibition.

Outside Olympia a giant inflatable sofa advertising this state of contentment wafts in the breeze; beneath it is a stand displaying a brand new Volvo estate, fitted with all the latest safety devices. Both are reassuring icons amid the insecurity of Nineties Britain. If only Volvo made furniture . . .

Like most of the punters here today, I've come for some inspiration on how to inject a little 'taste' and 'luxury' into my dowdy life. Naturally, I head straight for the show homes, Mecca for the upwardly mobile. The largest exhibit this year is provided by a home-building firm which is giving away ten of its homes in the *Mail*. But before you can reach this you have to walk through five mock-ups of houses which are meant to represent the last hundred years of home-dwelling. Although nothing so grubby is ever mentioned, these show homes are for very specific class strata – the lower middle class and the aspirational working class, the celebrated C1s and C2s.

'Welcome to our ideal home,' a recorded voice greets as you walk into the first, turn-of-the-century house. Plainly, this is an irony we are intended to taste: we can see that it is really quite ghastly – damp, draughty and, worst of all, without a breakfast bar. So it goes on: the Twenties house had a gas cooker but no insulation, in the Sixties home there is insulation but also lots of condensation.

After this depressing parade of the privations of previous generations, which inclines me to wonder why they didn't just do away with their sorry selves, we are ushered into the gleaming, brand new 1995 home. Clean and bright after the dinginess of the ancestral homes, it is a paragon of 'modernity'.

But it is also a monument to bad taste. Something quite appalling has happened to C1s and C2s since the Sixties – the Eighties. Gone forever is the endearing naivety, the charming lack of ambition of their homes, the reassuring sense of knowing one's place. Now there is a disturbing restlessness and hunger. According to a sign, British Home Stores, once the reliable purveyor of nice, homely tack, has been given free reign here, and it is frighteningly evident that they have gone 'designer'.

The master bedroom is an essay in beige that would best be left unwritten. The dining room has been painted a

110

'confident' green that fails to convince and makes Toilet Duck look a natural hue. The lamps are painted white and twisted into shocking tulip shapes. But the *pièce de résistance* is an ersatz Greek marble frieze of nude youths wrestling, which lines the dining-room wall. Really, things were so much better when the lower orders bought their art from Woolworths. This, Baroness Thatcher please take note, is what happens when you encourage ordinary people to have aspirations: they end up with dining rooms like Liberace's.

'Well, it's a nice house,' the male half of a middle-aged couple from Worthing tells me, tactfully declining to comment on the interiors. Another couple in their late twenties look shell-shocked.

'Absolutely awful. We just wanted to get out of there,' they gasp. But at least one woman is in raptures.

'A real dream home,' she exclaims and turning to her rather defeated-looking husband, 'wasn't it, John?'

'Yes, it was very nice, very nice . . .' he says, almost to himself.

This last couple are evidence that one of the traditional purposes of the Ideal Home Exhibition is to remind the men who's boss. Everywhere I look I can see men being dragged through show homes and carpet displays by wives who seem to grow more and more animated as their husbands grow more and more withdrawn. But then, the average *Daily Mail* married man is doomed to a life of servicing the mortgage repayments and putting up shelves. The best such a husband can hope for at the Ideal Home Exhibition is to be allowed to visit the Black & Decker stand. No wonder they want to reinstate the death penalty.

It goes without saying, of course, that there are some men here today who display an unabashed interest in fabrics and furnishings. Around the hall wander male couples whose enthusiasm and concentration is at least as intense as the women's. In theory, the Ideal Home Exhibition is all about 'family' and 'nesting', with no place for homos. In practice, it's a magnet for them. Maybe they're just taking after

111

Mummy again, or maybe it's a response to a hostile world, but lots of gay boys are desperate to create a snug, tasteful, private world with the boyfriend and the poodle (or just the poodle boyfriend).

I visit a show home with interiors by Maples. This one is very 'classy' – all luxury cream carpets, ruched velvet curtains and seasoned wooden furniture. It is as relaxed and confident as the previous show home was uptight and compulsive. A video constantly playing in the living room can be heard throughout the house. It shows a well-to-do, but 'casual' couple looking at various combinations of sofa, curtains and carpets, with a look of intense but refined concentration.

'The fine art of furnishing,' confides the smug, ever-so-slightly faggy voiceover, 'is knowing how to create the right look using texture, colour and form to create beautiful homes.

'Of course, part of the trick is knowing when it's not quite right.' He adds with an almost sinister final emphasis.

Knowing 'when it's not quite right' isn't part of the trick – it's all of it. Taste here is a polite euphemism for class, and having good taste is simply about not showing yourself up as common. This show home and the video are carefully targeted at those punters who live in terror of being found out – of using the wrong fork at the firm's dinner dance or having their choice of curtains criticised by the wives at the golf club.

There is no end to this self-improvement business. Once you have discovered how to make your home 'ideal' and to conceal how common you are, all you need to do is make the necessary arrangements with your bank manager to fill your domicile with labour-saving devices, which would be utterly pointless if they didn't serve the most crucial function of all – to make you feel important.

So I head for the Exhibition's upper levels which are crammed with stands demonstrating the latest gadgets. Here I learn about the 'fabulous' Quick Snack machine, a plastic device which *folds bread*, and an amazing Smart-Mop, which incorporates a *rapid wringing action* that promises to make you the envy of all. 'You'll be out of the door half an hour before your neighbour!' proclaims the enthusiastic young man demonstrating this marvel of modern science.

But I'm sold on 'the World's Best-Selling Steam Smoother'. A gaggle of middle-aged women are gathered around a demonstrator with hoop earrings, ski pants and a linen jacket, who has a fake tan and a phoney love-a-duck accent. She puts the device, which looks like a travelling iron, through its paces.

'You can iron your duvet on the bed, ladies, your curtains on the rail, your clothes on the hanger! No more unsightly creases!'

So, the boffins who came up with the Steam Smoother have finally made it possible for housewives to realise an age-old dream – now they can iron their entire home. In fact, with this fantastic labour-saving device they need never stop ironing. They can follow their husbands and children around with the Smoother, eliminating any wrinkly evidence of their existence.

Steam really seems to be the hot thing this year. A few yards away, another stand features a demonstrator extolling the benefits of the Steamcleaner.

'It's a twenty-first-century cleaning machine, ladies and gentlemen,' announces a balding, middle-aged man with a moustache and wearing a cheap suit with colour-picture fish tie. He has a slightly camp soft northern accent and a rather fey manner which doesn't really match the hi-tech seriousness of the product (but perhaps this is a deliberate attempt to make the technology seem friendly).

'The Steamcleaner, ladies and gentlemen, is safe, economical and environmentally friendly,' he chirrups. 'But most importantly of all, it's kind to your home: it *moistens*; it doesn't *dampen*.'

I struggle to comprehend the vital distinction between dampening and moistening, especially when it retails at £400, but I make a few enquiries and become engrossed in

113

conversation with the man. Like many of the demonstrators here today, he's an actor by trade.

'Musicals mostly,' he explains, 'although I have done straight stuff. I can move – but I didn't say I can dance!'

Does he enjoy this kind of work?

'Oh yes. You get to meet all kinds of characters. Some of the ladies can be a real scream. One stuck-up cow asked to see my attachments!

' "No good," she sniffed, turning her nose up when she sees them. Well, that put my back up, that did, so I said. "I'll have you know that this is the finest machine on the market." But she just said. "Oh, I already have one of those." She said she'd bought one for £39. £39! I ask you!

'There are a lot of women like that here,' he goes on. 'They pretend to be interested in your marvellous new product, but only so that they can turn around and tell you that they already have one anyway, which, *naturally*, they bought much cheaper somewhere else.'

June 1995

114

HARD SHOULDER

THE TRAFFIC THUNDERS past my outstretched thumb, racing to an appointment with its first traffic jam four miles up the road. Whining courier vans, hissing articulated lorries and purring Volvo estates with labradors bobbing in the back ignore my groovy request for a free ride. On a nearby lamppost other hitchers have recorded their despair among a liberal sprinkling of anarchy symbols, 'Jim and Alice were fucked here 11/7/93' and 'Jim and Alice fucked again 14/6/94'. Sometimes the callousness of the pollution-emitting, meat-eating, wage-earning world can prove too much to bear when you're signing on in three different cities. 'Stop, you bastards!' one freeloader has scrawled.

But it's a gloriously hot, sunny, lazy day at the start of the M1 in north London and I'm full of optimism about the road ahead and happy, as Blanche Dubois put it, to rely on 'the kindness of strangers' to take me to Newcastle (and I'm hoping that taking off my shirt will help that kindness express itself quicker).

I want to meet the great British motoring public, find out where they're headed and what's behind them, take in the view out front and check the rear-view mirror. I want to know what the British are looking forward to and what they're leaving behind. I'm not just hitching on the M1, you see; I'm hitching on the motorway of the British imagination. Motorways represent a virtual Britain, a Britain-in-limbo: they don't really exist anywhere – the hard shoulder

115

ten miles outside Glasgow looks much the same as five miles out of Exeter. And they're filled with people who all want to be somewhere else but aren't going to get there until well after teatime.

In this state of limbo you can almost believe in John Major's classless society. Standing at this very spot ten years ago, when I too was a sponger studying at the University of Life, a brand new Volvo Turbo came to a precision-engineered halt in front of me. Behind the wheel was a precision-groomed Max Hastings on his way home to Northampton. We talked, as you do, about the army and public schools and, all in all, we passed the kind of pleasant forty minutes together which class and cliques exist to prevent (so I hope that some readers of the *Daily Telegraph* will be suitably shocked to hear their editor has given free rides to loafers).

But today a dark blue Vauxhall pulls over and stops a few yards up the hard shoulder; the door opens. Less than ten minutes' wait. Not bad. James, a blond young man with pink skin, wearing a shirt and tie, is on his way to Nottingham. Once installed, I notice his car has been colonised by fluffy little trolls holding signs which offer such invaluable advice as: 'When the going gets tough, the tough go for coffee' and 'You don't have to be mad to work here, but it helps'. Something tells me he's not the editor of a national newspaper.

He is, in fact, a sales rep for an industrial products company on his way home for the weekend. Conversation proves a little tricky to start with. But, sitting in bumper-to-bumper traffic for an hour brings us on to the subject of how crap Britain is and my ride talks with real passion about the injustices that various British service providers have fool-ishly tried to foist on him. Apparently, he was even complaining about the food being cold in a restaurant when he met his wife.

So is there *anything* he looks forward to?

'Well, my wife and I are looking to emigrate to Canada or preferably America. There are more opportunities, and

116

people understand the concept of service so much better over there.' True, but it does seem rather a long way to go for a hot meal. But he's also looking forward to going to Mallorca on holiday – 'Just eleven weeks to go. Can't wait.'

Dropped at Nottingham East 'service' station I have a wander round and see why James wanted to take the first exit from Motorway UK. Service stations are also part of the classless society of motorways, but here the word 'classless' is interchangeable with 'clueless'. Smelly toilets, an amusement arcade with five-year-old games, a sad shop selling tabloid newspapers, tissues, fizzy drinks, chocolate and every kind of boiled sweet imaginable, and a sullen cafeteria that might have been specially designed to torture James. There's also a Burger King outlet with a lifesize cardboard cut-out of the Gladiator Wolf advertising a scratch-card competition in which you win a free coke if you guess his Gladiator pals' star signs. Meanwhile, families mill around with that glazed expression that comes from a combination of ennui and too many boiled sweets.

Standing by the exit road, waiting for my next pick-up, I watch the cars and lorries go by, just occasionally driven by someone I wouldn't mind getting to know better. Sex is, of course, an ever-present possibility in the course of hitching. The long-distance driver has little else to think about – hence the huge demand for chocolate and those sucking sweets. And sharing your car – a very intimate, private, personal space – with a complete stranger is, frankly, a form of promiscuity (though at least with casual sex you don't have to talk to your tricks).

But for me the possibility of sex has always remained just that. No one has ever made a pass at me, except for a Frenchman with acne near Perpignan. And he was so embarrassed by my refusal that he drove over 80km out of his way. Personally, I'm less inclined to take this as evidence of my unattractiveness, than as proof of the low number of homosexuals in the population – at least, those with cars (as everyone knows, homosexuals all move to London where they ride mountain bikes or sit in the back of taxis taking drugs).

That's not to say that there's no sexual component in a straight man's decision to pick up a strange young man with no shirt. It's just that for the most part they're probably unaware of that side of themselves, and I'm not about to put them in touch with it. There are enough men in London wearing Lycra already, thank you.

Another blue Vauxhall fleet car comes to a halt. In another context, its driver Stevey – a stocky man in his late thirties with cropped red hair and moustache – might be taken for a clone. But Stevey is, in fact, a Geordie. He's a communications engineer, which is slightly ironic as his thick Geordie accent and prolific use of expletives make him rather difficult to understand. But slowly, as he relaxes, the accent eases off and the 'f-word' count falls. I gather he lives in Halifax, and he's been divorced for five years.

'When my marriage ended,' he explains, 'I decided best thing was to gan out of fookin' Newcastle altogether, and I moved to Halifax. It's a smashing place, mind. Fookin' brilliant place to gan out on the town wi' the lads.'

Steve drinks Fosters Ice. What about brown ale?

'No way, man. We don't drink any of that piss anymore. Foreign lagers are the best. That Fosters Ice is nice and light, and you get pissed on it reet quick.

'An' being in a bottle you can carry on wi' a lass wi'out fookin' worrying about fookin' sloppin' it,' he says, winking at me. I wink back.

Steve was working in Birmingham last week, and he didn't like it there.

'It's full of fookin' niggers and pakis. Not that I'm prejudiced, mind,' he adds hastily. 'A lot of them are fookin' brilliant people. It's just wi' all those half-caste babies we'll soon be a fookin' broon country, man, instead of white, you know what I mean?' Ummm . . .

Stevey's looking forward to his tea. his girlfriend's made him chilli con carne – his favourite, after curry. He's also looking forward to his holiday in Spain (well, Benidorm): 'Only eight weeks to go. Can't wait.'

Stevey drops me off at a roundabout for the M62 and I thank him for the ride.

'See yer, Mark. I've really enjoyed your company, man.' Actually, I have to admit I enjoyed Stevey's company too. But I can't help wondering what the future holds for Britain when everyone – even slightly racist Geordies – wants to be somewhere else, eat exotic food and drink foreign lager.

Twenty minutes later another blue Vauxhall stops. Nick, a catering equipment salesman in his mid-twenties is on his way home to York, so he'll drop me off at the A1. Nick seems a mild-mannered chap, but he has a wild streak.

'I hate it when people cut me up,' he confesses. 'Sometimes I follow them for miles out of my way, an inch from their bumper, and just glare at them.'

Nick's looking forward to his holiday in Ibiza: 'Only six more weeks to go. Can't wait.'

My final ride in this voyage of discovery is on a lorry headed all the way to Newcastle with lads from the Isle of Sheppey: Steve and Mark. Both nineteen, Mark is driving, Steve is sleeping. Mark's blond with unnaturally bright, grey-blue eyes that seem to be laughing all the time. He's a bit overweight, but in a carefree, laddish sort of way. Actually, Mark's driving is also a bit too carefree for my liking; he keeps looking over his shoulder to talk to me as I sit bouncing up and down on the mattress in the back of the cab, next to a poster of Casper the friendly ghost. I notice he has some cuts on his left hand. How did he get them?

'Oh, putting my fist through the window a couple of days ago when my bird said she was leaving me,' he says matter-of-factly. 'Been seeing her three years and there's a three-month-old kid as well. We were having an engagement party next week.' So much for 'carefree', then.

Mark's quite unusual on Sheppey; he has a job.

'Most of the people I know deal drugs, or get into fights in pubs,' he explains cheerily. 'There isn't a lot to do in Sheppey. That's why I like this job – you get to leave the

119

island.' Steve's job also means he gets to 'go away'. He's just
served eight months for ram-raiding.

'He drove all the way to Southampton, poor bugger,'
laughs Mark. 'All the shops in Sheppey have reinforced steel
shutters and stuff – that or they're already empty.'

The lorry that is shaking our bones is a ten-year-old
British flat-bedder that's seen better days. 'It's been hammer-
ed,' says Mark. 'I can't get her to go over 50. I've tried
bending the accelerator pedal up, but it doesn't make any
difference. She's fucked.'

What does Mark want out of life?

'My old girlfriend back and a new lorry,' he says,
laughing.

Steve and Mark aren't going on holiday this year.

October 1995

FAMILY VALUES

IT'S A DARK, cold and foggy night across Britain but, by the miracle of televisual technology, families are enjoying the Californian sun, splashing in the water, playing a few rounds of volleyball and checking out the babes and dudes. It's Saturday evening and life's a beach as London Weekend Television begins its family entertainment broadcast to the nation with *Baywatch*.

All the same, things can get a bit hairy when you're out to relax and enjoy yourself. All sorts of horrid nastiness might befall you. You might forget your flip-flops, be attacked by a seagull driven mad by pollution, or knocked off a rock by a freak wave into water at least three feet deep!

But don't despair, because here comes David Hasselhoff running towards us with his squadron of young lifeguards cum guardian angels, all sweetly attractive. He sprints manfully towards the camera, breasts bouncing beneath their fur screen, a look of grim determination on his face. Unkind souls might look at Hasselhoff and compare his booby breasts with the pert pecs of Matt, the stud of a French lifeguard, or his wooden hair with the wavy, sea-breeze tossed blond locks of Logan the Aussie, and ask the question: *why*? But Hasselhoff is the star because he is the guarantee that this flesh-fest is *family entertainment*, that nothing seriously sexy or shocking will happen, that it will all turn out right in the end. Dull, deeply uncool, and a

121

bucket of sea-water over any beach party, Hasselhoff is Saturday evening TV's Dad.

Like pornography, family entertainment is difficult to define, but you know it when you see it. As Camille Paglia or anyone from the National Viewers and Listeners' Association will tell you, the family is there to defend us against sex and violence. Consequently family entertainment must protect its viewers not merely from unpleasant beach mishaps but from their own pleasuring desires. Family entertainment must be popular but wholesome, lusty but not lustful, heterosexual but not sexual – something all the family can watch without bringing up the subject of what Mummy and Daddy actually did to make a family in the first place. Family entertainment has to be safe. It must, like Daddy Hasselhoff, protect you from reality.

Of course, the TV Father Protector, unlike the real ones (who are either absent, or you wish they were) is peachy perfect. This evening's *Baywatch* storyline is called 'Father's Day' and features the hirsute one spending lots of 'quality time' with his son because his dad 'was really bad with stuff like feelings'. Meanwhile, Logan undergoes hypnosis to locate the cause of his mysterious flashbacks, the memory of a past event he has been blocking; cue footage of adorable little blond boy watching his lifeguard pop dying while rescuing people from a burning pleasure craft. An explosion rips through the boat and we see, in slomo his father's rather phallic float spinning in the air and landing forlornly at the feet of the little boy, who picks it up. And now he's a lifeguard too, so Daddy lives on – the family protects you even from death. But one of the greatest debts we owe to Hasselhoff and co. is for protecting us from the possibility of erotic contact between men. Homosexuality is most definitely not family entertainment. The stirring fantasy family romance presented takes care of that particularly icky idea, thank you very much. Young man! Don't stay at the YMCA! Don't hang around the bus station! – go surfing with Hasselhoff instead.

But LWT's next edifying offering, *International Gladiators*, almost lets the side down. You might find yourself gagging over the syrup-sweet sentimentality of *Baywatch*, but *Gladiators* has you choking over the size of some of the packets on display. This low-camp, high-budget, white-trash extravaganza would like you to think it's as straight as Hasselhoff's jean creases and as clean as Ulrika Jonssen's hair – especially since it goes out of its way to court children – but somehow the sight of waxed and tanned male bodybuilders posing in Lycra inviting you to guess their religion doesn't lend credence to this position. The 'theatricality' of the gladiators' bodies is only matched by the 'theatricality' of the games devised to make their muscle drag look practical and sustain the pretence that their bodies are there for a purpose other than to be gaped at. (Perhaps it shouldn't be so surprising: *Gladiators* is sponsored by Kellogg's Frosties, the people who brought you Tony the Tiger larking about with a horny baseballer in the locker room and a sweaty volleyballing Dean Cain).

Worse, this show sports some seriously butch women. While the female gladiators are usually femmed up with big hair and slap, as if to apologise for their muscles (but merely drawing attention to some curious similarities with the male gladiators), the female contestants are often much less – how shall we say? – conventionally glamorous. This evening, Eunice, a kickboxing champion from Merseyside, with an accent like a pint glass in your face, has to be physically restrained from going after one of the gladiators who made the mistake of getting in her way.

It might be easy to forget that this is family entertainment. Fortunately the show is liberally sprinkled with shots of the contestants' scary gene-pool in the crowd, holding placards and wearing T-shirts with slogans like 'Go, Dave, go!' As proof of the contestants' heterosexuality, shots of girlfriends and boyfriends are especially popular. In lovely Eunice's case, additional frequent shots of her baby were deemed necessary.

But hey, we're all one big family now. One big American

family watching the same American family entertainment in which all differences are erased. As one of the American gladiators in philosophical frame of mind confesses between games, *International Gladiators* has taught him that, for all his initial prejudices, 'the French and the British and the Russians are just like Americans'. Yes it's true, on Saturday evening telly at least, the whole world really does want to get into Lycra gymwear and make a tit of themselves.

On *Blind Date*, the next programme up, one of the male contestants is wearing a 'joke' Lycra outfit and Maria, one of the girls, enthuses about Dean Cain. She giggles: 'He's my ideal man. Lycra shows off a man's best features, you know.'

The three male hopefuls perched on bar stools this evening have no best features but are a classic line-up. No. 1's the creepy one from London with big, bleached teeth and snazzy jacket, who fancies himself something rotten – he's a 'personal development consultant' (how Californian can you get?). No. 2's the joker, wearing the Lycra and a pink baseball cap, a fat man from Jersey who works as an electrician and moonlights, of course, as a really wacky DJ! And then there's No. 3, the you-must-be-kidding one, a very precisely spoken young man with pursed lips from Ayrshire, wearing a padded jacket which, like his preciously styled thinning hair, is trying unwisely to draw attention to itself – he's an ex-air steward and 'professional male model'.

As you might expect and indeed hope, homosexuality proper has no place on *Blind Date*. But this is not just 'homophobia'. Homosexuals, as any viewer with half a brain can tell you, are probably invited on *Blind Date* more often than heterosexuals. What can't be tolerated, however, is homo*sex*. Unlike heterosex, it can't be sanctified and made sweet by hearts and cherubs, Cilla, a brightly lit studio and canned laughter. 'Romance' and the prospect of marriage don't perfume away the stink of bodily fluids when those fluids don't produce bawling, mewling tyrants that force you to spend half your life in Mothercare and B&Q.

Homosex may be forbidden to show its face but it's never far away, especially since heterosexuality can be so dull – as is shown by the fact that a week doesn't go by without someone, usually Cilla, making some jokey reference. This week Cilla introduces one male contestant as living in a '*four*-bedroomed house with *five* fellahs!' Ooo-err! But it's OK – he tells us he's sleeping in the *dining room*. Ha, ha! That was a close one!

Another elaborate homo joke involves No. 1's rehearsed response to Maria's Dean Cain question about what kind of superhero outfit the male contestants would wear. 'It would have to reflect my personality,' he intones, 'smooth,' (No. 2 in Lycra next to him strokes No. 1's thigh coquettishly), 'soft to the touch,' (No. 2 touches his thigh tenderly) 'and', he says covering his groin and leaning away from No. 2, 'hard in all the right places.' Of course the audience is shrieking by this point. In a queer irony worthy of *Blind Date*, the woman choosing, who of course can't see what is going on, mistakes this noise as a sign that creepy No. 1 is somehow irresistible and goes on to pick him.

Since *Blind Date*, for all its joshing and sniggering, doesn't *really* want to know about sex, it has to concentrate on 'romance'. Now, call me a cynical old tart, but I always thought the measure of 'romance' was how much money a boy spent on a girl before he fucked her. And it seems *Blind Date* does too. The most romantic locations are the most expensive and the most romantic men are the ones who buy the most gifts. Even Cilla is positively shameless about it all. This evening she introduces a boy from Ipswich with the line, 'Gary, yer've got a few bob or two haven't yer? 'Cos you're in business with your dad, aren't yer?' It reminds me of the words I once heard shouted out by a lass to her girlfriend at a disco in Liverpool: ' 'ere, Sharon, this one's gorra *car*!'

So when the winning numbers from the National Lottery are flashed up on the screen during the show it all makes perfect sense. In the cosy world of family viewing, only two things can change your life: money and love, the latter being merely a poor consolation prize next to the former. In both *Blind Date* and the National Lottery you have to pick your number and submit yourself to blind Fate, but with the difference that 'lucky' with the National Lottery is measured in millions rather than inches.

Blind Date and Cilla stagger off on their stilettos into the night. Up next: *Family Fortunes*, the last blast of family entertainment before the nine o'clock watershed. No bodies, no Lycra, no romance here – they were just gimmicks to soften you up for this, the ultimate distillation of family entertainment. Two tribes slog it out for the totemic 'four-door family saloon' and the accolade of being the most unremarkable family in the country. If anyone doubted that family viewing plus LWT equals human devolution, let them watch *Family Fortunes*. No skills, no knowledge, no personality and virtually no pulse required – all you have to do is come up with the most popular answer to market-tested questions such as 'Name something you would do in the event of a power cut'. (Surprisingly the top answer to this one was 'Look for a candle' and not 'Wait for the telly to come back on'.)

But there is a message for the Great British Viewing Public here and it is this: dream of frolicking on Santa Monica beach, imagine yourself abseiling in tights, fantasise about holidaying in the Seychelles with a millionaire, but please don't forget that you're a frowzy bunch of farts and appearing on *Family Fortunes* is probably the best you can hope for. And even David Hasselhoff's hairy bosom can't protect you from *that*.

May 1995

126

GRAN CANARIA? NEIN DANKE!

'WELCOME TO THE start of your holiday in Gran Canaria,' says a Northern girl's singsong but lifeless voice from the crackly speaker above my head, as the coach pulls jerkily out of the airport and on to the motorway. 'My name's Melanie, your rep for the duration of your holiday, and your driver's name is Juan.'

Why do they always do that? Why do they tell you the driver's name? What do you care what he's called? You're not likely to want to chat him up, unless you're into surly middle-aged Spanish men with BO. All you ever see of the driver is the back of his head and his sunglasses in the rear-view mirror. But maybe, judging by the way this one's driving, it's simple courtesy: it's nice and folksy to know the name of the man who is about to kill you.

No, the real reason they tell you the driver's name is to prove he's *Spanish*. This is a package holiday and the coach driver is the first and last native whose name you'll hear. The rep tells you what he's called to add a bit of local colour to the holiday, and to reassure you that the foreigners know their place and lovely Melanie's done all the nasty business of actually talking to them.

'I'm sure you're all going to enjoy your time in the wonderful resort of Playa del Inglés, one of the largest resorts in Europe,' adds Melanie, speaking ve-ry slow-ly because, although it's one of the largest resorts in Europe, there isn't much to say about Playa del Inglés, well not that

127

you'd want to hear on your arrival, anyway. Another reason Melanie is speaking slow-ly is because we are, after all, economy-class holidaymakers.

Apparently Playa del Inglés has a beach and a lot of hotels. In the unlikely event that you get bored with all these amenities, then you can go shopping. 'There are a number of shopping centres. Probably the premier shopping centre is the Yumbo Centre – by day. By night, however, I must warn you, it becomes the "alternative centre" of Playa del Inglés.' Melanie treats the word 'alternative' with audible rubber gloves and neat Domestos. 'It becomes full of transvestites and that type of thing,' she adds by way of helpful explanation.

'You may be wondering why I'm telling you this' – well, I am, Melanie, I am – 'but it hasn't been unknown for some lads to get a bit drunk and find themselves in the Yumbo Centre of a night chatting up some beautiful brunette, only to discover too late that the beautiful brunette was actually a bloke!' No! 'So I'm telling you this so that something like this doesn't happen to you!' 'Thank you, Melanie! Thank you! You've saved us from what could easily have been an embarrassing mistake . . .' I enthuse, until my travelling companion kicks me on the shin, hard.

But the clone couple sitting across the aisle from us, and the ones in the seats in front, and the bleached blonde Miss Thing with lace-up leather trousers and scarlet velour blouse sitting opposite Melanie at the front, all look grateful for the warning as well. Melanie was doing her job – protecting her tourists from the experience of difference, of anything out of the ordinary, of the 'alternative'. The package tour is one of the greatest exercises in self-delusion ever developed by capitalism. On the one hand glossy brochures tempt you with promises of 'getting away from it all' to 'exotic' locations, but on the other hand there is the tacit understanding that you will never really get away from it all, and that the tour company will do all it can to make sure that everything is as dully familiar to you as possible.

Gran Canaria itself is a lump of volcanic rock and silt off

the coast of North Africa. Its greatest claim to fame, is that its southern latitude gives fair-skinned northern Europeans an opportunity to cultivate their melanoma during the winter. Gran Canaria is Europe's Hawaii, a white trash playground but with less surfing and more polyester.

Of course, this isn't so surprising when you consider that most of the visitors to this island are German. In particular, Playa del Inglés (the beach of the English?) is overrun with sausage-eaters, and the bars and restaurants along the seafront mostly cater to their homesickness, with German names and beers and that international comfort food – chips. Mind you, it could be worse. It could be Benidorm; if there's one thing scarier than Germans on holiday, it's Brits.

To give it its due, however, Gran Canaria is responsible for fifty years of peace in Europe, keeping the Krauts happy by finally giving them the 'place in the sun' that they were denied by Britain and France. After failing, twice this century, to build an overseas empire of her own, Germany settled instead for the Canaries in the winter and every sun lounger in the Mediterranean in the summer. It isn't exactly a Third Reich, but then the overheads are so much lower.

Nevertheless, whatever the benefits to Europe in political stability, the sight of thousands of overweight Germans wearing too few clothes and too much facial hair is too much to bear. In Gran Canaria this winter, every German male over the age of ten is wearing a T-shirt with the legend 'Levi's 501 – the original'. Do they have Levi's in Germany? Do Levi's make elasticated stonewashed stretch jeans? A visit to Gran Canaria makes it so easy to understand the prejudice of Germans towards their East German brothers and sisters. I mean, the 'Ossis' have a command economy and a dictatorship to blame for their bad taste; West Germans only have themselves and Nena.

So I hope Melanie will understand why I couldn't help myself and flew in the face of her warning and, after experiencing Playa del Inglés by day, headed straight for the forbidden zone of the Yumbo Centre by night. Mainstream Playa del Inglés is the kind of place which makes you welcome anything 'alternative' with open arms and trousers (which is perhaps why all the gays here are such sluts).

The Yumbo Centre is basically a big oval-shaped hole that has been scooped out of the dirt. Into it has been poured a great deal of concrete that looks as if it is the surplus from some bankrupt dam-building project in the Third World. In it there are many duty-free shops, selling perfumes and aftershaves that are about as genuine as Playa del Inglés is Spanish. And lots and lots of bars. All full of Germans. But these ones wear leather, handlebar moustaches and Kouros. Very alternative. I search in vain for some of the transvestites Melanie warned me about. The nearest thing I find is Sean, a barman from the Wirral with a big Bette Lynch heart and even bigger hair. I ask him where I can find some beautiful brunette tranny that I won't guess has got a dick until it's too late. 'Search me, love,' he says. 'I suppose you might try and find one of the drag shows that some of the bars put on. But you don't see too many trannies round these parts and I've been here for six months now.' *Six months*!

I leave Sean's bar and wander down to the next level, past a café full of middle-aged German clones with cardigans over their shoulders, all sitting at little tables and all completely silent, except for the creaking of their necks as their heads swivel in synchronisation, following every piece of edible meat that passes them, exactly like Disney vultures. Soon, at the appointed hour, they'll fly wordlessly back to their bungalows and exchange their cardies for leathers and head for the backrooms of the upper-level bars. I make a mental note not to be there.

I don't find a drag show. But I do find Karl, a thirty-year-old, rather plain-looking shipbuilder from Hamburg, sitting in the corner of a disco bar. He looks so out of place and so glum that he could be one of the poor unfortunate straight men that blunder unwittingly into this place. 'Didn't your rep warn you about the Yumbo Centre?' I ask. 'No,' he says in a thick German accent. 'I am gay. But I hate this place. You are English. I verk in Leeds three months. It vas *scheisse*.' He spits, or something similar. 'This place too.

130

Scheisse.' 'Yes, but why are you here?' I ask him this hoping to find some answer to my own quandary. 'To have a good time,' he replies.

In another bar I start talking to another thirty-year-old who isn't from Germany. He's from Nottingham and he's here with his mother who 'doesn't know about me'. Of course she doesn't. Mothers of unmarried thirty-year-olds who bleach their hair and go on holiday with them have no idea that their son might be 'alternative'. 'I had to wait until she went to bed before I snuck out,' he confesses with an embarrassed expression. (How perfectly Alan Bennett-esque. I can't help imagining the scene: 'Don't you feel tired yet, mam?' 'Oh, no, son, I'm on holiday, and I'm going to stay up all night and keep you company!')

In desperation I visit a gay porn cinema, which turns out to be just a backroom without a bar. A tiny TV monitor flickers in the corner near the ceiling, while several men sit around in an awkward silence. The monitor is showing – yes, you guessed it – German gay porn. German gay porn, in case you're fortunate enough never to have seen any, consists of a series of clones with large noses, sausage-shaped dicks and orange bodies seeing if they can get their moustaches to stick to each other's pubes. All filmed lovingly in long shot next to an ornamental pool with plastic Ionic columns. So tasteful. I leave.

The Good Ship Yumbo Centre and its passengers turn out to be not so alternative after all, and anyway, completely out of gorgeous brunets. So I escape and head back out into Playa del Inglés, and find myself looking at the menu outside a 'young people's café' playing rock. I'm accosted by Sandra from Liverpool, an attractive blonde in her early twenties, chewing fiercely on gum. 'You from England, then?' she asks. 'Yes,' I, answer coldly, used to the hard-sell techniques of the touts Gran Canaria restaurants employ to drum up business. A pause. Sandra chews 'Are you having a good time?' 'Er, yes,' I lie, not looking away from the menu. Another pause. Sandra chews. 'Are you gay then?' she says matter-of-factly. 'Yes,' I reply, unsure whether to be upset that she spotted me so easily, or worried that this is a taunt because I'm not paying her the kind of attention an attractive blonde girl is used to from homesick British male holiday makers.

'You must be very sensitive to these things,' I joke, lamely. 'Oh no, I don't mind gays at all,' she says, chewing even harder on her gum. 'No, I didn't mean it that way. I meant you must be very good at spotting them,' I explain. 'What?' says Sandra. 'Oh, yeah,' she continues, not really understanding me. Another pause. 'Why aren't you in the Yumbo Centre, then?'

April 1995

SHAG NIGHT

'THEY AREN'T USUALLY stiff, but sometimes they do surprise you,' says Penny, and then turns to her partner. Sarah. 'Remember that one at the rugby club which whipped past my nose when I pulled his pants down and slapped you in the face? That was a bit scary, that was.

'But,' Penny confides to me, 'usually they're too frightened or pissed to get them up.'

I'm in the dressing room of a pub in Farnborough with Penny and Sarah, two stagshow strippers, whose job it is to make boys into men before their wedding day by getting their tackle out in front of their pals, whipping them, spraying their genitals with shaving foam and conducting impromptu proctological examinations. But, you'll be pleased to hear, no actual *sex* – no 'normal' intercourse – is permitted; they have to draw the line somewhere.

'We're straight girls,' explains Penny, but only succeeds in confusing me further. She's just come off stage and is sitting on a stool in front of me completely starkers. An 'irrepressible' brunette, she has been in the business for twenty years.

'We're not blue,' she insists, 'unlike some of the girls, who will do anything. We don't let them touch our privates, we don't touch their willies and we *never* do "extras". We use tongs and tie them up, but we never touch them.'

Ah, so that's what 'straight' means. It seems fair enough to me, but some men excited, at the prospect of seeing their best mate in full penetrative action, feel disappointed.

133

'I remember one show where afterwards this geezer came up to me shouting, "I thought you was going to get my mate! You didn't do nothing to 'im." He was so angry that we hadn't done more blue things to his mate that I really thought he was going to hit me.'

Perhaps you should have asked him why he didn't do it to his mate himself, if he was so keen?

'That was a bad evening,' recalls Penny, sensibly ignoring my remark. 'There was a huge fight – a four-ambulance number.'

What are the worst nights?

'Oh, football clubs are usually very bad,' says Penny. 'They're so rude and unhelpful and get very rowdy. So are police clubs – they know they can get away with murder. Rugby clubs are the best. They're usually very polite – they treat you special; somehow I don't think they get to meet very many women.'

The compère's voice introduces Sarah over the PA and she rushes out, blonde hair 'up' and clad in leather bondage kit she's been struggling into during my conversation with Penny. She's quite a 'stunnah' – and this is underlined by the huge cheer that goes up after she leaves the dressing room. After a few moments I follow her.

The pub is full of drunken men with ruddy faces in Armani jeans and loose-fitting shirts. They're cheering wildly, but good-humouredly, clinging to their pints protectively as Sarah picks on individuals, teasing them, getting them to play with her breasts. Watching them, I'm struck by how straight men, even when very drunk, have a tension about their bodies, a determination not to let knees touch, wrists sag, hips swivel. It's as though they want to fool the world that they have fewer joints than other kinds of human beings.

As Sarah struts her stuff, they laugh and show off to one another. She licks a lollipop with an unorthodox part of her anatomy and pops it in the mouth of one of the blokes sitting in the front row, who eagerly sucks it, looking around proudly, and thoughtfully hands it to his mate who also

134

sucks it and passes it on ('woman', it seems, is a flavour that brings men's tongues together).

Penny did a similar routine earlier, but instead of a lollipop she just used her fingers. Confectionery did, however, make an appearance in another part of her act where she made a couple of punters suck some polos for her. She then stuck them over her nipples and made the men kneel either side of her and suck them off.

Sarah 'climaxes' her solo act by spraying shaving foam on her crotch and rubbing a stocky farmhand's grinning face in it. The lads seem to like this especially, cheering loudly.

In the interval, the compère does his homo jokes. 'Are there any poofs here tonight?' he asks. Silence. 'Well, they say one in four blokes are gay,' (where does he get his statistics – OutRage?) 'so if you are out with three mates and none of them are gay, that means you're the poof!' Uneasy laughter.

After a few more jokes in this vein, the 'straight' girls come onstage together and perform a lesbian duo – no simulation. The men are so rapt that they forget to laugh and crack jokes; this is *serious*. They look like stray dogs at a butcher's shop window. If it wasn't for the backing music the only sound would be the swallowing of adam's apples.

Afterwards, Sarah is changing out of her bondage kit backstage and telling me how the lesbian scene is their *pièce de résistance*.

'I tell you, we could be rich if we marketed this number properly. The guys really go wild for it – they can't get enough.'

Why do you suppose that is?

'Well, because we don't simulate it. They can see everything.'

But why are lesbian numbers so popular with straight men?

'I don't know. All I know is that I really enjoy doing it – maybe that's what they pick up on.'

We're joined by Rick, the husband-to-be, and his best mate John, both in their early twenties. They have brought the girls some drinks as their backstage pass (they probably have a bet with their mates that they can screw the act). John, who is tall and dark-haired, has organised this stag night for his pal and smokes those horrid little Panatella cigars that young 'men of the world' smoke in pubs to impress their mates. Fair-haired and pint-sized, Rick is getting married in two weeks. He's wearing an L-plate round his neck and he's very, very drunk.

I ask them what is so exciting about lesbian scenes for straight men. John, the 'dominant' one in this duo, looks at me blankly. He's clearly never thought about this; no one was stupid enough to ask him this question before. At last, he says:

'Well, it's obvious, isn't it?' No. 'Well, it's because, well . . .' he trails off.

'. . . 'Cos it's two birds together,' he says exasperatedly. Yes, that's a working definition of a lesbian act, but what's the appeal?

'I dunno. It's just exciting.'

Rick appears to have thought about it a bit more. A bit too much, actually.

'It's like catching your mum in bed with her best friend,' he offers.

Before I can explore the implications of this particularly rich fantasy scenario, Sarah cuts in:

'But what about two blokes together? Doesn't that turn you on?'

The boys look like they've been goosed.

'Nah, that's not a turn-on at all. It's a total turn-*off*,' asserts Panatella man.

'Why?' Sarah perseveres.

'Because it *is*,' he replies, with impeccable masculine logic.

'But I really enjoy doing the lesbian numbers,' says Sarah. 'I find that a woman knows best what makes you feel good. It must be the same for blokes. A bloke must know best what you like, since he's got the same bits and pieces.'

John now looks like someone who ordered egg and chips and got nouvelle cuisine.

136

'Nah,' he says. 'That's wrong.' Clinching the argument with classic straight-boy reasoning, he adds, 'If you're a bloke you like shagging birds and they like being shagged, so it stands to reason that a woman's going to know best what you like and a man's going to know what a woman likes.'

'But I'm a woman,' counters Penny, 'and I have a boyfriend, but I enjoy sex with women more. I don't understand why straight men don't try it out with one another, I bet they'd really be surprised how much they enjoy it.'

'Yeah,' says little Rick, apropos of nothing and everything. 'I went home with a girl and her boyfriend a while ago. But, of course, I said to him, "If you fucking touch me, I'll fucking kill you".' Of course.

The boys, who initially thought I was the strippers' 'minder' and were buying me drinks all night, now know that I'm a journalist and want to know who I am writing for. I tell them. They ask what kind of magazine it is. I tell them. A pause. Both of them are a little thrown, but try to look cool. John is better at this than Rick, who can't stop himself asking. 'What, are you gay yourself?' I toy momentarily with refusing the dreadful little 'g' word, but then think better of introducing more queer theory to the discussion than the stripper Sarah has already done, and answer in the affirmative. Rick's eyes widen.

'But why is it, then,' he asks, with a burning curiosity which betrays years of frustration, 'that whenever you see gay men on telly they always have handlebar moustaches and leather caps?' Before I can tell him that he's a little confused (he's talking about lesbians not gay men), John, who is the protector in their relationship, realises the conversation is getting out of control and intervenes:

'I hope you don't think this is a normal stag night, 'cos this is seriously twisted,' he half-jokes. Before I can ask what is 'normal' about stag nights, John is busy trying to persuade the girls to give him their numbers so that he can call them direct, instead of going through their agent, to arrange a 'private show' for him and Rick. But I understand. After all, it's Rick's stag night and the stripper they want to shag is trying to persuade them to shag each other and a gay journalist is asking them why they like watching lesbians. I suspect that working out my relationship to Sarah is also doing their heads in. Before they hurriedly leave the dressing room, Rick turns to Sarah, gestures towards me, and asks: 'So, do you like the fact that he's a challenge, or what?'

Now it's Rick's big moment. On stage he is stripped bare by Sarah and Penny. They slap his face with their breasts, lower their crotches on to his face repeatedly, giving new and graphic meaning to the expression 'pussy-whipped'; shave his pubes, wank his willy with kitchen tongs and then tie it up with cord and lead him around the room by it (in symbolic imitation of married life).

Everyone laughs and has a good time, especially Rick, who is such a good sport. Then Sarah makes him bend over, bum to the audience, while Penny draws a smiley face on his buttocks. She lights a cigarette and puts it where the sun doesn't shine. Everyone laughs. Panatella man laughs. Rick laughs. His dad, standing at the back with a *'that's* my boy' beam on his face, laughs. Sarah removes the fag and sprays shaving foam in his bumcrack; Penny puts on an industrial rubber glove and, with a theatrical flourish, cruelly jabs a finger up Rick's poor abused ringpiece. Rick laughs even more than when he had a fag up his arse (well, what else can you do?).

Unfortunately for Rick, sitting as I am at the side of the stage, I'm the only person he can see when he looks up, laughing, to check that everyone else is laughing. Our eyes lock. This soon-to-be-married lad, this initiate into heterosexual, monogamous, holy wedlock who is losing his bumcherry in front of his mates, happens to catch the eye of the one admitted homo in the room. For a ghastly moment which seems to last an age, the smiles freeze and our laughter turns hollow. Self-confessed perverts, you see, tend to take the fun out of straight perversion.

August 1995

II

... I am right, for it is demonstrably true that desire can take as many shapes as there are containers. Yet what one pours into those containers is always the same inchoate human passion, entirely lacking in definition until what holds it shapes it. So let us break the world's pots, and allow the stuff of desire to flow and intermingle in one great viscous sea ...

Myra Breckinridge in *Myra Breckinridge* by Gore Vidal

Hollywood

WHEN DID YOU LAST SEE YOUR FATHER?

'I LOVE YOU, Dad.' 'I love you too, son.' Clichéd as it sounds to British ears, this dialogue (from *My Life*, released last week) is indicative of a new trend in Hollywood which quietly threatens to displace boy-meets-girl romance as the mainstay of the movies – father-meets-son romance.

That the Nineties are proving to be a decade of a 'crisis of masculinity' is now a commonplace. But, at the cinema, this idea is translated into the homely image of a crisis of fatherhood as what it means to be a man is examined through the prism of the father–son relationship.

Lambasted only last year by Michael Medved for single-handedly bringing about the ruin of the nuclear family, Hollywood appears to have taken up the 'Families Need Fathers' banner with zeal: even street-gang films like *South Central, Menace 2 Society* and *Boyz N The Hood* (1991) have all laid the blame for black gang violence at the feet of single mothers and absent fathers.

The father who is missing in all these 'paternity' films is not, as one might expect, the disciplinarian, but the father who knows how to love. In *South Central* the ex-con is saved from a wasted life by his love for his son. In *American Heart* another ex-con, Jack Kelson (Jeff Bridges), repeats to his son Nick the line 'You keep me straight and I'll keep you straight' like a mantra, but ultimately fails because he cannot express his love.

In *A Bronx Tale*, the young Calogero is saved from death

143

with his delinquent pals by a guardian angel gangster (Chazz Palminteri), who is able to show love in a way Calogero's hard-working father (Robert De Niro) cannot. And in *In the Name of the Father*, the failure of Giuseppe Conlon (Pete Postlethwaite) to express his love for his son Gerry is implicitly blamed for the delinquency which makes him an easy target for a frame-up.

This plea for a father who is not afraid of appearing weak by showing love for his son appears to be an inversion of the one which was offered during the decade which invented 'the delinquent' – the 1950s. In *Rebel without a Cause* (1955), 'mixed-up' Jim Stark (James Dean) was driven to hanging out with trouble-making kids by his revulsion for a weak father who doted on him.

But the very obstacles that make affectionate relations between fathers and sons so difficult in real life also make the representation of the relationship on screen a prickly and often unconvincing affair. And, in the mechanisms employed to overcome this, something is revealed about how far off the notion of a loving paternity still appears.

In the Name of the Father was fortunate inasmuch as the unusual and extreme circumstances of the plot, incarceration, forced father and son together: they shared a cell in the film (inaccurately). Other films have to be more wily. A favourite ruse is to employ 'fathers' who are not fathers, as in *A Perfect World, Man without a Face* and *A Bronx Tale*, or, as in *American Heart*, a father who has not seen his son since he was a baby.

Another strategy, which has become increasingly popular with films aimed at younger, media-literate audiences, is to exploit the very 'unreality' of the film medium. So action films like *Sidekick* (1992) and *Last Action Hero* (1993) self-consciously play the love a young boy has for his idealised screen hero against the failure/absence of the real father, and the impossibility/unreality of that love.

In *Last Action Hero* the boy's father is dead; in *Sidekick* his father is alive but a fat, nerdy computer programmer. In both films the young boy gets to meet his dream hero – but only long enough for the boy to learn how to be a man himself and realise that the superhero functions best as super-ego. In *Last Action Hero* the boy is gradually disappointed by Jack Slater/Arnold Schwarzenegger's lack of phallic ability in the real world. The message is not so much that 'guns are really dangerous', but that the young boy–older man partnership is 'really' dangerous. For no sooner is affection sought outside the home than the problem of the ambiguous sexuality of the substitute father raises its ugly head.

In *A Perfect World*, set in 1963, the sexual anxieties are initially very pronounced, because the 'father–son' romance here is fostered by an escaped convict, Butch Haynes (Kevin Costner), who kidnaps the boy, Phillip. These anxieties are raised right at the beginning only to be repudiated. A fellow escapee tries to molest Phillip and is summarily executed by Haynes. A little later the boy is embarrassed to change in front of Haynes. Haynes asks, 'Are you afraid I'll see your pecker?' Phillip nods and explains shamefacedly, 'It's puny.' Haynes gets Phillip to show him and pronounces it just the right size for a boy his age. It is the scene that transforms Haynes from potential perverter to masculine mentor.

Man without a Face, also set in the early Sixties, makes a great show of anatomising the origins of the corruption which blights relations between men and boys. Nick, a fatherless eleven-year-old boy suffocated by his feminist mother and sisters, turns for instruction to the 'wild man' of the town, the outsider McCleod (Mel Gibson), one side of whose face is hideously deformed. McCleod has a dark past, signalled by his scars: his face was burnt in a car crash that killed his passenger, a young pupil, cost him his career as a teacher and prompted accusations of sexual shenanigans with the boy. When it emerges that he is spending time with Nick, McCleod is hauled up before a star chamber of 'experts'. The psychiatrist (who is rather faggy, of course) asks 'Were you as *fond* of Nick as you were of Patrick [the

145

dead pupil]?' 'More, probably,' McCleod answers challeng-ingly and goes on to harangue the panel for their seedy minds.

What is on trial here, and in all these films to a greater or lesser extent, is the audience's own anxieties about close relationships between men and boys. McCleod refuses to allow all man–boy relationships to be judged guilty until proved innocent. But for all that, *Man without a Face* cops out: to spare the boy the 'probings' of a criminal investiga-tion McCleod agrees to forgo the opportunity to clear his name and accepts an injunction never to see the boy again – a metaphorical death. Like the ending of *Dead Poets Society* (1989) we are invited to feel anger at the cruel injustices which separate boys from their loved mentors, but also take secret comfort in the fact of it.

Loss and mourning are right at the heart of these films – which is why so many produce a corpse instead of a father unafraid to love (Bridges in *American Heart*, Palminteri in *A Bronx Tale*, Postlethwaite in *In the Name of the Father*, Costner in *A Perfect World*). They are an attempt to locate the source of the 'original sin' which makes the love they seek so elusive. Hence the fondness for the past, particularly the early 1960s, when America is deemed to have lost its innocence with the murder of its loving father, Jack Kennedy. *A Perfect World* even contrives to have Costner shot by an FBI agent on the eve of the assassination.

Death is yet again employed to make the expression of paternal love possible at the very moment that it becomes impossible in *My Life*. The most recent of the father–son romances turns out to be a wry comment on Hollywood's own role in the contemporary 'crisis of masculinity'. It is through the third party of his *camera*, videoing his life, that the dying Bob Jones (Michael Keaton) manages to make explicit his love for his unborn son, and through it learn to forgive his own father for his inability to show his love for him.

HUMAN, ALL TOO HUMAN

'THIS GAY RIGHTS plank does not ask for special privileges. It does not ask anyone to like us. What it does ask is that the Democratic Party recognise that we, the gay people of this country, are also human.' These words, spoken by San Francisco gay activist Bill Kraus at the 1980 Democratic Convention, when AIDS was a 'gay-related cancer' and only worth a couple of column inches, provoke a smattering of half-polite applause immediately followed by the headline portent: 'Reagan wins'.

This modest plea is clearly also intended to be taken as a 'plank' of *And the Band Played On*, particularly as it emanates from the mouth of Sir Ian McKellen who plays Kraus in the American HBO film of Randy Shilts' 'faction' bestseller about the early days of the epidemic and the conspiracy of indifference which turned it into the disaster we know today. McKellen's plea echoes the aim of *Philadelphia*, in which Tom Hanks' gay character is effectively put on trial before middle America to prove himself worthy of compassion and human rights. To both its credit and its debit *And the Band Played On*'s modesty proves false.

In pursuing a political rather than just a personal account of the AIDS catastrophe, *And the Band Played On* is more ambitious than *Philadelphia* and braver – it is not just one law firm that is indicted, America's institutions are in the dock. But it is also a vastly inferior film which points up just how smart and well-conceived *Philadelphia*'s cautiousness

147

was – despite the brick-bats hurled at it by gay critics angered by the muted nature of the Hanks/Antonio Banderas relationship next to the hetero lovefest of Washington and his wife. *And the Band Played On*'s overweening if earnest desire to make sense of the virus provokes a hubris which echoes that experienced by medical science.

The Band tries to negotiate what is unfamiliar territory for most American audiences – gays, retroviruses, politics – with an all-American format: a block-busting, star-spangled, detective story in mini-series style (the film was originally commissioned by HBO and is produced by Aaron '*Dynasty*' Spelling). So the virus becomes serial killer and Don Francis of the Atlanta-based Centre for Disease Control (Matthew Modine) doggedly tracks down the culprit, discovering on the way that people in high places are none too keen to see him solve the case.

The effect is rather preposterous, and only accentuated by constant flitting between cities and countries and an overly expository dialogue. One scene epitomises the trap-door which opens on the attempt to turn the Byzantine story of AIDS into a 130-minute gumshoe tale. Modine, stumped for a lead, sees his buddy playing Pacman. He frowns and then exclaims, with hilarious predictability, 'Of *course*! Something's gobbling up the white blood cells!'

The worthy intervention of names such as Richard Gere, Lily Tomlin and Phil Collins fails to rescue the film. *Au contraire*, their brief cameos make for a kind of Screen Actors' Guild Band Aid, in a film trying to tell us 'we are the world'. When Steve Martin makes an appearance I found myself waiting for him to puncture the pompous seriousness with a mad laugh. Only Alan Alda's potrayal of Dr Robert Gallo as a sleazy bully adds gravitas.

Perhaps this is why the most successful moment of the film is the most 'insane'. A CDC man trying to establish, through contact tracing, a sexual vector for the disease, interviews a dying young man. The lesion-covered patient paces around with his drip trailing behind him ranting about the number six, 'the sign of the Beast'. Shown a list of men and asked which of them he had sex with he sees only the number six in their telephone numbers or the date he met them. Madness, yes, but nevertheless an attempt to *explain* his predicament.

The look of numb awe and terror on the CDC man's face as he witnesses this echoes that of Denzel Washington watching a dying Tom Hanks translate with demented passion his favourite opera aria in the middle of a legal briefing. In both films this is the moment which comes closest to conveying the free-fall horror and confusion of the epidemic. In the midst of the serious can-do American business of investigation and litigation, the most 'meaning-ful' moment turns out to be an absence of meaning.

Of course, the moment is clawed back and presents instead the victory, of a sort, of heroic humanity. Not only are gay people at the end of both films vindicated as fully human but, at no extra cost, the human race's own humanity is reaffirmed. For all the callousness of institu-tions, employers, blood banks, *people* pull through.

And here is, paradoxically, the reason why AIDS films are generally so unsatisfactory and so mixed in their reception. AIDS is such a fragmented and fragmenting experience that no single narrative can begin to do it justice – least of all that offered by humanism. There are as many senses to it as there are deaths, and equally as many non-senses. This is some-thing most AIDS films seem unable to face, wearing instead their exegesis on their sleeves in an attempt to ward off uncertainty. Cyril Collard's *Savage Nights* (1993) was an exception, more nihilist than humanist, and the better for it – and was, inevitably, attacked for its 'irresponsibility'.

If in the latter part of the twentieth century we look to cinema to do our 'dream work' for us, calming the anxieties and stimuli of the day, it fails hopelessly when it comes to what is one of the greatest fears of our age. This is a particularly bitter irony for homosexuals. Excluded as they are from the dominant meanings of family and reproduc-tion, they have long looked to cinema as an alternative source of value and narrative in their lives – this in spite of its historical inability to represent them as anything other than

149

monsters. Now it only succeeds in portraying them as human and their lives as valuable at the very moment it fails in its desperate attempt to make some kind of sense of their deaths.

Guardian, 7 April 1994

FINISHING STRAIGHT

DON'T LOOK NOW, but upfront homo-eroticism seems to have arrived at the multiplex. Fancy a romp in the Australian outback with a troupe of drag queens? Try *Priscilla, Queen of the Desert*. Or perhaps an exploration of the ambiguous boundaries of human sexuality, a *Jules et Jim* for the Nineties? Try *Threesome*. Prefer your queer cinema with a bigger budget and bigger names? You won't have to wait long because coming soon is *Interview with a Vampire* starring Tom Cruise and Brad Pitt heavy necking.

Just what is going on at the movies? Only a few months ago, if you wanted to see same-sex desire that was a text rather than a buddy-movie type subtext in a mainstream film you would have had to make do with the spayed, no-touching-please portrayal of the Hanks–Banderas relationship in *Philadelphia*. After the commercial success of the New Queer Cinema and the popularity of 'lesbian chic' and *Go Fish*, has Hollywood decided that the public is ready for what was always deemed unshowable in mainstream movies: overt sexual passion between men?

Well, no. Not yet. What *is* playing at the multiplex right now is not upfront homo-eroticism but downright dissimulation, the product of a dizzying sleight of hand. The promise of queerness is used to titillate and fascinate but – don't worry – actually turns out to be *heterosexual*.

Threesome, starring Stephen Baldwin, Josh Charles and Lara Flynn Boyle, about the triangle between two male

151

college room-mates and a girl, is a classic of queer dissimulation. The film begins with a voiceover by Charles. According to his dictionary 'deviant' is 'one who strays from the path'. The story which follows, he tells us, is about how 'for a while all three of us were deviants'.

In fact, the film delivers nothing of the sort. The catch-line on the posters may be 'One girl, two guys, three possibilities', but there are only ever two: Baldwin and Boyle, or Charles and Boyle. The much-hyped third possibility is never seriously on the cards. Even the long-awaited 'threesome', when it comes (in tasteful soft focus), is an embarrassing repudiation of the threat that Charles poses to Baldwin's bubble-butt – Ms Boyle is sandwiched between them like a high-voltage insulator. When 'homo' contact is finally made, its purpose is to defuse. While kissing Boyle, Charles gingerly reaches over and briefly touches Baldwin's derrière. Baldwin takes Charles' hand and replaces it on his hindquarters (to fade out). So Baldwin graciously allows his fag buddy to touch his butt while he balls Boyle – the only 'homo' contact in the whole film is not about sexual ambiguity, or even sex, but about *tolerance*.

The irony of *Threesome* is that, for all its younger generation hipness and self-confidence, it is *Philadelphia* all over again: a film which is a plea for the acceptance of homosexuals but which cannot bring itself to show homosexuality. But *Threesome* cannot even be honest about its intentions. The only real deviance is when Charles, struggling against his homosexuality, sleeps with Boyle; here we are being didactically instructed that hetrosex is against *his* nature.

Moving hastily out of *Threesome* into the adjoining theatre where *Priscilla* is showing, we experience more disappointment. *Priscilla* is a curious example of a film which is both very 'gay' and very straight. Raucous drag queens, fierce frocks, blue language, and a hilarious collision of Sydney Culture with Outback Nature – but no homo-desire, thank you very much. Only Terence Stamp's sour and feisty transsexual Bernadette (i.e. a 'woman') is allowed a hint of a sex life. She starts a romance with a sheep farmer abandoned by his ferocious Bangkok bar girl wife (and here, not for the first time, *Priscilla* comes perilously close to the misogynist trap of Neil Jordan's *The Crying Game*, arguing that men can make better women than women).

The nearest *Priscilla* comes to same-sex contact is when Felicia, alias Guy Pearce of *Neighbours* fame, is nearly raped by a queerbasher; but the horror of the moment is not just in its violence but the notion of (queer) sex raising its head at all. Even Pearce's never-off-the-screen pumped body is a disavowal of homo-eroticism – no drag queen would virilise his body like this. Like his hammy queening, it serves to remind that he is dissimulating – it's really nice Guy Pearce, the straight surfer dude out of *Neighbours*. And the only tender scene between males in the film is between father and son. That the loving father is one of the drag queens is rather adventurous, but the fact remains that homo-desire in this film is sublimated into outrageous frocks and an ache for acceptance by heterosexuals.

So should we wait with baited breath for Neil Jordan's much heralded *Interview with a Vampire*, a film featuring some of Hollywood's most desirable young men chewing each other's necks? Surely a film with Tom Cruise as Lestat, Brad Pitt as his 'beautiful male companion' Louis, and Antonio Banderas as the older vampire with an interest in young Pitt, produced by America's first 'out' gay media mogul, David Geffen will 'come clean' about its homo-eroticism?

The signals are at best mixed – which in itself suggests that we may be in for more queer dissimulation. Rumours abound that when all-American hero Cruise accepted the part of Lestat he insisted that all the 'gay stuff' be excised from the script. However, Anne Rice, author of the original and avowedly homo-erotic novel, who loudly complained when the wholesome Cruise was cast, recently made an astonishing public recantation after viewing an early print, in which she stated that she was 'honoured and stunned to discover how faithful this film was to the spirit, the content, and the ambience of the novel'.

Nevertheless, Jordan himself recently complained to *Vanity Fair*, 'the homo-erotic stuff *is* what everyone talks about, isn't it? But these guys are beyond sex. Their lust is for blood.' *Of course*, – after all, a lust for blood is so much easier to portray, so much more *natural*, than lust between men. Cruise, apparently, has found his own way of sidestepping the issue. 'Lestat certainly loves Louis,' he admitted recently. 'He wants a companion ... But, also, Lestat created this creature that Louis has become, so he is very *fatherly* about it.' In other words: it may look queer, but it's OK – this is really just heterosexuality again.

CLEAN-CUT CRUISER

'THE LAST GUY you ever woulda guessed' was the general response to the discovery that Rock Hudson was gay. One echoed by the reaction to the idea of Tom Cruise – the all-American boy with the million-dollar smile, Mr Top Gun, Mr Born on the Fourth of July – as a bitch-queen with a craving for fit young men's necks.

When Cruise was cast in the role of the vampire Lestat in Neil Jordan's interpretation of Anne Rice's openly homo-erotic novel *Interview with a Vampire* last year, the world was equally divided between those who gasped and those who laughed.

But when *Vampire* opened in the US last month, Cruise surprised everyone again with his performance, gaining plaudits and congratulations on his 'versatility' and 'cour-age' in taking on such a 'challenging' role.

And certainly Cruise has been transformed: he's shed those muscles, bleached his hair and let it grow. The sturdy American boy has been replaced by unnatural androgyne. But this is not so much a departure for Cruise as a queer revelation – a revelation about the sexually ambiguous nature of his screen appeal in even his most wholesome-looking screen appearances.

Right from the start, Cruise's body was at the centre of his success as a Hollywood boy (although he is thirty-two he still plays boys). He was one of the original 'brat-packers', the moody, sexy young toughs of the early eighties whose greatest claim to fame – whose *only* claim to fame – was stripping off at the drop of a clapper-board. In his first major film, *Taps* (1981), he played a 'troubled' cadet at a military academy obsessed with military regalia, working out and showering.

But it was *Risky Business* (1983), in which he played air guitar bouncing around in his underwear on his parents' sofa and giving good ass that his career really began to take off. It is worthy of note that the producer for this movie was David Geffen, also producer on *Vampire*, and also the man responsible for bringing together Marky Mark and Calvin Klein and thus the sexploitation of another American boy in his prime and in his underwear.

The after-burners kicked in, sending his career ballistic, with his performance as Maverick, the gung-ho fighter ace in the definitive eighties movie: *Top Gun* (1986). Cruise perfectly and literally embodied the new individualism and male narcissism of that decade, while the military setting, patriotic tone, and Reaganite politics helped to pass off the startling revolution in the way men's bodies were being displayed as something reassuringly 'traditional'.

Maverick, the Reaganite youth role model, tells us repeatedly that 'I'm used to going out and getting what I want'. But clearly what he wants is Val Kilmer, who plays the hot-stuff pilot Iceman; Next to the adrenalin-rich, ecstatic airborne frolics of Iceman and Maverick, the ground-based, soft-focus antics of Kelly McGillis and Maverick look rather unconvincing.

In another military role, *Born on the Fourth of July* (1989), Cruise plays Ron Kovic, a corn-fed mid-Western boy who loves his mom and prefers baseball and wrestling to girls. The Vietnam war costs him his fine body, castrating and crippling him, but he finds love nevertheless (after leaving Mom) in the form of anonymous black men. It is a black man who saves his life when he is wounded in Vietnam: it is a black male nurse giving him an enema who first tells him the truth about the Vietnam war ('You can shove it up your ass!'); it is a black man who rescues him

156

when he topples out of his wheelchair during a police charge at a demonstration. In *Fourth of July*, Cruise brings together the old and the new American homo-erotic tradition, the cinematic and the literary: he is Huck Finn saved by his devoted 'Nigger Jim'.

In *A Few Good Men* (1992) Cruise dons the military drag yet again, this time as an immature Navy lawyer who can't think without his baseball bat pacifier. He becomes a man by facing down the castrating bully, Marine Colonel Jessep (Jack Nicholson). He is encouraged to take on the role of ethical Oedipus by his superior officer, played by Demi Moore. But unlike McGillis in *Top Gun* (also Cruise's superior), Moore is not an example of 'the feminine' which exists simply to be conquered; there is no triumphal sex scene. When Nicholson leers to Cruise in front of Moore: 'You know, you just haven't lived until you've received a blow-job from a superior officer,' the legacy of *Top Gun* crashes and burns. Cruise is a new type of man; Nicholson the old, discredited variety.

Which is perhaps why on the rare occasion Cruise has appeared in films heavily based around heterosexual romance, such as *Far and Away* (1993), his performance is so unconvincing. Nevertheless, even in this nineteenth-century period piece, in which he plays a never say-die-Irish-American immigrant and boxer Cruise is still coded sexually passive. It is Nicole Kidman (his real-life wife) who makes all the moves and it is *his* body which provides the voyeuristic thrills. While he is asleep Kidman steals not one but two giggly looks under the sheets at his wedding tackle; later when he is dressing she checks out his buns.

Likewise, in *The Firm* (1993) the hottest sex scene is where Cruise is seduced and rendered helpless by a prostitute who goes down on him.

The masculine/feminine, active/passive troubling conundrum of Cruise's body is not lost on the actor himself and finds expression in curious vanities. The shot of his bum was cut from *Far and Away* on his insistence, reportedly because he was unhappy with how it looked. His lack of height troubles him, threatening to reveal his lack of masculine presence; Kelly McGillis complained of a bad back for weeks after *Top Gun*: she had to stoop to rest her head on his 'manly' shoulder. In *Vampire* he is reputed to have worn built-up shoes because he was worried about being over-shadowed by Brad Pitt.

The real transformation for Cruise in *Interview* is not the homo-eroticism, nor the ambiguous messages of his body and his screen presence, but his 'coming of age'. *Vampire* is the first film in which he plays a man. In an ironic twist on *The Color of Money* (1986), Cruise is Paul Newman to Brad Pitt's Tom Cruise, in a classic man-boy 'Greek' pedagogic relationship. Or perhaps the reference is more *All About Eve*. Today's trade, as nasty old pre-liberation queens used to say, is tomorrow's competition.

Guardian, 7 December 1994

Television

THE STRAIGHT MEN OF COMEDY?

RECENTLY SOME US fundamentalist ministers decided to 'out' two much-loved characters from the children's TV show *Sesame Street*. 'Bert and Ernie are quite obviously gay lovers,' they declared. 'They cook and tend plants together and even share a bedroom.' By way of clinching the argument they added. 'Sometimes they even do a bit of sewing.'

It must have come as something of a surprise to the millions of parents who consider *Sesame Street* an entertaining and innocent form of education for their kids, to discover that it was promoting homosexuality all along. Needless to say, Children's Television Workshop, the makers of *Sesame Street*, were unhappy with this interpretation of the private life of two of their most popular stars and refuted their charge as 'ridiculous'. Later they issued a terse statement which simply stated: 'Bert and Ernie do not portray a gay couple and there are no plans for them to do so in the future.'

Of course, things are no longer that simple. In this media-literate age almost everyone prides themselves on their ability to 'read' the 'real' meaning of films and TV shows – one always opposite to the official one. As evidence of this, even square old Bible-bashers are having a go – and poor old *Sesame Street* is feeling the effect of their 'reading'. Now that the allegations about the 'true' nature of Bert and Ernie's relationship have been aired, who can watch Bert and Ernie

161

curling up in their matching, side-by-side beds underneath a portrait photo of them arm in arm in quite the same way?

Actually this contretemps over the sleeping habits of male comedy duos is nothing new. There have been outings/readings before – from the other side of the political fence. The gay film critic Vito Russo, in his book, *The Celluloid Closet*, claimed that the classic male comedy duo Laurel and Hardy were gay, pointing out that in films such as *Their First Mistake*, in which Ollie's wife sues him for divorce, naming Stan as 'the other woman', they exemplified the 'perfect sissy–buddy relationship, which had a sweet and very real loving dimension'. He cites the French critic André S. Labarthe's observation that the classic silent short, *Liberty* – in which the fat man and the thin man escape from prison only to hurriedly pull on each other's pants by mistake and spend the rest of the film trying to swap trousers in alleyways, the back of taxis and even a building site always interrupted by shocked passers-by – as offering 'to anyone who can *read* the unequivocal sign of unnatural love.' [My italics.]

Then, like now, many reacted indignantly to the suggestion that there could be anything filthy or 'unnatural' in the relationship of two men who were taken to be the epitome of purity. 'There is something rather absurd about discussing this seriously at all,' harrumphed the critic Charles Barr in his book, *Laurel and Hardy*, insisting that because the pair had 'the minds of nursery children' it was only 'natural' that they should 'share a bed like nursery children'. In other words, the fact that our heroes shared a bed was taken as the very sign of innocence itself.

Actually, as this piece of circuitous reasoning shows, the shared bed, *de rigueur* for Laurel and Hardy and the male comedy duos that followed them, from Jerry Lewis and Dean Martin to Morecambe and Wise, was the contradiction at the heart of the genre, managing somehow to accommodate the audience's curious ambivalence towards non-heterosexuality – both hungering for it and loathing it.

162

The shared bed signified both the innocence of the relationship – oh, look, they sleep together, how sweet! just like brothers! – but also and at the same time (but held under the 'innocence' idea) its *queerness*. If this wasn't the case; if, as Barr *et al* argue, their intimacy was only 'innocence', where would the gags come from? After all, we laugh at what we fear.

Even in Laurel and Hardy's day the audience knew well enough what two men in a bed signified. And this is precisely why the shared bed was so popular, because through comedy, the audience could enjoy in a 'carnivalesque' fashion 'queer pleasures', witnessing a touching relationship between two men that would otherwise be branded perverse. Jerry Lewis' and Dean Martin's relationship had all the hallmarks of institutional homosexuality, with Jerry as the defenceless, immature ever-so-slightly effeminate young 'punk' seeking the 'protection' of his older, wiser, bigger room-mate Dean (this in the Fifties, when much of America was familiar with military service and its 'situational' homosexuality). Those British suburban family favourites Morecambe and Wise exhibited more Sixties signifiers of homosexuality than a Soho drinking club; in addition to sharing the same bed they were cardigan-wearing bachelors with a passion for Shirley Bassey and musicals who lived in a spotless interior-decorated home (without even a housekeeper or maid to save their masculine reputation); Ernie was a vain wig-wearing playwright; Eric was obsessed with Ern's 'short fat hairy legs'; one of their most loved sketches has them in dressing-gowns making breakfast together.

The 'ticklishness' and the discomfort that these deliberately queer images produce is always released in laughter – 'How *absurd* it all is, thank God', the audience says by laughing (and how absurd of me to think that there was anything funny *peculiar* about this, it half says to itself, wiping the tears from its eyes).

But no longer. Now that homosexuality is so much more visible, and thus much more in the front rather than the back of people's minds, this disavowal is no longer enough. As

163

David Ashby, the Conservative MP who shared a bed on a holiday with his rugby pal discovered, 'doubling up' with another man can no longer be presented as the sign of innocence itself – it *only* connotes queerness. This is partly why it is no longer gay critics who 'out' comedy couples – but instead fundamentalist ministers who once upon a time would have been goggle-eyed at the *sick* notion that Jerry might be rubbing more than Dean's back at the end of the day or that Stan might suck more than his thumb in bed. Bert and Ernie don't even share the same bed, just the same bedroom. But such is the paranoia of this homo-obsessed age that just two men living together – even on a children's TV show – is taken by many as an irrefutable sign of deviance.

The flip side of the visibility of homosexuality is that relations between men are now so suspect, so scrutinised, so policed that the instant men betray any intimacy or 'unmanliness' they are instantly labelled gay and 'other'.

This is why contemporary heirs of Laurel and Hardy, such as Rik Mayall and Adrian Edmondson in *Bottom*, may live together and clearly be all that each other has in the world, may fail to show any real interest in women beyond impressing one another, but are nevertheless sentenced by modern sensitivities to sleep in separate rooms. Nor are they allowed any of the tender moments that Ollie and Stan enjoyed in between the nose-twisting and the foot-stamping; instead the spiteful spats are cranked up to full-blown sado-masochistic rituals; their violence is emphasised far more their 'love'. (Nevertheless Rik and Adrian remain together and their tainted, twisted love survives an equally tainted twisted world.)

Others are allowed to share bedrooms, but only if they make a 'knowing' display for the audience, which signals 'I know you know I know what this means'; 'irony' replaces 'innocence' and there is no longer any subtext, everything is 'read' for you in a deliberately vulgar fashion. This is exemplified in *Terry and Julian*, in which one very straight and one very gay man (Julian Clary) are made to share a

164

single- bedroomed flat. The very first episode featured a gag based around the (mistaken) idea that Julian was masturbating under the covers while Terry looks on aghast. *Terry and Julian* also illustrates the strange contradiction of modern attitudes towards queerness, that while homosexuality has become more difficult to disavow as it has become more public, it has also become less scary – and therefore less funny. Hence *excess* is required from Julian Clary, forcing him to camp it up with *single* entendres about warm hands on his entrance, to the point where he threatens to vanish in a puff of pink, fragranced, ironic smoke.

Beavis and Butt-Head also act out a knowing, playful irony, this time where the joke is at the expense of a whole *genus* of American males, represented by two teenage MTV-addicted Midwestern metal-heads who share a sofa instead of a bed (although they use it as one) and who are forever trying to assert their heterosexuality by miming sexual excitement whenever 'babes' appear and expressing contempt for 'wussies'; but so hysterically – psychiatrically and comedically – that it is always self-defeating. They are obvious virgins (as far as the female sex is concerned, although there is a faint suspicion that they may have indulged in 'circle-jerks' and 'willy-measuring' in the past) and even when they try to assert their heterosexuality vicariously when watching pop videos they fail abysmally, often mistaking male performers for female ones. Their favourite topic of conversation is butts – each other's, about which they are, *naturellement*, inordinately sensitive. Like the characters in *Bottom* (also, as the name suggests, obsessed with the masculine *arse*) they are spectacularly cruel to one another and forever talking about 'chicks' but in fact only have each other (the only person we ever see generate a truly loving response from them is a heavily muscled young sadist who locks them in his boot and drives over rough ground). While the profile of this group of American teen males is scathingly accurate, their 'homosexuality' is part of their humiliation and punishment for being so crap at being men, which contrasts unfavourably with the

165

usual male comedy duo scenario in which homosexuality is offered as a kind of *reward* for being so unmanly.

Knowing irony mixed with surrealism, however, makes it possible to stick closer to the original queer romance formula. Reeves and Mortimer recently performed an Xmas show which included a shared bed moment. The shared bed had nearly visible quote marks around it and was explicitly 'knowing' in both its references (Morecambe and Wise) and its meaning (homosexuality). Nevertheless what is most interesting about Reeves and Mortimer is the way that their act is based upon what is essentially a romance between them, which is, beneath the noisy brashness, quite clearly of the tender variety which has all but disappeared. And like some of the great comedy homo romances, theirs is also a rather wistfully infantile affair, with their boy–boy love-in conducted in an imaginary world with an imaginary language which excludes everyone else (but of course, their appeal is based on the fact that everyone wants to join them in that snug little world). Just as important as the surrealism here is the alibi of laddishness, nicely reinforced by authentic North-East accents.

Those seafront perennials Cannon and Ball are also able to get away with presenting a boyish tenderness, largely because they are aimed at an audience that is both working class and elderly – homosexuality is something that afflicts other classes, and other generations. In one of their most requested 'serious' routines, Cannon serenades Ball with 'You are the Wind Beneath My Wings', who falls asleep and Cannon carries him offstage 'to bed'. The audience adore this because it allows them to enjoy the signs of queer love but at the same time deny its existence. But even Cannon and Ball acknowledge that times have changed – and reinforce the distinction between their 'pure' masculine love and the 'travesty' of it contained in homosexuality by the jokes about 'pooves' and that dreary, meticulously bad impersonation of effeminacy as much a part of working-class culture as saveloy and pickled onions, which is designed both to ridicule homosexuality and point up how unable a real man is to perform it even when he tries.

But by far the greatest, most dangerous, most *passionate* queer comedy lovers ever to hit the screen are Ren and Stimpy, whose love affair apparently breaks all the rules. Not only do they share a bed but they regularly demonstrate their intense affection for each other: Stimpy regularly showers Ren with sloppy, big-lipped kisses, and in the very first episode Ren pines for an absent Stimpy, weeping inconsolably and making a fetish out of his fur balls. That Ren is a chihuahua and Stimpy is a cat should defuse the threat somewhat, but in director John Kricfalusi's hands this becomes itself something queer, connoting other transgressions: miscegnation? bestiality? Their cartoon antics are even 'zanier' than Reeves and Mortimer but again this hardly comes across as a strategy to make them safe for the consumption of children (the target audience) but rather something that makes them even more disturbing. This is also the case with the stunning violence which outdoes *Bottom* and *Beavis and Butt-Head* in its sheer sadism but is itself something *perverse* rather than a distraction from perversion (as one particularly fabulous episode, 'Nurse Stimpy', a kind of no-holds-barred doctors and nurses, demonstrates all too well).

The queerness of the relationship between the floppy 'bottom' Stimpy and ruthless 'top' Ren is simultaneously so explicit and so innocent that it is as breathtaking as it is endearing. In their regular bedtime ritual the back-flap on Stimpy's pyjamas pops open as he climbs into bed, prompting him to proffer his bottom and ask sheepishly, finger in mouth, 'Oh Ren, could you button me, please?'

With its flagrant anality (Stimpy's 'first material possession' is his cat litter) our cartoon lovers, like all the best queer comedy romances, tap into the nostalgia and sense of loss adults feel for the infantile attachments and pleasures which they are required to abandon in order to 'grow up'. At times *The Ren and Stimpy Show* seemed to go further than this and become a glorious insane revenge on 'adult society'.

Like 'The Big Baby Scam' in which Kricfalusi's heroes, down on their luck, substitute themselves for a couple of babies so that they'll be pampered: 'I tell you, man,' says Ren, 'babies have got it made!' (Naturally the adults don't notice their children have been replaced by a cat and a chihuahua.)

How did he get away with it? How could chaste, respectable Bert and Ernie be fingered by fundamentalists when mad, bad and totally pervy Ren and Stimpy escaped without censure? The sad fact is that in the end Kricfalusi *didn't* get away with it. After only two seasons, and despite enormous success, Nickelodeon fired Kricfalusi because he refused to 'tone down' the content of his cartoons. Ren and Stimpy were put in the hands of a new director more willing to toe the line and consequently Ren and Stimpy are no longer nearly so funny nor nearly so lovable.

Ultimately, what makes the queer romance of comedy duos so appealing is precisely that it is so unconventional and that the lovers themselves are so thrillingly *unmanly*. In the end both the fundamentalists and the gay critics can claim that Bert and Ernie, Laurel and Hardy or any of the other male comedy duos are 'gay', but this 'reading' is almost to miss the point – which is that they are not *straight*. As Charles Barr argued, these male–male romances are indeed 'innocent', 'childish' and 'pure' – but only in the sense that they key into the audience's nostalgia for the easy and less repressed pleasures of infantile sexuality, which indeed, are innocent, but only of sexual differentiation; male comedy duos can be queer because they exist in a space which pretends not to know what homosexuality is.

If they have to be called anything, perhaps it is better that they are described as 'queer'. Reading them as 'gay', either as part of an attempt to raise the visibility of homosexuality so as to help the cause of gay rights or as part of an effort to protect the nation's youth from 'unwholesome' influences – i.e. an alternative to compulsory heterosexuality – is equally mean-minded. The unmanly romance of male comedy duos is no one's exclusive property: its queerness, its departure from gender-appropriate behaviour, its transgression against convention, is something available to everyone, gay or straight. The punchline is that male comedy duos are so popular because hetrosexuality *and* homosexuality are the biggest jokes of all.

Attitude, December 1994

THE GENERATION X FILES

TONIGHT THAT ERA of human history ushered in by the Enlightenment comes to an end. What's more it's the Beeb that's scheduled it. 'It's a whole evening devoted to the uncanny, the bizarre, the peculiar – and the downright freaky,' enthuses Michael Jackson, Controller of BBC2, of his channel's 'Weird Night'.

Featured attractions include items on visions, such as the woman who 'saw a troll in her bedroom' (well, we've all been there), 'spine-tingling' coincidences, urban myths that turn out to be true and a review of the year by *Fortean Times* – 'April: Heather Woods of Lincoln suddenly bleeds with the marks of crucifixion on her hands, feet and ribs. Her doctor is mystified.'

What would Lord Reith have made of it all? No need to surmise – the answer to that question will no doubt be provided very shortly in the form of a televised seance.

Of course, it isn't just the BBC that has embraced obscurantism. Over on ITV, Michael Aspel, the man with the Face You Can Trust, does his best to give superstition a good name in *Strange But True* with 'investigations' into visitations by angels, spontaneous combustion and 'near-death experiences'. But it is the BBC, *the* vehicle in the twentieth century for enlightened liberalism which has decided to celebrate the decline of reason so ostentatiously.

Why? Why now? A clue is given by the fact that one of the featured programmes in 'Weird Night' is an episode of *The*

170

X Files deemed 'too scary' to show in its regular slot. A runaway ratings success for BBC2, regularly pulling in over six million viewers, *The X Files*' phenomenal popularity marks a watershed not just in how people watch TV but how they see the world.

Apparently a cross between science fiction and the detective genre, *The X Files* in fact undetermines the traditional narrative of both, confirming simultaneously the popular feeling that science knows both less and more than it is letting on. Two FBI agents, Malder and Scully, unearth evidence of paranormal and alien 'happenings' but their superiors refuse to accept their reports, pointing out that they have 'contravened procedure'.

Programmes like *The X Files* and *Strange But True* appeal to people's experience (or is it hope?) that there are more things in heaven and earth than are dreamt of in rationalism, that the empiricism of science is undermined by empiricism of popular culture.

More than this, the show is a kind of post-modernist *Scooby Doo*. Scary things happen, disturbing the equilibrium, the kids investigate, but instead of discovering that behind the ghost mask all alone was nice Mr Grimaldi the ice-cream man, the FBI agents merely find more mystery. So, we discover that the Space Shuttle malfunction was caused by a space demon, or those gruesome murders were caused by an alien with a taste for human liver – but more questions are raised than solved; equilibrium is never restored.

And this is why this kind of show is so popular as we approach the end of the millennium. Not just because of the well-documented historical pattern of 'end of the world' hysteria at such times, but because the end of the twentieth century is also the end of what the French post-structuralist Jean-François Lyotard has called the 'grand narratives' of modernity. The accounts of the world produced by the Enlightenment, such as 'rationalism', 'progress', 'socialism' and, crucially, 'science' no longer inspire the kind of faith they did (compare the wide-eyed evangelism of the old

171

Tomorrow's World with the current light-weight magazine format).

The new state of science in the popular mind is best epitomised by the *Paul McKenna Show* in which the 'science' of hypnosis is presented as a near-mystical power over the uninitiated – explanation and enquiry into the phenomenon are not wanted here, just mysterious spectacle.

But obscurantism is not senseless, quite the reverse. To some extent we are all Malders and Scullys now, attempting to find our place in the world with outdated maps. We are like someone with AIDS who turns to alternative remedies: they may not cure the illness but they can help to make some kind of sense of it where science failed.

Of course, the rise of obscurantist TV has another, more prosaic explanation. Leaving the viewer uneasy makes them more likely to stay tuned for the next programme: unresolved problems make for unlimited viewing. In 1951, the classic science fiction movie *The Thing* warned the world: 'For God's sake, watch the skies!' Today the exhortation might be: 'For God's sake, watch the telly!'

Independent, 17 December 1994

OOH, NO MISSUS!

'CAMP', WROTE SUSAN Sontag in her famous 1964 *Notes On Camp*, 'is the answer to the problem: how to be a dandy in the age of mass culture.' While the old-style dandy despised the vulgar, pressing a perfumed hanky to his nose, she argued, the new-style dandy, the camp aesthete, 'sniffs the stink and prides himself on his strong nerves.'

You certainly need strong nerves to watch TV these days. In fact, camp seems to have conquered the airwaves. On Channel 4's 'good morning campers' extravaganza, *The Big Breakfast*, Scouser drag queen Lily Savage acts as agony aunt. On BBC1's *The Weekend Show* and *Pets Win Prizes*, Dale Winton – a mass culture dandy if ever there was one – holds court as a connoisseur of the trivial. Meanwhile the fey mannerisms of male children's TV presenters, quite understandably, drives Gary Bushell to fulminate in the *Sun* about pervert plots to corrupt the nation's youth.

But for all Bushell's sphincter-clamping anxieties, the victory of the 'gay sensibility' on TV doesn't quite signal a triumph of homosexuality. The fact is, the gay sensibility isn't gay any more: straights – clutch the pearls – seem to do it better.

For proof of this, look no further than BBC2's lesbian and gay lifestyle programme *Gaytime* TV. Here the attempt to use camp – Dayglo sets and the arch look-my-cheek-has-my-tongue-in-it presentation of Bert Tyler-Moore and Rhona Cameron – to lighten the heavy burden of worthiness that

173

curses community programming and offer the audience a point of identification, merely piles on the agony. The presenters, the show and even homosexuality itself come across not so much as swell swishers at the forefront of mass culture as sorry victims of it.

Gaytime TV, taken with the now defunct dreary *Out* series on Channel 4, is evidence not just that the gay sensibility has nothing necessarily in common with the gay identity, but also that the earnest political demands of the gay identity are probably irreconcilable with camp's essentially amoral aestheticism. The sad irony is that the modern gay identity is something that Oscar Wilde wouldn't be caught dead wearing.

Alas, homosexuals are generally better at camp in the closet, at least as far as TV is concerned. The careers of Larry Grayson, Frankie Howerd and especially Kenny Everett, whose best work was in the late seventies before he came out, demonstrate this. The Stonewall riots may have kicked off gay liberation but they also helped kill off the connotative importance of camp; you can't flirtatiously allude to something that you're supposed to declare.

It isn't impossible to combine camp with a gay identity – it's just very difficult. Simon Fanshawe fails absymally, perhaps because he mistakes luvviness for campness; Julian Clary succeeds triumphantly – if only by giving an ironic nod to an audience's idea of The Homosexual. But even Clary's brand of excessive campness is overshadowed by Vic Reeves and Bob Mortimer, comedians whose intense over-investment in trivia and 'worthless' mass culture is extraordinarily camp in a way that their heterosexuality merely accentuates.

But there is still a great attachment to the notion of camp as a gay sensibility on the part of many gays. 'Postmodernism is straights catching up with camp,' the gay critic Andy Medhurst recently suggested. In fact perhaps the stiletto is rather on the other foot: what passes for camp among gays today might really be nothing more than gays catching up with postmodernism.

Other gay writers, such as Moe Meyer, the editor of *The*

Politics and Poetics of Camp (published by Routledge last year) have recognised the postmodernistic divorce of the gay identity from camp: but blame it on 'straight appropriation'. In a classic piece of self-serving reasoning, he argues in his introduction to this po-faced book that camp is only ever camp when it signifies queerness. So when straights do camp it isn't real camp – just like when whites sing the blues, it isn't real blues.

Meyer locates Susan Sontag's essay as the beginning of the 'corruption' of camp. 'Camp became confused and conflated with rhetorical and performative strategies such as irony, satire, burlesque and travesty and with cultural movements such as pop.'

Of course, it is precisely because camp is so nebulous a concept, so easily 'confused and conflated with irony, satire and pop' that it has become the sovereign sensibility of television and perhaps of postmodernism itself. And camp can also be deployed as a deconstructive device, pointing up – celebrating, in fact – the gap between surface and content.

In the hands of someone like Armando Iannucci this can be enormously liberating, cruel fun. His *The Day Today* series was a parody of media styles which brilliantly illustrated the pompous vacuity of TV news shosw and the manipulative assumptions built into its techniques.

It's worth noting, however, that Sontag, the author of the famous 'failed seriousness' definition of camp, drew a distinction between 'pure' or 'naïve' camp (failed seriousness) and 'deliberate' camp, or 'campness', suggesting that the latter was usually 'less satisfying'.

But this distinction depended upon camp being a marginal sensibility. The proliferation of media and consumer culture, largely through TV, in the three decades since she wrote her critique has not only ended the gay claim on camp but also the innocence that made 'pure' camp possible. No one could make *Crossroads* today without being able to resist signalling to the world that they knew it was 'really camp', by showing close-ups of the walls wobbling or Noele

Gordon's upper lip trembling nobly (which is, of course, what Victoria Wood's spoof Acorn Antiques was all about).

To a certain extent campness has become a knowing postmodern excuse for crap (e.g. *Gaytime TV*). Producers of TV programmes have cottoned on to the fact that almost everyone now wants to have good taste in bad taste; a nose for the vulgar. But as the great fraudster himself, Oscar Wilde, put it in one of his camp aphorisms: 'In all unimportant matters, style, not sincerity is the essential. In all important matters, style, not sincerity is the essential.' Or was it Edina who said that?

ARMY DREAMERS

WHAT IS IT about men in uniform? In the last few months there have been no less than three documentary series on BBCTV about life in the military. *HMS Brilliant* (about the Navy), *In the Company of Men* (about the Army), and now *Redcaps* (about the Military Police). Over on ITV the highly popular military soap opera *Soldier, Soldier* continues its tour of duty and a glamorous series about the RAF is on its way. Even *Top of the Pops* is khaki-fixated these days, with *Soldier, Soldier*'s lovably dull NCOs, played by Robson and Jerome, hogging the number one spot with the kind of tacky old love songs squaddies whistle in their draughty barracks.

So why is the nation apparently gripped by a prime-time uniform fetish?

The answer is, of course, nostalgia – nostalgia for a lost Britishness (they know who they are because their cap-badge has a crown in it), a lost order (they know their place because of the stripes on their battledress), and a lost class consciousness (the officers know their responsibilities; the ranks know their duties). But most of all, what is at stake is nostalgia for a lost masculinity. The world of TV soldiers is largely presented as a world where feminism never happened, a world where female employment is not outstripping male employment, a world where men are 'in the company of men' and women are camp followers. So, in the fictional *Soldier, Soldier*, the women are all wives and girlfriends; the exist only inasmuch as they are dependent and doting on the men. The men go to work and war; the women bear them children and try to work out what their emotionally illiterate husbands want.

Of course, this fantasy doesn't correspond with the reality of military life today – especially since the integration of women in the early nineties. Men in the military are undergoing a crisis of identity just as pronounced as men in the 'real world' – perhaps more so, given that many men joined the military precisely because it took them away from women and into the company of men to do manly things.

This came out in the documentary *HMS Brilliant*, where many of the male ratings expressed intense dislike of women ratings being allowed on board. 'It's a man's job,' they kept saying. 'Women can't do the work – they're not up to it.' In fact, it was apparent that the problem was precisely that women *could* do the job, and in doing so demonstrated that it wasn't a man's job any more – just a job.

The arrival of women in workplaces previously the preserve of men has coincided with the disappearance of the kind of employment – in the factory, the pit, the army – that used to give them a job for life, make them attractive marital propositions, keep women at home and men together. In a world where most employment opportunities are not in the King's Own Fusiliers but at McDonalds or the local electronics factory where eighty per cent of the workers are female, and where women are increasingly independent of men, men are less and less likely to find their sexual validation in their work or in their relationship to women – who are becoming too powerful for men to feel manly around.

So image culture has stepped into the reality breach, providing men with somewhere masculine to escape to and the sight of men doing manly things together – all from the comfort of their armchair. Hence the boom in TV pro-grammes on the military and the enormous growth of football-related media (football being at least one thing that women will never be able to do properly – or likely to want to). Hence also the New Lad consumerism of a magazine like

178

Loaded, which offers men a chance to buy into a culture of manliness that they are excluded from by economics, history or just bad asthma. In short, men are looking more and more to one another for their sexual validation and less and less to women. Indeed they seem to be showing a certain independence of the female sex, and consumer capitalism has cottoned on.

However, while men are more likely to look to one another for their masculine affirmation these days, they are still very much afraid that this will result in them being labelled gay. The line between being interested in manly things and being interested in men is as incoherent and inconsistent as it is necessary to pretend that it is clearly and easily drawn – the punishment for not religiously observing this pretence is exile from the very company of men that was sought.

This is, of course, the official policy of the military: homosexuality is still grounds for instant dismissal. The purity of military camaraderie, i.e. male intimacy, must be preserved by the scapegoating of queers. But even here there is a growing sense that this obsessive patrolling of the line between homosociality and homosexuality generates paranoia which is itself a fearful obstacle to male intimacy. This was the theme of the successful West End play *Burning Blue*, which was not so much a play about gays in the military as about masculine friendship and how homophobia not homosexuality poisons it (using the rather crude ploy of making the investigator the obvious 'perve').

That the film rights to *Burning Blue* were snapped up so quickly suggests that someone believes there is a larger audience for this message. In the meantime, you can catch *Crimson Tide*, Tony 'Top Gun' Scott's paean to the virile-but-pretty submariners of the US Navy, a study of tense handsome young necks and sweaty faces softly illuminated by dials and flickering screens, set inside a huge penis, and ask yourself whether Hollywood is interested in drawing the line between an interest in manly things and an interest in men any more.

In the saloon-bar world of British newspapers, however, the line is still being chalked out – perhaps only because it is such good copy. The is-he-or-isn't-he? David Ashby court-room soap opera is a case in point. The Tory MP's attempt to sue the *Sunday Times* because it suggested that he was homosexual after he shared a bed with a male friend on holiday is a battle over what is and is not acceptable in relations between chaps.

But the case is also an example of how homophobia has historically been employed to keep men from neglecting their reproductive/marital/familial responsibilities. The fear was that as a kind of 'free sex' or pleasure without obligation, homosociality plus homosexuality equals neglected women. Mrs Ashby allegedly shouting 'poofters! poofters!' through the letter-box at Mr Ashby and his male friend is the sound of that fear.

Confusingly, an avoidance of intimacy with men is likely to provoke accusations of homosexuality too – from the men you refuse intimacy to. 'Bachelor' Blackburn Rovers striker Graeme Le Saux is apparently called a 'poof' by his team-mates for his preference for antiques and reading the *Guardian* instead of getting drunk with the lads and wearing his trousers round his neck – leading to blows on the football pitch and prompting an appearance of his 'stunning' girlfriend on the front page of the *Star*, reassuring us that 'He's no homaux – he's all man'.

But despite the continuing comic panics over the ground-rules for men together – made even more panicky by the increased profile of homosexuality in recent years – we still have the rather startling image of Robson and Jerome crooning old love songs while looking into one another's eyes on *Top of the Pops*, and telling interviewers that they try to say 'I love you' to each other at least once a day. And still no front page 'pooves in uniform' expose in the tabloids or homosexual witch-hunt in *Soldier, Soldier*.

Perhaps this is because in the nostalgic, unreal world of TV khaki Robson and Jerome represent, homosexuality hasn't been invented yet. Or, then again, it might just be that the popularity of the TV squaddies' sentimental love-affair – far more sentimental than that permitted between men and women these days – is a sign that the desire for images of masculine romance is now greater than the fear of homo sexuality.

Guardian, 9 December 1995

Pop Stars

THE PERSUEDERS

I HAVE SOMETHING to confess. When I listened to Suede's eponymous debut album last year I was disappointed. Disappointed that it turned out to be as good as the hype had trumpeted it to be. This was an album which went gold on its first day and sold 100,000 copies in the first week, by a group whose canny PR people secured them no less than nineteen magazine covers. Suede were everywhere and everyone was hailing them as the greatest thing since The S****s. So I'm sure you can sympathise with my frustration on discovering that I couldn't loftily dismiss them as paste imitations and actually had to admit that *Suede*, at once savage and tender, sleazy and sublime, was one of the greatest first albums ever.

Suede, the bastards, they had it all. They had the press, they had the material, they had the success. And to cap it all they had a dangerous, scandalous edge in the form of Seventies androgyny queered up for the Nineties. It was there in their songs – 'We kiss in his room to a popular tune' 'The Drowners'; 'In your council home he broke all your bones and now you're taking it time after time' ('Animal Nitrate') – and an album cover which featured two lesbians snogging. Most of all, it was there in the sissy shape of front man Brett Anderson. With his irritating girlish fringe, weedy pointy shoulders and pigeon chest, his swinging, child-bearing hips (to which he insisted on drawing attention by swishing around and banging the microphone against them) and his Seventies blouses baring a waspish waist and nibblesome navel, Anderson was the most offensively, delectably unmanly pop star since Morrissey.

But I needn't have fretted. Even as Suede were being feted, a backlash was brewing which would unmask them as fakes. What finally unleashed it was *that* remark – the one Brett made about considering himself 'a bisexual who had never had a homosexual experience'. So Suede were frauds after all! All that mincing of hips and meeting of same-sex lips was phony, a sham! How satisfying!

Gay critics fired the first salvos, denouncing Suede as shameful expoiters of their culture. 'Is there any real difference between what Brett from Suede is doing and what the Black and White Minstrels once did?' demanded one furious gay music journalist in *Melody Maker*.

Meanwhile, those straights who had been discomfited by the queerness of Suede, were given a green light to ridicule them for being big girl's blouses, now that they had no fear of being called 'homophobic'. After reading one gay critic's attack on Anderson, 'comedians' Newman and Baddiel included a typically witty sketch in their last tour which derided him for his poofiness.

Interestingly, no one bothered to ask just what was so 'gay' about Suede. Unmanly? Definitely. Androgynous? Yes. Bisexual? Perhaps. But *gay*?

What is this thing called 'gay culture' anyway? Kylie? Advertorial for designer underwear? Water-soluble lube with vitamin E? Talk of 'exploitation of gay culture' might make some sense with boy bands who, with their shaved chests and nipple rings, are 'gay' to the point of parody. But when it's applied to rock and roll, something that has always fucked with the signifiers of gender and sexuality, it just sounds like whingeing.

Worse, it's about maintaining a fictional, neat and tidy sexual status quo. Many straights are even keener than some gay critics to perpetuate the lie that homo-eroticism – and indeed anything that is not blokeish heterosexuality – has a gay copyright. After all, anyone with common sense knows that what's not one thing must be t'other.

Now, more than a year later, as Suede prepare to release their second album, *Dog Man Star* they seem as cursed as they were blessed last year. Second albums are always a test, but after such a debut album as *Suede* it becomes a trial. Gone is the honeymoon with the press, and gone also is Bernard Butler, the band's guitarist and Marr to Brett's Morrisey, in an acrimonious and very public separation. What does the Posing Sodomite have to say about *that* remark now?

'It was completely misread,' he says, the annoyance registering in his voice. 'I was talking about the way I write and the way I generally feel about life. I don't feel 100 per cent akin to the male world or 100 per cent akin to the female world. I was trying to express in a sexual perspective something that was more spiritual. Lots of things I write about are third person but written in the first person. Basically it was about not wanting to be pinned down.'

Brett Anderson is perched awkwardly on the arm of the sofa opposite, his body angled slightly away from me. Is he afraid of being 'pinned down' as Someone Sitting on a Sofa? Is he, in fact, occupying some more artistic, ambiguous space between sitting and standing? Simon Gilbert, the band's drummer who came out as gay last year, is also here, facing me with his knees apart, apparently happy to surrender to the definite, fixed position of sitting on the sofa (albeit in the middle).

Brett continues in his fast-talking, surprisingly laddish South Coast voice: 'I don't think that anyone should have to be pinned down, even if they are definitely in a category – definitely gay or definitely straight. Because you happen to engage in certain sexual practices you shouldn't have to be that and nothing more. I was trying to state something universal while everyone wanted to read something specific.'

He has a point. OK, so the refusing to be pinned down, 'I don't want to label myself' thing is, in a sense, laughably adolescent. But isn't that what pop is for? To be wilful, self-

absorbed, self-important, pretentious? To refuse the definition, the certainty, the common sense, the maturity, the
lifelessness of adult life, however hopeless such a resistance
might be? But gays and straights did not appreciate Suede's
irresponsibility. Like most who advocate the possibility of a
third position in the Sexual Identity War, Anderson was
caught in the cross-fire between the two camps of heterosexuality and homosexuality.

'The gay side thought it was a cop out and the straight side
weren't happy with it either,' he complains. 'Everybody
wants you as a figurehead for their party; the world is just a
series of tribes that want you to speak out for them but I've
never felt myself part of any tribe. I don't intend to be a
spokesman for any of them in particular. I'd like to think
that individuals have got a bit more intelligence than to be
happy with belonging to a glorified football team.

'I was seen as a whipping boy for people who wanted to be
right-on as well. I happened to lay my defences open. Before
I did people had thought: he probably is homosexual so we
can't criticise him on those grounds because we won't be
seen as right-on. Newman and Baddiel wouldn't have dared
do the same sketch about Andy Bell – although I'm sure they
would like to – because they know they would have been
slated as homophobic. I think men who are perceived to be
gay but who aren't actually don't have the political defences
to fall back on that gay men do.'

But then you were a rock star making this statement.
Wasn't it a rather cynical thing for someone in your
privileged position to say, exploiting for your own ends the
good old-fashioned 'ambisexual' appeal of rock'n'roll?

'Perhaps, but that would only be true if it were a charade. I
think it would be impossible for me to act any other way. It's
not a ploy.'

So you refute the accusation that you were appropriating
gay culture by 'posing as a somodite'?

'I wasn't "appropriating", it – that sounds like stealing. I
thought I had a kinship with it. My own sexuality aside, I'm
quite deeply involved in the gay world because a lot of my

friends are gay and because of this feeling of kinship. But like I said, I didn't actually feel as if I was part of any particular group and didn't want to be, so I didn't feel a fraud at all. I wasn't "posing as a sodomite" – I felt completely justified in what I was doing.

'I think it's more to do with the way the press decide to portray us that caused the gay community to turn against us. In the *NME* there were cartoons representing us as limp-wristed Lord Fauntleroys. We weren't trying to come across that way at all, that was the way the media decided to perceive us. Now I think we've gone beyond that – but that's not to say that I've turned my back on what I was talking about then, it's just the way my mind works.'

But surely you can't just blame the press for your image as effete fops?

'Look, any pop band can get some success by wearing pink feather boas and some make-up – "Ohmygod, they're *outrageous*" – we're doing the opposite. We never felt we fitted into any categories. I think that the music we make is a metaphor for everything including our sexuality, the way I've always tried to avoid barriers. Simon's the same . . .'

'I have to say that I really sympathise with Brett's position,' Simon chips in. 'I come from the other side of the fence, if you like. I've called myself a bisexual person who's never had a heterosexual experience. I never wanted to fit into the stereotypical image of what a gay person is. I think that it's a lucky accident that brought me together with Brett because we really do share a similar outlook. Of all the bands I've been with, it's only with Suede that I felt able to be honest.

'But I don't want to be defined by my sexual preference, to be put in this category which is to all intents and purposes a clubby crowd. I never felt like I belonged in the straight world before I came out. After I came out I didn't feel like I belonged in the gay world either.'

Actually, Simon doesn't exactly look like he belongs in Suede either. His hair – which is short, spiky, and an angry red-purple – is somewhat at odds with the louche Suede-boy coiffure. Apparently, people often thought that he must be 'the straight one' because he had short hair. As he continues talking, it becomes apparent where his image comes from. Like many young outsiders growing up in the late Seventies, Simon had found a home in punk.

'It seemed to express something about me and I really enjoyed the ambiguity of the lyrics – like The Clash's "Stay Free", which I interpret as a love song from one man to another. I'd never identified with politically gay bands and performers like Jimmy Somerville. I think that a song should speak to whoever's listening without hitting them over the head with rhetoric that's bound to turn some people off.'

But all the bands Simon had belonged to had displayed sufficient casual homophobia to persuade him to stay firmly in the closet.

'They all had their puerile anti-gay banter which I had to sit through without saying anything. Suede were different. One day somebody asked if I was gay and I just said, "Yeah". For a moment I thought, Oh shit, what have I done? I'm out of the band now. In fact, the way everyone reacted was brilliant. It felt so right after that. I think it has a lot to do with the similarity between Brett's outlook and mine.'

Have either of you consummated your 'bisexuality' since last year?

Simon: 'No.'

Brett: 'Not physically.'

Simon: 'I'd say the same.'

What does that actually mean, though?

Simon: 'It means that I can relate to a woman without actually getting into bed with her. In the same way as Brett does with men.'

So superficially there's a neat symmetry between you in that you both want to avoid categorisation, aspiring to be something more and less than what you might be seen to be . . .

Brett: '. . . yes, there is . . .'

Simon: '. . . I'd agree with that . . .'

. . . but perhaps only superficially. Some might argue that

you, Brett, were claiming a certain credibility without actually putting your iron in the fire or, probably more to the point, allowing someone else to put his in yours.

Brett: 'Mine's a kind of active statement and Simon's is a kind of passive statement? Yeah, I know what you're saying. There's a huge history here which I'm kind of attaching myself to, or people assume I'm attaching myself to. I don't really see how to get away from it – I'm not saying that I never said it, but . . .'

Now Brett is swallowing water. I throw him a line: Perhaps you were attacked for merely putting into words what has been the unofficial formula for truly great rock'n'roll all along?

'Yeah, I'd agree with that.'

Does he think that his crime was more explanation than exploitation?

'Yes, I think that's been my problem all along – giving too much away. It would have been very easy for me not to mention my sexuality at all and people would draw their own conclusions. I've been incredibly honest. I've never said anything that wasn't true.'

As a result of Brett's honesty, some sections of the indie press slated Suede for being 'inauthentic' poseurs – possibly the worst crime in the indie universe. Perhaps this had something to do with the notion among some sections of the music press that masculinity is equivalent to authenticity, and also working-classness?

'Yeah,' Brett agrees. 'Indie does have this huge emphasis on authenticity: everyone has to play and it's a case of all the lads together. But the whole indie thing is so much a fucking fake itself!' he exclaims with real vehemence. 'It's actually the children of the landed gentry with guitars! I can name quite a few names – but I won't – people with extravagantly rich parents who have decided to go for this scruffy image.

'None of us have ever been part of that sort of gang at all. We made music from the other direction: we're from a scruffy background and aspired to something much more . . . *ambitious*. I've always wanted to make pop music, I've

191

always wanted to have hits, I've always had a really *pop* ethic and loved the bands who were just out-and-out Motown. These other people are the reverse: they're coming from successful backgrounds and want to have this authenticity and avant-garde appeal by slumming it. I want to make good songs that everyone can understand and really . . . *shine.*'

This is the moment to mention those lovable dog-racing cock-er-nee geezahs (or so they'd like you to think) who have risen to fame since Suede's disappearance from the scene. Brett pauses at the sound of their name – maybe *bristles* would be a better description. 'Ummmm . . . I don't really have anything to say about Blur.'

He looks at Simon.

'No, there's not much to say,' concurs Simon, on cue. 'A lot's been made of our supposed spat with them but it's all hype really.'

Brett: 'They do their thing and we do ours. The press make out that there's this big rivalry between us, when there isn't really.'

I try to explain that all I want is a kind of 'compare and contrast' angle on Blur. Brett shifts uneasily, moving even more of his bodyline away from me, flicking nervous sideways glances in my general direction, head close to his chest as he speaks – like a painfully shy boy making his first pass or telling the police where he hid the body.

'Look, any of these bands that have been getting all this attention lately have made it because we haven't been around [*flick*]. That sounds really big-headed I know, but I don't think that anyone has had the track record that we've had. Most people only know our singles – that doesn't reveal the depth to our musical style [*flick*]. Things like our B sides. We've never made a duff B side. Some of our B sides are better than our album tracks. Without being really, y'know, conceited [*flick*]. I don't think that there's anyone who has produced such a body of work in such a small amount of time. Not even some of the great British groups of the past

192

[*flick, flick*]. I think that the next album will completely ground everyone else [*flick*]. I think.'

His speech over, Brett shifts his bony bum around on the sofa arm a teensy bit more towards me.

'I hate all this big-headed crap, y'know?' he confesses. ' "We're the greatest", blah, blah. We've never gone around with this attitude' – now his voice is almost plaintive – 'we just happen to think that our music is great and that it has real depth to it.'

Did he face away from me because he was embarrassed at having to sell himself; or was it because he was embarrassed by the 'real' Brett Anderson – someone fiercely ambitious, competitive and egotistical? Whatever the reason, there's more than a certain amount of truth in what he's saying. It wasn't until Suede came along and showed that the body of pop wasn't quite as cold as everyone had taken it to be that groups like Blur had any chance at all.

The few tracks I've heard off the new album suggest Suede have indeed taken a new direction. Toned down is the raw energy of the first album; anger is here replaced by melodrama and, astonishingly, it comes off. Emotions are painted on a larger canvas with more unabashed extravagance than British pop has had for years. Some will denounce it as self-indulgent and pompous. But at least one track, 'Still Life' – a ballad that grows into a breathtaking orchestral production, is going to be huge. It's so expansive, so gorgeous that no one will be able to resist its goose-pimpling embrace. It will be played on Radios 1 and 2; housewives will hum distractedly to its bitter-sweet melody in kitchens while their sons weep disconsolately to its wailing angst in their bedrooms.

'I think that we've successfully combined those things which we've always been good at before,' claims Brett. 'We've always been able to produce those bubblegum singles like "Animal Nitrate" and "The Next Life", and on this album we've been able to blend the cockiness of these with something more wistful. "Wild Ones", for example, is for me the most successful thing I've ever written. It's incredibly catchy and poppy and at the same time it's something quite beautiful. I think,' he intones solemnly, 'it's really, really rare for pop music to produce something beautiful.'

Do I detect something of Ravel's 'Bolero' in the finale of 'Still Life'?

'Yeah, we ripped it off a bit. If people just heard that track off the album they'd be quite misled because it is very orchestral. We wanted to go for something quite heroic. It's very easy for a pop band to get a bit of money and pay for an orchestra to accompany them. I think that song justifies it because if you hear it on its own, as an acoustic vocal, it builds naturally anyway. The orchestral embellishments just suggest themselves.

'It is quite pompous, especially the end part. But pop music has always been about being pretentious – you can't be worthy, there's no point. That's the crappy thing about the indie scene: it doesn't go any further than a bunch of people slapping each other on the back going, "Yeah, that's worthy".'

Like the Manic Street Preachers, Suede are a pop group who have that loyalty to pop music that most fans don't have time for any more. Suede are from an era where there were only three TV channels; two were showing football and one was showing a documentary on fly-fishing. They are from an era of youth-club discos and smoking behind the bike sheds, when the idea of a good time was rattling around in a battered Cortina without tax or insurance, or beating up the local queer. It's also an England that arguably no longer exists or, if it does, is fast fading away.

Simon disagrees. 'Since I came out, I get a lot of letters and I can tell that life in small towns hasn't changed much. People tell me about getting beaten up in the school playground and stuff. Mind you, Stratford, where I grew up, is really weird. The first time I went back to Stratford after coming out I expected people to be really put off about it – y'know, "Oh, here's that fuckin' queer". But not at all.

194

People were saying, "Why didn't you tell us when you used to hang around with us? It would have been cool."

'It's easy to say that things have changed sitting here in London as a member of the media elite. This world just carries on and on, no matter that there are smart people walking around with black briefcases. [Brett glances at my black briefcase.] There are kids out there who desperately need something to cling on to. Yeah, it is an old-fashioned idea, but it's what we grew up with. I think it's easy to talk about the advancement of society when you live in a big city but I don't think things have moved on from 1954 once you get outside it.'

But isn't this a rather patronising view?

'Yes, it is quite patronising, but I also think that it's quite true,' he says rather impatiently. 'It's patronising towards the people who inflict it on the ones who don't want it. But they deserve it. Like all my family. They're living in a different age. It's all lino and corned beef, like something out of *Look Back in Anger*.'

Brett and Simon grew up in those corners of Britain where Thatcherism, satellite TV and Sega Mega-Drives never happened. For Simon it was the tourist/rural limbo of Stratford-upon-Avon; for Brett it was Haywards Heath, a dormitory town north of Brighton. Both men wanted to be pop stars for as long as they can remember. 'When I was about four I used to imagine being Paul McCartney,' confesses Simon. No wonder he became a punk.

I put it to Brett that yes, Britain is still dowdy and desperate – perhaps more so – especially in those forgotten corners. But the world that produced a passion for pop has gone.

'Yes, that's true – the world has completely changed in that sense. That's why I think the new album is a step forward because it is not as caught up with the inverted nostalgia. Where the last album was retrogressive; the new album is much more wistful and in love with the modern age.'

195

Brett admits, however, that his new optimism is somewhat stifled by certain local realities. 'The Suede backlash was partly to do with a reaction against success. Anyone in this country who achieves success is struck out against. You're allowed to go only so far and no further. This or that song will be dismissed as a "pile of shit" because it's not avant-garde enough, not because it's actually any good or not. America's very different – it seems to be more hopeful.'

But isn't that part of the deal? That the melancholic, repressed twistedness that your music has fed off can't be separated from the bitterness, envy and narrow-mindedness?

'Yes and that's where the dichotomy lies. This band is caught up in its own history and that's what makes us what we are. Yet there's that desire to reach a kind of spiritual state and shed your skin and go on to another plane . . .'

Isn't this where you end up following in Morrissey's steps, who also celebrates the mundane and the desperate in Britishness and yet tries to transcend it?

'I don't think he's expressed any desire to escape it,' replies Brett quickly. 'After fifteen years in the music business there's been no development in his intention, and I intend to develop. He's found his niche and seems content within it. That's fair enough, that's the way he feels. I don't want to come across like that. We want to do different things and even over the space of the last two albums I think we've made quite giant leaps.'

Brett seems rather keen to put some distance between himself and Moz. Maybe this is because he was mocked by the Glum One himself for his hero worship of Bowie and Morrissey (Morrissey reportedly said: 'His reference points are so close together that there's no space in between').

But talking of 'giant leaps' actually encourages the comparisons. The world gasped at the recent discovery that Morrissey *liked a game of footie* and now I can exclusively reveal that Brett was *good at sport at school*.

'Sport was the only thing I did. I held the record for the 800 metres at my school, Oat Hall Comprehensive, for five years,' he says in a studiedly casual way, obviously enjoying the turbulence this fact creates in the wake of his Prince of Fey image. 'They used to feed me a special high protein diet at school because I was the only one good at sport.'

Simon was not such a prized pupil. 'I hated school for the first year but then I became a punk and got respect – perhaps because I was the only one in Stratford. I wasn't any good at sport but I was very good at forging my mum's handwriting on the off-games chits.'

Just before the end of the interview I ask Brett about his relationship with pigs. References to things porcine abound in his work, including the track 'We Are the Pigs' on the new album. What do porkers mean to him?

'I don't know really,' he says looking away with a half-smile on his face. 'The cover of *Animals* by Pink Floyd is probably one of my favourite images in the world. It's a metaphor for sexuality and brutality, stuff like that.'

I suppose that pigs are very . . .

'Human.'

Yes . . .

'And pink.'

Absolutely. And in touch with their bodily functions.

'Yes. They're supposed to smell but they don't.'

And so the truth is out at last: Brett's thing for pigs and pig culture is not so much exploitation as identification.

Attitude, October 1994

OH, MY SHIFTLESS BODY

Celebrity is a form of revenge . . . but what else do I have to offer?

Morrissey

1983, *The Tube*, 'This Charming Man'. A thin, ethereal youth in a blouse open at the neck, revealing a junk jewellery necklace and skin almost translucent from a diet of cakes, biscuits, baked beans and the occasional tangerine, is waving a bunch of gladioli around his head and simpering into the camera. 'Why pamper life's complexities/when the leather runs smooth on the passenger seat'. The 'outrageous' frocks of the New Romantics and the 'gender-benders' have been discarded in a rumpled pile; the plastic necklace is an anti-accessory, it says goodbye to rock 'n' roll drag – it's time to frighten the horses with the Truth.

And it's all there in that simper: a simper full of threat, a simper that could as easily bite your head off as cover you in kisses, a simper that is the product of years of frustrated ambitions. It says, 'Aha! *I have you now.*' He's waited his whole life for this moment. Sequestered in his bedroom reading Capote and Wilde; plotting and planning, scheming and dreaming, like a seed waiting for spring, full of fond thoughts of how beautiful a bloom it will make, he waited for The Smiths. Now his moment's come and he's coating the world in petals and poison, dusting a fragrance of rebellion everywhere. Now that falsetto yelp, of delight, of

198

triumph: 'Yow!' Provoking, imploring, beseeching, teasing: 'Will Nature make a man of me yet?'

In January 1984, subsisting in Manchester in the sad, unemployed-and-unemployable, bedsitting lifestyle which was so fashionable and so romantic in the 'alternative' early Eighties, I used to spend a great deal of time staring out of the single, small window in my room at a neighbouring brick wall and thinking 'alternative' thoughts. As is often the case with dreamers, I was Unhappy With the World, and With People in General, but most of all, I was Unhappy With Myself.

It will hardly come as a surprise to you, then, to discover that, like countless other unlovable adolescents, when I came across The Smiths' debut album my reaction was like Robinson Crusoe discovering Friday's footprints in the sand. 'Does the body rule the mind/or does the mind rule the body?/I dunno . . .' wailed Stephen Patrick Morrissey over Johnny Marr's sad-happy chords in 'Still Ill', perfectly encapsulating the dilemma of the terminal neurotic and promptly becoming the No. 1 idol of my life.

But there was more. Not only was this man clearly a self-loathing, self-loving, cynical, romantic, over-intellectual, over-intuitive mess, but also, best of all, he was queer-but-not-queer: his sexuality was the most glorious contradiction in a whole panoply of unresolved and – thankfully – irresolvable contradictions.

Mozza's extraordinary significance to a whole generation of young people, like myself, who could not decide whether they were inadequate to the world or the world was inadequate to them (or whether there was any difference), was not simply his 'sexual ambiguousness'. It wasn't Joe Dallesandro's chest on the sleeve, nor lines like 'You can pin and mount me/like a butterfly' ('Reel Around the Fountain'), and 'I'm not the man you think I am' ('Pretty Girls Make Graves'), 'And if the people stare, then the people stare/I really don't know and I really don't care' ('Hand in Glove'). it was that in his lyrics and his life Morrissey refused the

199

differentiation of desire on which the adult world is built: Morrissey was a one-boy, guerilla campaign against the Oedipus complex.

1985. *Top of the Pops*, 'The Boy with the Thorn in his Side'. He's wearing just a black cardigan and dark flannels (secondhand, of course), swinging his hips around, all abandoned gestures and awkward angles – elbows jutting like arched eyebrows. Again, no lipstick or eyeliner to hide behind, just one word felt-tipped on his neck: 'BAD'. This is the most sublime moment in the history of pop – beyond the rebellious dreams even of his trashy glam-punk idols, the New York Dolls: a strumpet pansy, a flaming nancy-boy, stands before the nation, hands on hips, knees together, performing 'The Boy with the Thorn in His Side'.

He's camping it up in the most frightful, exhilarating, vindictive way, a way you'd forgotten camp could be – a withering, intelligent violence in every flick of his wrist. This is the kind of camp that mugs you in alleyways, but it's after your heart not your wallet. Clutching his bleeding side in the style of a vaudeville actress, he delivers his pain to the camera like a fist: 'The boy with the thorn in his side/Behind the hatred there lies/a murderous desire for love/how can they look into my eyes/and still they don't believe me?'

Morrissey is Britain's most famous celibate after Cliff Richard. But unlike Cliff he has made it absolutely clear that his celibacy is not a case of 'waiting for the right girl' but a kind of perversion – a refusal of the 'sexual aim' and a renouncement of manhood. Many find it remarkable, not to say incredible, that a man whose lyrics are among the most sexually knowing ever written could seriously be, to all intents and purposes, a virgin. In fact, he has had, he claims, fleeting encounters with both men and women in the past but they have always ended in disaster. That he doesn't take on the tag 'bisexual' is probably something to do with the fact that it would only multiply the error, carrying with it, as

200

it does for many, the idea of 'double' the attraction and opportunity instead of double the disappointment.

He recently confessed, 'Desire is excruciating to me, and as far as I know that's all there is. I can't imagine being loved by somebody whom one loves.' It is precisely this intimate knowledge of the disappointment of sex which makes him such an ironically potent lyricist of desire. His celibacy marries the brassy surface optimism of pop to the deeper, darker currents it carries with it from its blues origins. Morrissey draws attention to the dangerous shadows around sex in a sunny, 'pro-sex' age which sees genital friction as an absolute good to be engaged in by all. That he should do this as a pop star – the individual who has, more than anyone else in the modern age, come to stand for the idiotic idea that sex equals freedom – only makes his position all the more precious. Morrissey's invocation of desire is unrequited and unrequitable, a yearning to yearn – that's all there is, he says. It's not surprising that for many this is not enough. We've all heard the rumours about Moz's sex life. But I, like many others, shall continue to believe in his celibacy – much like Catholics continue to believe in the Virgin Birth.

Of course, for some gays, Morrissey is someone who has been 'really gay' all along – he's either a mere hypocrite or 'hasn't come to terms'. There is no irresolvable contradiction – all he has to do is 'come out', preferably on stage at Gay Pride, join the Gay Community and everything will fit into place and Morrissey won't be miserable any more. And if he won't come out as gay then he should come out as straight. One gay music journalist decreed in *Gay Times* that if Morrissey didn't come out he should stop 'ripping off' gay culture. 'To steal the things that are ours and throw them out into straight society, like pearls before swine, is divorcing these things from their meanings,' he scolded. 'This is cultural imperialism of the very worst kind.'

But, it almost goes without saying, it is precisely because he 'divorces things from their meanings' and discovers new, more interesting ones along the way that Morrissey is such a great artist and pop star and why millions of young people Unhappy With the World love him. It's why bequiffed hod carriers are in the habit of flinging themselves at him on stage, kissing him passionately and then dropping to the floor in a dead faint.

'I don't believe in heterosexuality or homosexuality,' Morrissey once said. 'I think to even recognise those terms is to demand sexual segregation. I consider myself a prophet of the Fourth Sex. The Third has been tried and failed.' The response of some gay critics to the Morrissey phenomenon shows just how complete that failure has been, how the loudest demands for sexual segregation can come not from straight 'swine' but gay 'pearls'. In the gayist world view, there is no space for the outsider. He must be Out, he must join the Club, he must be in other words, an *insider*.

Fortunately, Morrissey is not about to record 'Glad to be Gay'. He'll continue to explore the margins and wastelands of desire and identity. He will continue to draw the fire of those pedants disguised as music critics who are uncomfortable with indeterminacy – sexual or political. For example, his recent pillorying in the *NME* as a 'racist' for daring to write songs like 'The National Front Disco' which don't contain the correct, wholesome and unambiguous 'moral'.

It was probably Morrissey's desire to 'divorce things from their meanings' that drove him to kill the skinny boy with hearing aid, gladioli in his back pocket and NHS glasses held together with elastoplast. 'The Living Sign' realised by the end of the Eighties that everyone thought that they knew what he represented – who he *was*: 'That Morrissey, 'e's that wailing big girl's blouse, innee?' So, being the perverse creature that he is, he ritually murdered the boy with the thorn in his side and put in his place something previously unthinkable: Butch Morrissey.

1992. *Your Arsenal*. With a crash of crepe-soled bullying from his lead guitarist Boz Boorer, Mozza grabs you by your glands, breathes beerily but clearly into your face with all the promise of a Bank Holiday ruck in Brighton. Even when crooning in his more traditional fey way, you can't help but glance nervously at the 'gold' knuckle-dusters he's sporting on those fingers with their new-look glam rockabilly manicure. We are all mods to Morrissey's rocker and we'd better effing watch out. *Your Arsenal* is easily Mozzer's most physical album, the cover sleeve advertising this with a shot of what was once the boniest body in pop looking almost – gasp! – *muscled*. The critics that had pronounced him long dead from anaemia caused by a diet of insubstantial self-parody are now lying bleeding on the pavement. Is he eating meat?

The vegan bedsit creatures who reverently chant his lines at sunrise and sunset will be astonished to find no lyric sheet in this album. These tracks are less likely to explain themselves than a football hooligan. And with titles like 'You're Gonna Need Someone on Your Side', 'Glamorous Glue' and 'The National Front Disco', you know you're in danger of forfeiting your front teeth – which is exactly what happens in 'Certain People I Know', where Mozza sings merrily about breaking a billiards cue over your face. He's a man with nothing to lose – everything he valued has been lost already: The Smiths, pop music, Britain.

Butch Mozza may take some getting used to (and may be a tad unconvincing), but it makes a heroic kind of sense. He has become, by dint of will, one of the 'ordinary boys' he used to envy for their masculine ease – an ease he felt belonged to a different planet from his own. He has created a rockabilly band – a world – composed of lads that look like the working-class heroes he made into icons on his cover sleeves in his Smiths period and now his own face stares out from the sleeves of his solo records.

Morrissey's current obsession with the 'homosocial' world of skinheads ('Suedehead'), gangster boys ('Last of the International Playboys' and 'Spring Heeled Jim'), sailors ('Billy Budd') and young toughs ('We'll Let You Know') was there from the beginning: the grease in the hair of a Speedway operator is all that a tremulous heart requires

('Rusholme Ruffians'). But now it is a world which he can feel part of, with his rockabilly band of tattoed-on-the-neck sexy toughs, new-found enthusiasm for boxing, football and his stocky skinhead companion Jake. As with his earlier incarnation as the prophet of the 'Fourth Sex', he navigates a world of nameless passions, reminding us that the 'masculine' in a man can be as queer as the 'feminine' in him. Morrissey's reincarnation as a 'lad' is as disturbing and as offensive, in its own way, as his gladioli manifestation.

Mozza started off as the boy who would not become a man; but like many narcissists before him he discovered that this strategy was too vulnerable to the outrageous slings and arrows of Old Father Time (pretty girls may make graves but pretty boys dig their own). So, he decides, rather than become a laughing stock I will become a man – but in *excess*. Oedipus is rebuffed again as Moz refuses to take his position in the Triangle (Mum, Dad, Child) which states you cannot *be* what you desire and you cannot desire what you *wish* to be, and makes a flagrant bid at becoming what he desires and desiring what he has become.

It was all there at the beginning. The cover sleeve of *This Charming Man* charted the future. A still from Jean Cocteau's *Orphée* depicted the young and beautiful Jean Marais prostrate, cheek pressed longingly against his reflection in the pool. The Charming Man of the song is both his daydream lover and himself as he might wish to be: 'It's gruesome that someone so handsome should care'. Now, through the alchemy of pop music, Morrissey has the one that he can't have and it's written all over his face.

Attitude, February 1995

Interview With Oscar Wilde

How does it feel to be the world's most famous bugger?
OSCAR WILDE: Perhaps I merely reveal myself to be a hopelessly deluded old fool, but I would prefer to think that my fame in the latter part of the twentieth century is a result of my linguistic rather than my pederastic activities; that after the passage of time, when people talk of my legendary tongue, the image it conjures up is more associated with a theatre, a salon, or a first-class restaurant than a bordello.
Yes, of course. But you've become a hero to millions of queens . . .
A hero? In what way?
As the first gay man, the one who gave gay men their sensibility, who gave them a name and a face.
I can assure you I was not the first gay man. There were plenty of other dissolutes, although, admittedly I was for a while perhaps second to none in the sheer athleticism of my indulgence.
No, no, you misunderstand me. Today 'gay' means homosexual, er, what you would have called 'Uranian' or 'Greek' love. It's no longer used to suggest vice.
What? You have no other word for the greatest love of all than 'gay'? How dreadful! How do you distinguish between the pure and noble and the filthy and depraved? Where is one supposed to find ideals? In the gutter? Where is the room for the love that inspired Michelangelo, Shakespeare, Alexander? Is everything to be trampled in the dirt?

205

Certainly, I looked for love in the gutter – and that was my error; but since when have the errors of one individual meant to be taken as a manifesto? Has the love that dare not speak its name really become the love that will not pull its pants up?

But surely your speech from the dock about the love that dare not speak its name and how it was intellectual rather than physical, cultural rather than carnal, was just a necessary subterfuge . . .

On the contrary, it was probably one of the most sincere moments of my life. Or rather, it was one of my least insincere moments. It moved the jury. It almost moved me. On the other hand it was not my greatest work. All art, if it is to be art at all, must be quite useless. I was sincere, but it was bad art. That was the tragedy of my life after my ruin.

Well, nevertheless, you remain a hero to gay, er, Uranian men for bravely resisting the homophobia of the British State.

I'm not sure what this 'fear of the same' is that you refer to. I was loathed for being an outsider, for being Irish, for being an upstart, and most of all for being clever. The English are a generous race, they can forgive you everything except being right. I committed the cardinal sin of climbing to the top of the social ladder and parodying the conventions that took me there. People never bring you garlands for puncturing their illusions; they always come after you with knives. On the other hand, perhaps in me English society recognised itself all too well. You see, I was a fraud, a dissembler, a plagiarist and a charlatan – all the essential virtues which made England great.

Yes quite, but I think you misunderstand me again. 'Homophobia' is the fear and loathing of homosexuals, those attracted to the same sex.

Ah, so 'homophobia' is convention?

Yes, of a kind, but it can be challenged today. Today there is something called gay pride. Gay men show the world that they are proud to be gay, that they're no longer ashamed. You helped to make that possible.

Pride is something I know about. Pride is something I made a special study of. Pride is what led to my downfall. I invited disaster into my life and set up a table for it by my endless vain indiscretions, most particularly with Bosie. Yes, the Marquess of Queensberry was quite mad, but in allowing the even madder Bosie to provoke him I was quite the maddest. I then compounded my error and sealed my fate by suing him for calling me what I was. In a plot development which Shakespeare himself might have penned, disaster descended on me when I tried to prove a fool a liar. Fools speak sooth – even the dimmest student of drama knows this. But pride goeth before a fall, the clerics parrot to us in their nauseating way. And alas, like too many religious clichés with the meaning wrung out of them through over-use, there is more than a drop of truth left in it.

But it is through gay pride that gay men overcome the oppression and prejudice which ruined you.

Rotting in prison after my sentence and ebbing away in Paris like a cheap watercolour in the rain I had time to consider the hubris that was visited upon me and reinterpret it as a kind of justice. I thought myself the Lord of Language, I thought that I could breathe sense into clay such as Bosie, take meaning where I pleased, find beauty in any place I cared, no matter how sordid or polluted, that truth and falsehood were preoccupations of those without imagination enough to tell a pretty lie. I saw insincerity as a way of multiplying my personality.

But today we celebrate you as a postmodernist, a playful wearer of masks, the pope of inauthenticity. You're one of the creators of what we call today the 'gay sensibility'.

I do not know what this 'gay sensibility' is that you speak of. Aestheticism was my guiding principle. But I tell you this about inauthenticity: pride is a mask. Behind it you will always find something else; sometimes another mask, more often than not merely sorrow. Sorrow is not a mask for anything, sorrow merely *is*. That is its truest hardship. It is also its greatest virtue. In sorrow you are forced to see things

207

and people as they really are. After my fall, sorrow was my only personality.

But that is why gay pride is so important. Gay men come out to the world and announce who they really are and demand that the world accepts them, so that they cannot be pilloried as you were.

Are you telling me that you do to yourselves, of your own volition, that which it took the full majesty of the law, the gutter press, the Marquess of Queensberry and the Government of the day, to do to me? That you put yourselves in the dock and drag your own private life out for the world to see?

Well, yes, but it isn't like that. You showed that visibility was the important thing. You gave the love that had no name a name and an identity. Within a few generations, a movement had developed which was strong enough to encourage people to be open about their sexuality.

Extraordinary. You admire my insincerity and claim it as part of this thing you call a 'gay sensibility' and yet with your strange ritual of 'coming out', you seem keen, like religious zealots, to strip yourselves naked before the world; a strange way for any debutante to behave. Suddenly Anglicanism seems quite appealing. My dear young man, my 'coming out' cost me everything I owned and valued. But most of all, it cost me my wife and my family.

Today, gay men don't get married.

You do not marry? There are no women in your lives? How do you propagate yourselves?

We don't. We leave it to straights.

To *what*? – Oh never mind. You have no children? But that is too terrible for words. Of all the incredible things you have told me about your time this is the one I find most shocking. My children were the most precious things in the world to me. When the courts took them away it was the bitterest blow – bitterer by far than the humiliation, imprisonment and bankruptcy. No children! I take it, then, that these 'gay' men today are all artists?

Well, no. Not the kind of artists you mean.

But what do they leave for the world? If they have no

children and no art, what do they contribute? What is their legacy for posterity? With what promise of immortality do they warm themselves in their old age?

Well, I don't think that concerns people today so much. Gay men just enjoy life and take each day as it comes. And some of them maybe try to make things a bit better for the next generation.

So pleasure is all there is?

Well, it's part of being gay in the Nineties. Pleasure is how gay men validate themselves and their sexuality in a world which has done much to denigrate them.

I am appalled. Where does a concept of sin fit into this world of pleasure? In the period before my arrest I allowed myself to become a corrupt pleasure-seeker, a slave to my own appetite. I betrayed my wife and family. I betrayed my gifts, my country and my ancestors. I thought only of how to satisfy my lust and was always on the look-out for new ways of indulging it. I was utterly, utterly lost. It did not validate me or this thing you call my 'sexuality' – it quite undid me. The Lord of Language was not even the Lord of his own soul. I grew fat and bloated on vice; like some Ottoman potentate I devoured whole sub-continents but was left hungry. If I hadn't been arrested I would probably have exploded into a porridge of corruption. Towards the end I only wrote for money, and the money was only to slake my unquenchable thirst for sensual ease. To cure the soul by means of the senses is a doomed project.

But didn't you once say that the moralist is one who lectures on the dangers of sins of which they have grown tired? And that pleasure is what one should live for, since nothing ages like happiness?

No, Lord Henry Wotton says it in *The Picture of Dorian Gray*. But, yes, Lord Henry was me – or rather, one of the masks I wore. However, these sentiments are pure style; only a fool would take them literally.

Is there any message that you would like to pass on to your admirers?

No, except one thing. Don't make love to boys whose

209

fathers cannot spell 'sodomite'. Their education is likely to be very poor and their manners even worse.

Attitude, February 1995

STRAIGHT MAN OF POP

WAY BACK IN 1984, Bronski Beat had a hit with a cover version of Donna Summer's disco classic 'I Feel Love'. The video of the two singer-freaks – front-man Jimmy Somerville and guest vocalist Marc Almond – makes strangely compelling viewing. Jimmy, in baseball jacket and jeans, hops awkwardly from one foot to the other, looking all of twelve, singing in his falsetto-cum-castrato; Marc is doing his Maria Callas in leather routine. But these freaks are telling us they feel love. Which one do you believe?

The early Eighties was a good time to be a freak. Lots of people made a good living out of it. Marc, Jimmy, Pete Burns and Boy George are just a few who are still hacking it. Ironically Jimmy was at once the most freakish and yet the most straitlaced of that crew. Not so much small as miniaturised, with a large head and high forehead, like Marvin the Martian (well, at least I didn't make any reference to root vegetables) and with a voice which brought dogs running from miles around, Jimmy was not what you might call the boy-next-door type.

And yet Jimmy went out of his way to present himself as normal and down-to-earth. The others flirted with glamour and mystery, playing on their ugliness and transcending it, but Jimmy offered just 'himself'. Instead of using his freakishness the way that the others did, as another special effect in the distorting lens of stardom, he seemed keen to use stardom to tell the world how ordinary he was.

211

In the sexual sphere, Jimmy was equally unambiguous. The others were coy and enigmatic about their sexuality, Jimmy stated it bluntly, developing a reputation for impatience with other pop stars less forthright than he was. After 'I Feel Love', Jimmy had a bust-up with Marc over his Bishop-of-London tendencies, then a run-in with the Pet Shop Boys and Andy Bell. A more unpleasant person than myself might have described Jimmy as an Eighties lesbian trapped in a Seventies gay man's body.

Even when stars finally come out they are still not worthy: 'I hope I'm not going to get lumped in with Melissa Etheridge, Neil Tennant and kd fucking lang,' Jimmy said recently. 'I've never been scared from the outset of specifying that I love men, or hidden the gender in my songs.'

Are there any gay performers he admires?

'Och, I was wondering when you were going to bring that up,' he groans, in a surprisingly deep, no-nonsense Glaswegian voice. 'I don't really know . . . It's funny because I did an AIDS benefit in Vienna and Marc Almond was there and we did this version of "I Feel Love" and we got on fine.'

I put it to Jimmy that the others may have been closeted but they were undeniably different, while Jimmy was very conformist in his appearance, as if trying to be his own positive image. 'Yeah, yeah, they were different, but they were in drag,' he argues. 'It wasn't anything new. People weren't threatened by it and forced to discuss it. Basically George took over Danny La Rue!'

Perhaps there is some truth in this, but why should pop 'threaten' us? Can't it just inspire us? Why should it be political? Jimmy's 'politics' are always there. The use of male pronouns in his lyrics – commendable as it may be (and virtually no one else does it) – even makes some gay people wince. Is this 'internalised homophobia' or is too much riding on it for it to work as pop?

'But what am I supposed to do?' retorts Jimmy. 'I'm a gay man. There's no room for ambiguity in my life because I suspect it would stop me from being a happier man. By refusing to deal with ambiguity I'm at least trying to find out what kind of person I am, what it is that makes me what I am. If I go through life clouding the issue I don't think I'm going to get anywhere.'

It's interesting that while Jimmy may consider himself the existentialist pop star whose art is about identity – denotation not connotation, authenticity not duplicity – he made a career largely out of cover versions. Covers, moreover, of Seventies disco records whose sexuality and gender is often confused. He argues that gay men turn to these songs because there are no other 'gay' songs (apart from his own). 'There are just so few with openly gay lyrics,' he says. 'When I do gay gigs the atmosphere is amazing because everyone gets off on finally having some songs that speak to them.' But many gay men – more than those who buy Jimmy's records – identify 'inauthentically' with heterosexual divas and torch-song singers.

And Jimmy does it himself in every hit single he's ever had. For all his 'truthfulness', Jimmy sings *falsetto*. 'I enjoy falsetto. It's grown with me and I have a lot of control over it.' Significantly, this is the only feminine quality he exhibits – everything else is resolutely butch. So who is the 'real' Jimmy Somerville – the one who sings in a 'feminine' voice, or the one in front of me with a Glaswegian accent deep enough to fry haggis in?

'I'm not sure,' he demurs. 'Sexually I'm completely passive. I've only ever fucked about four men in my whole life. Maybe that's because when I was younger I was abused, although I don't have a problem with being passive. But out of the bedroom I'm quite an aggressive, dominant person. I don't give up until I get my own way.'

Would he like to be looked after?

'In my head I'd really like a relationship where I didn't work – I love doing housework and being at home. But then, I don't really need a relationship. The relationships I have with my friends are the relationships that I want and need. When I have a relationship with someone, it's more lust than love, and that wears off very quickly, and then I just want to move on to the next thing. I think that we are conditioned by

213

straight society to have heterosexual expectations in relationships, expectations which aren't suitable for gay men.'

Perhaps. But then, even queers are of man and woman born and maybe they shouldn't pretend that they can forget that.

Jimmy's father was a roofer and his mother a cleaner. It seems his father was a distant but all-important figure. Asked if his parents are still alive he replies, 'No, my dad's dead. He died when I was twenty-four.' Almost by way of an afterthought he adds: 'My mum's still alive.' He told her about his gay feelings when he was fifteen. 'She was great about it, actually, but she didn't understand. Still she told me I was still her son, and all that.' But it was his father's indifference which seems to have preoccupied him. 'I found out later that she told my dad and he just said, "well, leave him to find his own way" – which I kind of resented. No one was giving me any directions about where to go, what to do or what was going to happen.' Perhaps Jimmy would have preferred even a harsh paternal response to the indifference he got, and it seems he never forgave his father. What did he feel when he died? 'I don't really know. I don't think I felt anything; I felt I had to be part of this ritual of "family loss", but I didn't really know him.'

Jimmy's resentment is understandable. Living in a small working-class Glaswegian home, he shared a bedroom with his sister until the age of twelve, when it was decided that he was too old to continue sharing. So he was moved into the house of the family living downstairs, who were 'old family friends' – but they still weren't family. 'Because I was moved out, and what was going on in my head sexually, I become a loner and never developed any close emotional attachment to my family,' he says.

Growing up short, strange-looking and queer is difficult anywhere, but growing up these things in Glasgow in the late Sixties and early Seventies must have been nightmarish. 'Pretty much my whole youth was spent in tears. That was a lot to do with the fact that I became aware of my sexuality at a very early age – that really determined how I was treated in

214

my youth. I can understand the argument for coming out later – sometimes I wish I hadn't come out until I was twenty-three instead of thirteen.'

Who to?

'Well, at the time, anyone actually, because I'd just discovered the bus station!' he says, laughing. 'But looking back on it I was being abused. I was being used by these older men as a thing, purely for their own sexual gratification.'

From an early age, sex proved to be something that separated Jimmy from human intimacy rather than brought it to him. The unspoken fear of heterosexual incest ejected him from his family, and his homosexuality left him isolated – even from the people he was having sex with. So Jimmy, like a thousand working-class queer boys before him, with no prospect of a grant-assisted escape to university with a nice gay soc, ran away. 'I had to leave because I was hanging out with really nasty, dodgy, horrible people,' he says with feeling. 'We would run around the centre of Glasgow, pissed on cheap lager, terrorising everyone. I discovered some terrible things about them and decided to leave. I got on the train for Euston, and ended up sleeping in the station for the first five nights.'

London turned out to be much kinder to Jimmy than Glasgow and saw the launch of his pop career with the electro-pop band Bronski Beat. But after two top ten hits ('Smalltown Boy' and 'Tell Me Why') Jimmy left in 1984. He lasted longer with The Communards, with the keyboard-ist Richard Coles, scoring nine top thirty singles and a number one with 'Don't Leave Me This Way' before moving on. 'Working with Jimmy was very difficult but rewarding,' Coles recalls. 'There were lots of tears before bedtime, and I could have quite cheerfully killed him on more than one occasion, but it was worth it. I've never worked with anyone more talented.' After the Communards, Jimmy left Britain to live in San Francisco, but he came back six months later, having discovered that America was not to be his home after all.

So has the runaway found a home yet? 'No, I don't think I

have,' Jimmy admits. 'But does anyone, really? It's kind of frightening, but it's also exciting, because it makes me think. Seeing close friends die from AIDS has made me realise that there are only two certainties in life: birth and death. When I was a kid we lived opposite this big hospital which is now the leading hospital for AIDS in Scotland. It's funny to think that I was sleeping opposite that hospital all those years. I've called the new album *Dare to Love*, because I think that the thing to do is to just go with it – because whatever you do, you're going to end up dead!' Jimmy laughs nervously or challengingly, I'm not sure which.

Nevertheless the title track from the new album is actually a 'political' song about the persecution of homosexuals. Unfortunately, as the preachiest track on the album, this is also the least appealing and, frankly, doesn't make homo-love very attractive, characterising it once again in terms of oppression. Is he still using politics to stand in for feelings?

'A lot of the songs I've written in the past have talked about "we think,' and "we feel" – but I suddenly realised, who is this "we" – it's what *I* think and feel. The first half is about me and the second half is about the age of consent. I was once really depressed and the family doctor convinced my mum that I should see a psychiatrist, so I ended up in a psychiatric hospital. So it's dealing with the political, but in a personal way.'

But isn't it ironic that his latest album should be called *Dare to Love*, when he himself had admitted that he doesn't really love so much as lust, repeating the pattern which made him a loner in the first place? 'Maybe,' grants Jimmy. 'But I really feel that my relationships with my friends are what is important. I can't stop myself from kidding myself some-times that what I want is a one-on-one relationship – but deep down, I know that isn't what I want.'

From 'I Feel Love' to 'Dare to Love' it seems that the honest, upfront, split-me-down-the-middle-and-am-I-not-gay? honest pop star has nasty contradictions and unresolved ambivalences which might have made him more of a, well, pop star, if he hadn't refused to 'deal in

216

ambiguity'. Funnily enough, Jimmy is quite proud of his moment with Marc back in 1984. 'I think that song was really one of the most subversive moments in pop,' Jimmy tells me. Oh really? 'Yes, because it was a huge hit, but it was just one big gay threesome – me, Marc and then halfway through, this guy called Johnny.' Indeed, they do look painfully uncomfortable together, like two gay men repelled by one another but thrown together by a mutual shagging interest: 'Johnny Love, Johnny Stardom, Johnny Tomorrow – Johnny, remember me.'

I'm convinced they both feel love, but I'm wondering which one posterity will remember. Ironically it might be the one who told us that he was just an 'ordinary bloke' – if only because no-one will ever be able to listen to Sylvester again without thinking of Ian Hislop.

Attitude, July 1995

Shopping

DEVIANCE SELLS

'FIVE PEOPLE IN this cinema have appeared in a porn film,' accuses the man on the screen. 'Seventeen of you are wearing nothing under your jeans ... One of the women in this cinema was born a man.' A strange way to advertise whisky this, accusing your audience of being freaks and pervs. But nowadays this is *flattery*. 'You look like ordinary people. But then you think I'm drinking ordinary whisky.' The ad closes with the product shot and the words: 'No ordinary whisky.' The message is clear: despite appearances, you are really interesting people; buy our extraordinary product and you will realise your extraordinary potential.

Everyone wants to be different these days. Or so advertisers seem to think. A sado-masochistic scenario between two men is used to sell Tennent's lager; Carl Lewis in red stilettos promotes car tyres and Levi's sells its 'super loose' jeans with a poster of some decadent, druggy-looking party-goers in leather. The sleazy production and 'superloose' legend all convey an 'anything goes' attitude. Quite a break from the clean-cut images of America which Levi's has become famous for.

Maybe it shouldn't be so surprising. The prime 'yoof' slots on TV have long been exploiting younger people's fascination with the bizarre. Programmes such as *The Word*, *Eurotrash*, *Penn and Teller* and *Viva Cabaret* owe their success to their ability to deliver taboo-breaking images. What *is* surprising is that advertisers have taken the

221

voyeuristic, transgressive appeal of these shows and exploited it as an aspiration of the youth market.

Advertisers have good reason to believe that deviance sells. The recent Demos Genderquake report suggested that most young people welcomed the decline of old certainties; that young people are now 'in favour of androgyny', rejecting 'fixed gender roles' and moving away 'from attachments to authority, puritanical codes, security and parochialism'. But advertising agencies had already learnt this from their own market research. A year ago the ad agency Collete Dickenson & Pearce in its 'Lost Generation' survey claimed to have identified a group of people dubbed 'New Realists' who could be appealed to by 'daring to be different'. In other words, 'Deviance' has become for many young people a distinctive style with which to navigate a world without reliable landmarks.

'Daring to be different' has thus become a mantra in advertising aimed at young people. In a TV ad for Irn-Bru a young girl with attitude turns a handsome (and rather loathsomely 'nice') prince back into a toad followed by the words 'Think different' flashed on the screen. In another soft drinks ad a strange young man harangues the camera about being 'different' and urges us to 'see what works for you'. And the famous Tango ads also appeal to young people's attraction to the odd; what could be more different than a fat, bald orange man in a nappy?

Advertisers have always appealed to young people's taste for rebellion. But this rebellion used to be ritualised and uniform. Young people were expected to want to be different from their parents but not from other young people – in fact they were supposed to want to be *just like* other young people; in terms of what they wore, how they cut their hair and what they listened to. The glossy ideal of rebellion that 'the kids' were supposed to aspire to was, in fact, anything but. In the mid Eighties this peaked with the nostalgic, heritage-industry 'rebellion' of cool retro Fifties style, of Levi's jeans, white T-shirts and old rock 'n' roll.

But with the proliferation of new media and new lifestyle

the youth market began fragmenting and with it went the certainties about what young people wanted. The young's interest in rebellion became less ritualised, less bound up with the branding of commodities, more about attitudes. Advertising began to abandon its traditional 'marketising', the creation of homogeneous markets to sell to. 'Trying to create a "cool" image around a product with glossy production values no longer works,' says Charlie Sampson of the ad agency Cowan Kemsley Taylor which has a special interest in the youth market. 'Nowadays, advertisers have to be where young people's heads are at rather than their wardrobes.'

Roy Edmonson of Shilland and Co., PR for Levi's, claims that the Warhol party 'super loose' ad continues the Levi's tradition of rebellion, but, he admits, something of a departure. 'This is probably more contemporary than before; perhaps the rebellion it represents is more to do with lifestyles than with what you wear.' None of the people in the ad are apparently wearing jeans.

The Levi's and Canadian Club are also rather 'queer', relying on one of the most intensely felt forms of 'difference'; sexual deviance. In the Eighties, homosexuals embraced the once derogatory word 'queer' precisely because it celebrated their difference. Queer politics revelled in the deviant cachet of homosexuality, expressing itself loudly and stylishly through S&M chic, 'Queer as Fuck' T-shirts, and ACT-UP/ OutRage 'kiss-in' stunts.

This stylisation of transgression, like all post-modern avant-gardism, was soon assimilated into the mainstream. Madonna's *Sex*, with its homage to lesbianism and S&M was the first example. Now it is commonplace, albeit in diluted form. In addition to the 'fetish' connotations of the Levi's 'super loose' revellers, and the jokey sadomasochism of the Tennent's Lager TV ad (where a thirsty masochist without a pint begs a sadist to take another sip from his – he refuses, naturally), S&M chic has made some surprising appearances. An award-winning ad for Dunlop tyres used footage of glamorous creatures in leather masks and spiky rubber outfits to the strains of Velvet Underground's 'Venus in Furs' ('Shiny, shiny, shiny boots of leather/Whiplash girl child in the dark'). Little wonder then, the ad was the subject of a complaint to the Advertising Standards Authority on the grounds that it promoted sado-masochism.

But, like many ads exploiting the appeal of difference, its message was ambivalent. 'Prepared for the unexpected' was the end line, suggesting Dunlop would keep you 'on the straight and narrow' when faced with queer attractions. (Likewise, when the Canadian Club cinema ad tells the audience it looks ordinary, this is partly a reassurance.)

Nevertheless the celebration/exploitation of difference in advertising continues apace, even in ads, like Uniroyal, not specifically targeted at young people. A Smirnoff ad shows the cool, respectably bourgeois sophistication of a 1920s cruise liner distorted through a vodka bottle into something weird and wonderful (and dangerous), while a McDonald's promotion of a free Bic razor finishes with a shot of a lucky male recipient shaving his legs in the bath.

Some might see all this as merely a sign of *fin de siècle* decadence, of how jaded appetites have become under the relentless titillation of popular culture. Perhaps. And then again, perhaps it is just that advertisers have to try a little harder to inspire punters that can no longer be relied upon to conform to expectations any more.

Whatever the truth, there is certainly evidence of desperation on the part of advertisers, especially where the new uncertainties of the youth market are concerned. The most shocking accusation in that shocking Canadian Club ad is undoubtedly 'Seven people in this cinema aren't paying any attention to me at all.'

Guardian, 11 November 1995

METROSEXUALS

'IT'S BEEN KEPT underground for too long,' observes one sharply dressed 'metrosexual' in his early twenties. He has a perfect complexion and precisely gelled hair, and is inspecting a display of costly aftershaves. 'This exhibition shows that male vanity's finally coming out of the closet.'

And it's busy filling the new-found space in there with expensive clothes and accessories. 'It's a Man's World – Britain's first style exhibition for men', organised by *GQ* magazine in London last weekend, shows that male narcissism has arrived and we'd better get used to it.

With pavilions representing top men's fashion designers such as Calvin Klein, Ralph Lauren and Giorgio Armani and all the latest 'grooming' products, It's a Man's World is, as Peter Stuart, *GQ* publisher, describes it, 'a terrific shopping experience'.

Metrosexual man, the single young man with a high disposable income, living or working in the city (because that's where all the best shops are), is perhaps the most promising consumer market of the decade. In the Eighties he was only to be found inside fashion magazines such as *GQ*, in television advertisements for Levi's jeans or in gay bars. In the Nineties, he's everywhere and he's going shopping.

Metrosexual man wears Davidoff 'Cool Water' aftershave (the one with the naked bodybuilder on the beach), Paul Smith jackets (Ryan Giggs wears them), corduroy shirts (Elvis wore them), chinos (Steve McQueen wore them), motorcycle boots (Marlon Brando wore them) and Calvin Klein underwear (Marky Mark wore nothing else). Metrosexual man is a commodity fetishist, a collector of fantasies about the male sold to him by advertising.

Even the title of the exhibition reveals how much times have changed. Not so long ago the expression conveyed the idea that the world belonged to that half which shaved; Nowadays, it seems to mean that you have to have the right *après-rasage* face cream.

On one of the stands at It's A Man's World men lie supine while attractive women in white coats rub luxurious moisturisers into their faces; cameras display the beauty treatment in close-up on banks of screens. Behold the metrosexual pampered by women, technology and capitalism; behold the metrosexual as star.

'It feels nice. Basically you get a free facial out of it,' says James, a nineteen-year-old in natty jeans and Italian dadshirt, face aglow. 'This stuff is a bit out of my price range as I'm a student,' he confesses. 'But if I had the money I might well buy the stuff.'

Is all this attention to appearance a good thing? 'Yes,' says another young man, casually-but-carefully dressed in Caterpillar boots, pristine Levi's, T-shirt, sweatshirt and bomber jacket. 'If women take so much trouble over their appearance it's only fair that men should take a bit more care themselves. My girlfriend would certainly agree!'

But is it really about fairness, or is it about the way you feel when you look in the mirror? 'I suppose it's mostly the way you feel,' he admits.

A twenty-one-year-old stock manager in Gap jeans agrees. 'Men are just as vain as women and it's a good thing that we're able to show it these days.'

One of the major interests behind metrosexual pride is, as the impressive list of sponsors of this event shows (Dunhill to Porsche, Timberland to Simpson's of Piccadilly), big business. Metrosexuals are the creation of capitalism's voracious appetite for new markets.

Heterosexual men used to be the world's worst consumers. All they bought was beer, fags and the occasional Durex; the Wife or 'Mum' bought everything else. In a consumerist world, heterosexual men had no future. So they were replaced by the metrosexual.

The promotion of metrosexuality was left to the men's style press, magazines such as *The Face*, *GQ*, *Esquire*, *Arena* and *FHM*, the new media which took off in the Eighties and is still growing (*GQ* gains 10,000 new readers every month). They filled their magazines with images of narcissistic young men sporting fashionable clothes and accessories. And they persuaded other young men to study them with a mixture of envy and desire.

Some people said unkind things. American *GQ*, for example, was popularly dubbed 'Gay Quarterly'. Little wonder that all these magazines – with the possible exception of *The Face* – address their readership as if none of them was homosexual or even bisexual. Little wonder that 'It's A Man's World' organiser Peter Stuart found it necessary to tell me that 'all the men will bring their girlfriends'.

The 'heterosexual' address of these magazines is a convention, there to reassure the readership and the advertisers that their unmanly passions are in fact manly. Nevertheless, the metrosexual man contradicts the basic premise of traditional heterosexuality – that only women are looked at and only men do the looking. Metrosexual man might prefer women, he might prefer men, but when all's said and done nothing comes between him and his reflection.

Metrosexuality was, of course, test-marketed on gay men – with enormous success. It's a Man's World is billed as the first man's style exhibition – but the Gay Lifestyles Exhibition, which features fashion shows and a whole range of 'men's products', is already in its third year. It was in the style-obsessed Eighties that the 'gay lifestyle' – the single man living in the metropolis, and taking himself as his own love object – became a model for non-homosexuals.

Perhaps this is why *Attitude*, a style magazine launched

earlier this year, felt able to break with convention, and address itself openly to gay men and what it called 'strays' ('gay-acting' straight men).

The New Lad bible, *Loaded*, for all its features on sport, babes and sport, is metrosexual. Just as its anti-style is a style (last month it carried a supplement for 'no-nonsense' clothes, such as jeans and boots), its heterosexuality is so self-conscious, so studied, that it's actually rather camp. New Lads, for all their burping blokeishness, are just as much in love with their own image as any other metrosexual – they just haven't come to terms yet.

Nor is metrosexuality a vice restricted to the poncey Southern middle classes. Working-class boys are, if anything, even more susceptible to it. For example, Newcastle men between the ages of eighteen and thirty-five, apparently spend more money per head on clothes than any other men in Europe. If you live with your mother, as do many working-class boys until they marry, and, crucially, you have a job – your disposable income and your metrosexual tendencies are likely to be high.

And metrosexuals have an amazing sense of solidarity. Back at It's a Man's World, Steve and Paul, two fashionably dressed men-about-London in their late twenties, admit to spending 'a substantial amount' of their income on male cosmetics and clothes, and think that the exhibition is 'great'. But they're worried that they might be letting the metrosexual side down.

Says Steve: 'It's a shame that you picked us because we're gay and people might think that a show like this is just for gays and wouldn't come. The thing is, straight men are just beginning to discover the joys of shopping and we wouldn't want to scare them off.'

Independent, 15 November 1994

LEVI'S

REMEMBER THOSE LONG, dull, pining years when you were a kid and there were no nude men on telly? How women had a monopoly on 'sexiness' and men were only allowed bodies to kick balls around or kill one another? Even *Grandstand* might be worth watching all afternoon if it included a short post-match changing-room interview. And remember how avidly you watched Tarzan movies and eagerly cut out those illustrated classified ads for thongs and bullworkers from the Sunday colour supplements, before your mum began to ask awkward questions about the holes in the paper? (Or was that just me?)

All that was before Nick Kamen's striptease in the launderette. In 1985, the year of Kamen's laundry run, advertising discovered the male body and hasn't been able to leave it alone since. Surprisingly, ten years on, the industry whose job it is to redefine the word 'fickle' several times a day has yet to grow bored of pneumatic pecs and washboard stomachs, which are used to sell everything from ice cream to cleaning fluid. Young queer boys today must be bored flaccid with seeing men get their kit off and probably long for the romantic days when the nearest thing to male nudity was the underwear section of Littlewood's mail order.

Nevertheless, when Kamen shucked off his jeans, peeled off his T-shirt and threw them into the washing machine (didn't anyone ever tell him to wash his colours and whites separately?) he changed the world. The agency behind that

229

Levi's campaign and all those that have followed – Bartle Bogle (now Bartle Bogle Hegarty) – managed, through the innovative flair and confidence of their commercials, to make the new exploitation of men as sex objects that characterised the Eighties appear as if it had been invented by them. As a measure of their success, their audacious 1985 campaign increased sales of Levi's by 800 per cent in five months.

It may appear ironic that advertising for men's clothing sold male nudity to the world, until, that is, you consider that what the advertisers did right from the beginning was to fetishise a certain type of masculinity and attach it to the commodity. This was the tough-but-tender, 'authentic' masculinity of Fifties America, rock 'n' roll, James Dean in *Rebel*, and Marlon Brando in *The Wild One*, a masculinity, in other words, which gay men had enthusiastically worshipped and attempted to appropriate by, well, wearing Levi's. Advertising sold, to its target audience of straight males aged sixteen to twenty four, a 'gay' fantasy about a commodity which had for years been the 'gay jeans'.

For this reason, and the fact that representing men as sex objects had previously been the preserve of gay porn, many Levi's ads looked rather queer. Of course, by making sure that those seen to be enjoying the naked model are always female – see 'Launderette', 'Fridge' (1988), 'Tackle' (1993) and 'Creek' (1994) – the ads try to ward off this possibility. But doing so merely serves to highlight the 'non-heterosexuality' of the ads, that in Levi's-land sexual difference no longer calls the shots, men are the passive object of women's gaze, and masculine does not automatically map on to 'active' and feminine on to 'passive' – something acknowledged in 'Drugstore' (1995) in which it is the girl who buys the condoms and takes the boy out.

In a sense, what is being sold with Levi's jeans masculinity is the 'gay lifestyle' itself: one of the key features of Levi's man is that he is a single young man taking his pleasures where he pleases – Nick Kamen, let us not forget, was doing his own washing, where was the 'little woman' in his life

230

who was supposed to take care of these things? Even when he does have a girlfriend he leaves her (see 'Parting').

But perhaps the most fascinating aspect of the Levi's ads is the way that they push the commodification of the male body to its logical conclusion. There has always been more than a hint in Levi's commercials that the jeans are intimately associated with the ultimate male accessory – the penis. In 'Parting' (1987), the girlfriend who pulls on her soldier-boy's jeans is using them fetishistically as a sexual substitute. In 'Creek' this is deftly played up by tracking down the apparently naked cowboy's body towards his groin as he rises out of the water and showing, instead of his prick, the (wet) product.

The suggestion that the jeans are a type of phallus which can be put on and taken off also implies that Levi's are a kind of drag and that gender itself has been commodified. Again, the advertisers seem hip to this and take the implication to its ironic limit in 'Taxi' (1995), where the all-American masculinity of previous Levi's advertising is sent up by a black drag queen who deceives the macho taxi driver who thinks he's in control. Cue the punchline: 'Cut for men since 1876'.

Launderette (1985) Kamen takes his kecks off, starting a fashion for boxer shorts and a panic among launderette owners about rocks in their machines. After a short-lived pop career, Kamen disappears from view; by today's standards, his much-praised 'hunky' body looks surprisingly scrawny.

Bath (1985) Young stud does chin-ups in his humid Fifties apartment, wearing only a pair of Levi's. Camera zooms in on the product/his arse when he squats, stroking the denim around his buttocks. Sensibly, he decides to cool things down by taking a cold bath, but sadly he keeps the jeans on.

Parting (1987) Soldier boy leaves girlfriend for 'Nam. As he steps on a Greyhound Bus he hands her a package which turns out to be his Levi's. Later, lying on her bed, she pulls them on slowly, eyes closed, a rapturous look on her face.

Fridge (1988) Ramshackle diner in the middle of a baking desert, gorgeous babe behind the counter. Hunk with fabby blue contact lenses saunters downstairs wearing only his boxer shorts. Babe opens fridge and hands him a pair of Levi's. He pulls them on slowly, eyes closed etc, etc (that soldier's jeans sure get around) to the sounds of Muddy Waters' 'Mannish Boy'.

Pick-up (1989) Girl rescued from breakdown with nerdy bloke by hunk in pick-up truck who takes off his jeans (natch) to use as tow rope. The legend 'Levi's: separates the men from the boys' would be more convincing if the man didn't have perfectly gelled hair, Clinique skin and a red neckerchief which looks positively starched.

Pool Hall (1991) *Color of Money*-inspired ad has sexy bloke in Levi's play fat ugly bloke in rancid trousers; sexy bloke has no money so bets his jeans, turning out his empty pockets as the camera goes close up on his surprisingly large packet. Unfortunately, the sexy bloke wins and forces fat bloke to take his pants down. A cruel pricktease.

Camera (1991) Brad Pitt in shirt-tails is released from a Mexican prison, but when he comes to claim his property his jeans are missing (that'll teach the pretty blond gringo to wander around with no pants on). Luckily, his girlfriend arrives with a spare pair and they manage a successful photo shoot outside the prison before driving off in her *Thelma and Louise*-style convertible.

Swimmer (1992) Based on the film of the same name starring Burt Lancaster, a young man wearing only a pair of Levi's swims through a series of private pools, watched admiringly by the frustrated wives of unattractive old men. Ends with him diving from the high board with a female swimmer. One of the unattractive old husbands is coded slightly faggy by the way he camply motions with his hand for his security guards to leave the swimmer alone.

Night and Day (1992) A girl tries to find a man who fits a pair of Levi's dropped at midnight (a role reversal of Cinderella). Each of her prospective candidates is a mock-up of a famous man-as-sex-object photograph, and the one

232

who finally fits the jeans is a facsimile of Herb Ritts' screamingly camp tyre boy.

Camp Fire (1993) A group of cowboys have their picture taken around a campfire by a female photographer. We see, through her eyes, the crotch of the cutest one, crouching by the fire, legs apart. Eventually her 'castrating' gaze proves too much and he leaps up, yelling and fanning his crotch.

Tackle (1993) An American football player gets debagged in front of an admiring female spectator (who is almost as pretty as him) eating melted marshmallow (Phnarr, phnarr!). Worse, he almost gets his hair mussed.

Creek (1994) Two 'innocent' Amish girls can't believe their luck when they come across a muscular young cowboy bathing, apparently naked. But, not knowing this is a Levi's ad, they're being clit-teased something rotten.

Fall (1994) A Freudian delight: a man falls off an oil derrick (so phallic) and breaks his leg (so castrated). In hospital he stops an older female nurse from cutting off his jeans – so she pulls them off instead, and as the music crescendos he looks about to swoon. But before she can have her way with him, a middle-aged doctor rushes in. Dad? Or just a jealous fag?

Drugstore (1995) A boy buys condoms from drugstore owner and then knocks at his door to take out his daughter. 'Sister' ad plays trick on you by revealing at the last moment that the condom buyer is a Twenties riot grrrl and her date the drugstore owner's well-groomed son. The latter version is, of course, more in keeping with the world created by Levi's advertising.

Taxi (1995) *The Crying Game* in a Yellow Cab. Stunning black woman takes a ride in a taxi. Grinning, repellent driver ogles her in rear-view mirror, his toothpick making lewd gestures. Glamourpuss passenger takes out face compact and . . . *electric shaver*; starts trimming chin stubble. Driver does double-take, eyes pop and toothpick sags. Tranny leaves cab triumphantly – without paying her fare.

Attitude, August 1995

233

GAYSPIRATIONS

THE CONRAN VENETIAN blinds on the windows are quite gay. And so are the pretty rows of imported bottled beer behind the bar. The stainless steel bar-top is gayer, though. The silver-framed Herb Ritts prints on the wall are definitely gay – especially the one with the model pretending to be a tyre-fitter. The pin-spot lighting is *very* gay. And the rainbow Freedom flags and the neon sign on the wall which says 'YOU CAN BE ANYONE' are *painfully* gay.

It's a quietish Sunday night at Jo Joe's, Birmingham's and perhaps Britain's newest gay pub. But this is a gay pub with a difference. Just opened by Ansells, part of the Allied Domecq group, this pub – the first of a series of outlets – is the first brewery-owned pub to be explicitly marketed as a gay pub.

In the past breweries have been more than slightly closeted about their gay pubs, despite the enormous profits they make from them (a recent survey in one gay magazine found its readers visited bars at least ten times a month). The thinking was that if such bars were known as 'poof-pubs', they would lose out with the non-poof punters.

But now Allied Domecq has decided the gay pub should go mainstream. The company has woken up to the power of the pink pound and is eager to foster an association that previously dared not speak its name. 'We believe the time is now right to adopt an overt and open stance,' the company says. In keeping with this, Jo Joe's is not a sticky-carpet joint in the 'gay ghetto' of Birmingham's Hurst Street area, but a high-profile outfit on the main thoroughfare of Queensway Smallbrook.

And the clientele? Well, they're straight – or at least the group of trendies in their late twenties I'm talking to is. 'We were just passing and we liked the look of the place,' one of the chaps explains, almost apologetically. 'It beats most of the watering-holes in Birmingham. Anyway, we like gay places because they're more relaxed and more fun.'

Gay is now, in other words, just another pub theme. Like Olde Worlde, Spit 'n' Sawdust, High Tech or Cocktail, Gay has become simply an environment for the consumption of alcohol. The much rumoured Gay Guinness ad may never have existed, but its popularity as an idea, connecting beer and homosexuality in a way that was previously unthinkable, gave a hint of what was coming. Jo Joe's shows that gayness has finally been commodified; homosexuality has been made consumer friendly, if not actually soft and furry.

To be fair, there are also some gay customers and most are quite sanguine about becoming a marketing niche. 'I think it's great,' says one late-twenties gay man in baggy shirt and jeans and brown Kickers, clutching a very large and very continental-looking schooner of pale lager, chatting with his straight female friend. 'At last there's a place you can drink in Birmingham that's gay-friendly and top class, and where you can bring your friends along.' But doesn't he feel his homosexuality is being, how shall we say, prostituted? 'No. Not at all. Homosexuality isn't my life – it's just a part of it. I'm all in favour of barriers being broken down and if this bar helps, then that's great.'

The sound of barriers coming down is also the sound of cash registers ringing up profits from the opening up of new markets. Jo Joe's is the brainchild of a think tank within Allied Domecq called ADventure, set up to monitor cultural change and identify new business opportunities. They quickly targeted the youth and the gay markets as priorities, the gay market because of its role in 'style and fashion leadership', particularly in the pub/club sector. In other words: if you've got the gays, then you've got young people and the future is yours.

So it comes as no surprise to find that Jo Joe's is situated next door to a rave club called Tin Tin, which, like most of the best rave clubs, describes itself as 'gay' but locals assure me is mostly straight. In the rave world gayness represents to young people an aspiration, a partying, feelings-driven lifestyle. And also a very effective way of keeping away the ' 'Ere! Are you lookin' at my bird?' type of heterosexual male no one seems to want any more. And lo, on Saturday and Sunday mornings, when Tin Tin closes, the ravers troop into Jo Joe's to sip their fruit juice spritzers and admire the 'YOU CAN BE ANYONE' aspirational neon sign and Allied Domecq scores another cross-over victory with its strategic demographics.

The punters on Birmingham's traditional gay scene, though, are not so sure about barriers coming down. 'Nobody can get in,' a casually if dully dressed gay man in his thirties told me earlier at the Jester, Birmingham's oldest gay pub. 'They turn you away if you don't look right. I think you have to be young and trendy. I must say, though, the bar looks very nice. What you can see through those shuttered blinds,' he added tartly.

It seems that despite all the commercial hijacking of gayness, not everyone is invited to the postmodernist party. The plundering of the margins by the mainstream has ironically left some homosexuals looking very dreary indeed.

Some have decided not to wait to be refused admission and have tried rallying the faithful against this appropriation of their sexuality. There have already been demonstrations outside Jo Joe's complaining about their allegedly discriminatory door policy. 'I for one won't be drinking in that establishment,' fulminates one lost patron in the local gay freesheet. But most gay male customers at Jo Joe's are unperturbed by the demos. 'Well, in the end, this is a commercial establishment,' says one young professional. 'And a very nice one at that. And if the management wants to keep out shaven-headed lesbians with I AM A DYKE tattooed on their foreheads, then why shouldn't they? No one's being turned away for being gay – they're being turned away for being tasteless.'

Watching the glamorous trannie bar staff dancing in the middle of the pub, shaking their tambourines and wiggling their hips to the impeccable sound system belting out 'I Wanna be Free, Gay and Happy', it strikes me that mass consumerism has achieved something miraculous. Gay is something that everyone can now buy into. Which is, if you have the money, rather liberating.

You really can be anyone, just don't be unfashionable. Or poor.

Observer, 3 September 1995

Men

BACKS TO THE WALL

AT THE HEIGHT of the age of consent debate in the House of Commons, Nicholas Fairbairn reminded the Honourable Members of just what was at stake. 'What we are talking about here,' he intoned gravely, 'is the putting of a penis into a man's arsehole.'

At moments of national crisis you can always rely upon crusty old colonels and medievalist politicians to put into words what everybody else is thinking but is too shy to mention. In their bluster about 'sodomy' and 'buggery', Fairbairn, Paisley and the other monsters of the Id who stalk the House of Commons encapsulate perfectly what the issue had come to represent symbolically – the sanctity of men's bottoms.

What was under review was not the *gay* age of consent, but the *male* age of consent, and whether or not the powers of the state should be mustered to protect male cherries for a longer period than the female variety. In this scenario the rich diversity of male homosexual behaviour was reduced to the single, terrible image of boys being buggered. The debate was not over homosexuality *per se* (after all, lesbianism has effective parity with the heterosexual age of consent), but *masculinity*, and the ways in which boys are made – whether they like it or not – into men.

One of the arguments put forward by those opposed to equality was that boys mature slower than girls – this despite the fact that the BMA itself supported equality. This is

241

because it articulates a cultural 'truth' rather than a scientific one. Put crudely, women are 'made' to be penetrated while men are not. It worried MPs that the law might treat male and female orifices alike, and no longer privilege masculinity as a priceless phenomenon that must be nurtured by society and the state.

Homosexuality is still seen by many if not most, as the worst possible failure in the process of masculinisation, widely equated with the ruin of the family and Western civilisation. Why? Precisely because of its *attractiveness*. Official heterosexuality is so deeply unfulfilling and unrewarding a lifestyle that boys must be forbidden even considering the alternative. As Warren Farrell has pointed out in his book, *The Myth of Male Power*, when boys enter adolescence and realise what kind of performance is required of them as men, their suicide rate increases by *25,000 per cent*. This is why homosexuality must be described as 'unnatural' and 'perverse', and why the state must persecute it. Otherwise, boys might have a choice between quick death by their own hand, or the slow death our society calls 'manhood'.

You can see this thinking in the Home Secretary Michael Howard's argument against equality, in which he admitted that medical opinion considerd that sexual orientation was fixed by the age of sixteen in most cases, but "there would be some young men for whom homosexual experiences after that age would have potentially disturbing effects."

In other words, while we acknowledge that most of those boys who are going to fail as men have already failed at the age of sixteen the possibility, however slight, that some young man who is otherwise heterosexual might develop a taste for non-heterosexual behaviour is a 'disturbing effect' for the state to consider, and criminalising all young men who have sex with men before they are eighteen is a price well worth paying to prevent it. Thus the lives of and liberty of young gay men are worthless, compared to the 'successful' masculinisation of one heterosexual man.

But this is also why the unequal age of consent for

homosexual activity is not simply a gay issue. The legal persecution of homosexuality is part of the larger process by which all men are denied choice and coerced into performing a desperate and airless definition of masculinity: exclusive heterosexuality, marriage, alienation from 'feminine' feelings and, above all, the imperative to always be a 'fucker' and never a 'fucked'. This is a tragedy for all men. After all, what boy in his right mind would *choose* to grow up into Nicholas Fairbairn?

Time Out, 19 March 1994

NEW LADS AND OLD MEN

MEN ARE IN danger of extinction. The economic revolution of the last two 'post-industrial' decades has hit them badly. As traditionally 'masculine' heavy industries have dwindled, two million men have disappeared from the work force, and it is forecast that by the end of the century more women will be employed than men. Men are also being given their cards at home: more and more women are opting for divorce or starting families without men. At the same time, the ascendancy of feminism has made masculinity problematical, portraying it as the root of all evil, from rape and war to joyriding and wet toilet seats.

The phasing out of traditional masculinity by capitalism, its redundancy in many modern families and its undesirability in the social sphere has resulted in what has been termed a 'crisis of masculinity'. Not surprisingly, this crisis has produced a 'masculinist backlash'. By the end of the Eighties a 'men's movement' had emerged in America, which claimed that feminism had robbed men of their self-respect and rights as fathers and individuals. (Women and feminism, of course, were easier targets than a faceless capitalism.)

Some of the more spiritual leaders of the men's movement, such as the poet Robert Bly, argued not so much that feminism was the enemy, but that there was a need for men to get in touch with their 'deep masculine'. Modern man, he argued in his bestseller *Iron John*, was cut off from masculine culture and confused about how exactly to be a man. While women had gained from the sexual and economic upheavals since the war, becoming more assertive and powerful, men were sadly lacking in confidence and energy. He offered the parable of a boy smothered by his mother's influence who finds Iron John, a hairy 'Wild Man' who lived deep in the forest, and who learns from him how to get in touch with his 'deep masculine', overcome his mother's power, win battles and generally become a successful guy.

The mainstream impact of the men's movement's philosophy in the USA was demonstrated by the phenomenal popularity of *Home Improvement*. A so-so sit-com about a husband who is obsessed with all things virile and confused by the demands of the 'female' world (his wife and family) and receives advice over the garden fence from a Robert Bly figure who happens to live next door, it became the top-rated comedy show on American TV within weeks of its launch.

In Britain, despite an equally deep sense of crisis, the men's movement failed to take root. With the exception of a few embittered male journalists such as Neil Lyndon and David Thomas, no leadership emerged. British men turned out to be too self-conscious in talking about 'men's issues' to adopt the American approach. Instead of the men's movement, what developed in Britain in the late Eighties and early Nineties was the phenomenon of the 'New Lad'.

Ostensibly a reaction against the woman-dominated 'New Man' image, this movement, which had no real leadership or organisation, took up many of the principles of the American men's movement. But instead of weekends in the forest beating drums and rapping in the sweat-lodge, British men went to watch footie.

The new fashionability of football coincided with the discovery by men (often engaged in 'feminine' jobs) that football was a way of getting in touch with their 'deep masculine', without being ribbed by their mates. Unlike the USA where the men's movement cut across classes, initially the New Lad movement was a predominantly middle-class phenomenon with literary and journalistic roots. Britain's Robert Bly was Nick Hornby, his *Iron John* a book entitled *Fever Pitch*, which garnered astonishing literary plaudits. Hornby writes about being a man, but obliquely, through the medium of the man's world of football. *Fever Pitch* told the story of a boy, awkward and lonely, separated from his dad, raised by his mother, who finds salvation in football – the same underlying narrative as *Iron John*.

Hornby explains how, on his very first trip to a football match, he fell in love with 'the overwhelming *maleness* of it all; the smell, the spitting, the swearing'. Football was a traditional way of celebrating masculinity which fitted into the British ethos of conformity. No self-absorbed, silly American prancing in the forest for the British Wild Men; instead the reassuring, beery, joshing mateyness of the football crowd, and the mildly self-deprecating humour of the terraces.

Like the American men's movement, however, the British New Lad 'revolution' was actually founded on a reactionary romanticism. It wanted to turn back the tide, instead of facing up to the new realities facing men in today's economic and social climate. Football suited this romanticism perfectly: its eulogising as 'the beautiful game', which has accompanied the rise of 'New Ladism' is very much about the 'beauty' of masculinity that writers would feel awkward about referring to directly – either because they would be afraid of being thought to be homosexual, or because they would be attacked as sexist. In football, however, this swooning passion for virility can be safely exercised without restraint.

Hence the adoration for Eric Cantona, very much *the* Wild Man of British Football, particularly for the quality press. Paul Gascoigne served for a time, but Cantona was a far superior vehicle for their aspirations. Here, at last, was a hero: dark, brooding, passionate, handsome, manly and unpredictable – a man in touch with his 'deep masculine'. He was even willing to pose as an intellectual and styled himself

246

a 'philosopher' and 'poet'. In fact, in *La Philosophie de Cantona* it sounds as if he has been reading Robert Bly:

'I have this passion in me that I can't handle,' he writes. 'It's like a fire inside you which demands to escape and which you have to let go. Sometimes it wants to get out to do harm . . . But I can't be what I am without the other sides of my character.'

Of course, this 'other side of my character' – what Bly calls the 'warrior within' – is never very far from violence, as Cantona's recent karate exhibition at Selhurst Park showed. Interestingly, it was the quality press which rushed to defend Cantona, while the tabloids condemned him. The *Guardian* described his attack as a 'truly moral outburst'. The sheer scale of the incident's coverage in the quality press, never mind the gushing and sycophantic nature of much of it, showed just how important symbolically he had become to the New Lad literary tendency.

What the Cantona incident really underlined about New Ladism is its essential immaturity. His 'truly moral outburst' might be more accurately described as a truly childish one. This was the behaviour of the school playground – down to the straight-to-video karate kicks in retaliation for the alleged taunt about Cantona's mother.

New Ladism, for all its fan-love of masculinity, is actually an avoidance of manhood, a celebration of immaturity in a world where being a man has become an extremely compli-cated and uncertain business. Since the romanticisation of football is about a nostalgic attachment to traditional, pre-feminist masculine values, it should not be so surprising that it has at its heart a longing for the certainties and irresponsi-bilities of boyhood. As Eric put it: 'I wish that I had remained a child; that I never had to grow up.'

But boys have to grow up: however painful it might be, it is generally less painful than remaining a child, a softy, a Mummy's boy. Just as the boys in the playground doing their karate moves are also demonstrating their indepen-dence – that they are tough young men, not Mummy's little baby any more – so New Ladism is a kind of arrested masculine development. These are grown men indulging a fantasy of independence (while actually remaining utterly dependent on their mothers or their proxies).

This arrested development of New Ladism, in fact, brings male heterosexuality alarmingly close to male homosexuality: according to some (admittedly controversial) psychoanalytic accounts, male homosexuality is caused by an unconscious fidelity to the Mother, masked by partial attempts to prove that you can live without her (for example, by never marrying, and by being scrupulous about personal hygiene and keeping your flat painfully tidy). In the case of New Ladism, however, the illusion of independence from the all-encompassing power of women is achieved through the opposite strategy – by keeping your room messy.

Which is where the New Lad journal *Loaded* comes in. With 'For men who should know better' as its tag line, *Loaded* is by far the most commercially successful manifestation of New Ladism; its studied, if sometimes witty desire to shock is the equivalent of the wilful teenage boy's untidy room in mother's well-kept home. This resistance to feminine hegemony merely reveals its own futility (even if it is enjoyable). With features extolling the attractions of large breasts, football, beer, vindaloo and vomit (though not necessarilly in that order), it holds up an aspiration to Laddishness which most of its readership can afford only when their girlfriends or wives let them go out to play with their mates.

But at least leaving it lying around, open at a particularly 'sexist' picture, can be relied upon to wind up your feminist girlfriend, just as the clothes on the floor of your room, or the cigarette smoke on your breath, did your mum. So desirable an effect is this, apparently, that in the year since *Loaded*'s launch, practically all the men's style press have tried, to varying degrees, to 'do' the New Lad.

The new straight male masculinity's parallel with male homosexuality does not end with a fixation on proving independence from women. There is something ironically excessive and artificial about it, which can't help but end up as a kind of failed seriousness. In other words, it's rather camp. New Lads are, by definition, Lad wannabes – contradicting the first rule of laddishness: either you *are* a lad or you aren't. New Lads are just as much a 'phony' marketing phenomenon as New Men. *Loaded* is as much a brochure and manual for living as *Cosmo*. All in all, the New Lad-ism of *Loaded* looks to much like Edina-and-Patsy meets Liam and Noel Gallagher. The 'crisis of masculinity' becomes a crisis of fashionability: 'Let me see – I've got my Blur T-shirt, Umbro sweatshirt, posters of Pamela Anderson, Eric Cantona and Ollie Reed. Am I a New Lad yet, darling? Or do I need an Arsenal away strip as well?'

Admittedly, perhaps there is something exhilirating about the fact that anyone can be a 'Lad' these days – if they really want to. Just as the proliferation of lifestyle-ism has meant that anyone can be 'Gay' – if they really want to. Nevertheless, it is still a bitter irony that the cultural reaction to the changes driven by capitalism which have unmanned men ends up co-opted back into the process of emasculation itself. The consumer revolution which has made the old masculinity obsolete sells back to men an adolescent dream of a world in which they are still a vital force, rather than just another market segment. Women, meanwhile, get on with the business of taking over the world.

Attitude, August 1995

DRAG ADDICTS

DRAG IS THE drug! proclaimed the surprise hit film of 1994, *Priscilla, Queen of the Desert*, a flounce around the Australian outback with a couple of female impersonators and a transexual Terence Stamp. A year later Hollywood seems to have picked up a serious habit, developing a craving for men in frocks that shows no signs of abating. Johnny Depp is dragged up to the nines in *Ed Wood*, a film about the famous transvestite Fifties B-movie director. Even action heroes like Wesley Snipes and Patrick Swayze can't resist the urge, donning dresses and slap in *Too Wong Foo, Thanks For Everything, Julie Newmar* as if they'd been doing it all their lives. Apparently Hollywood's leading men were scratching each other's eyes out for the chance to frock it up. Scriptwriter Douglas Carter Beane told *Variety* that 'James Spader was gorgeous, Matt Dillon was breathtaking and Rob Lowe could be the new L'Oréal girl.'

Of course, Hollywood has only just got hip to an intoxicant that rock 'n' roll has been inhaling for years. In the Sixties there was the Rolling Stones in drag for their single 'Have You Seen Your Mother Baby?', in the Seventies there was Bowie and glam rock, and in the early Eighties Boy George and the 'gender benders'. In the Nineties Nirvana were among the first to mainline eyeliner onstage, British group James 'did' Laura Ashley for the cover of *Laid* and even U2 dabbled for a promo (but then changed their minds). Not wanting to be left out, female performers flagged how hip they were to drag's groove – and not just fag hag Maddy. Cyndi Lauper used a line of drag queens in her video for the remake of 'Girls Just Wanna Have Fun', but Gloria Estefan in the promo for 'Everlasting Love' recently took the whole thing to its logical conclusion and bowed out to a collection of female inpersonators performing her entire back catalogue of images.

What makes the Nineties fixation unique, compared with other transvestite fads, is not just the fact that Hollywood is now coming out of the closet wearing its entire contents, but the scale of the interest in drag and the way in which it seems to be conquering all forms of media simultaneously – cinema, rock and pop, even TV (Julian Clary continues his single-entendre costume career and the BBC has given London gay drag act Lily Savage her own show). The fashion world is also getting in on the act, dusting off the old 'men look marvellous in skirts' line, while Jean Paul Gaultier's shops last year reportedly sold more of his men's 'kilts' than trousers.

Why now? Why has drag so suddenly and completely caught the imagination of the age? You could do worse than start with Camille Paglia, American stand-up academic and self-confessed drag queen groupie. Like many others, she sees the rise of the drag queen as a sign of our 'sexual crisis', but one that has surprisingly impressive antecedents. Thus the drag queen is 'a pagan priest whose ancestry is in the ancient cults of the Great Mother', and she 'defies victim-centred feminism by asserting the dominance of the woman in the universe'.

Of course, some might argue more prosaically that with the increasing power of women in all spheres of life – not just the reproductive – men's eagerness to put on frocks is merely a survival strategy. Forced, after the bobbing of John Wayne Bobbit's John Thomas, to choose between their trousers and their trouser snake, it isn't so surprising that many men have chosen the latter.

But there is more to the appeal of drag than simply wishing to join the winning team and hang on to your

251

trophies. The recent film *Junior*, in which Arnold Schwarzenegger becomes pregnant, is a kind of 'biological' drag in which a man 'puts on' the reproductive ability of women. Echoing the escalating anxieties of men in all walks of life, Arnie the fertility scientist is replaced by a female scientist (played by Emma Thompson who clumsily lands *on top* of him on her arrival) and so in turn decides to usurp the woman's role by giving birth. But the film also provides an ironic commentary on another kind of drag which Hollywood has been exploiting for years – muscle drag, or bodybuilding.

Bodybuilding is itself an attempt to usurp the 'female' role of narcissist, of a thing to be looked at – her 'enchanting' power of *glamour*. The most obvious way for a male to achieve glamour is by donning female clothes and make-up – but until now, unless you were a rock star, this was unacceptable unless you were looking for gags. However, in the late Seventies Hollywood discovered that the male film star was able to become a thing of glamour narcissim *and* hang on to his virility by accessorising himself with flesh rather than silk and satin. Consequently the vehicles for these bodybuilder drag artistes were hysterically macho and action-packed – to disguise the 'feminine' passivity of their exhibitionism. It seems that Hollywood's interest in 'real' drag in the Nineties was prepared for by Arnie and Sly in the Eighties and by the subsequent failing glamour of such bodybuilders.

Curiously, in real life bodybuilding drag is more likely to cost the man's virility than plain old-fashioned transvestism. Sustained use of steroids (male hormones) can bring about the atrophy of male genitalia and the growth of breasts. *Junior* offers an ironic comment on this. To become pregnant, Arnie, the most famous bodybuilder in the world, takes a cocktail of *female* hormones. Checking into the maternity clinic disguised as a woman, he explains his bizarre appearance as the result of 'being forced to take steroids when I was a member of the East German swimming team'. The closeness of the link between man's envy of woman's reproductive and glamorous power was further underlined in *Frankenstein*, in which Kenneth Branagh (Emma Thompson's husband) in the title role shows off his new gym-pumped body and is engaged in creating his own 'baby' – the monster.

However, drag's enormous popularity is more than just a function of man's wish to identify with woman's power – reproductive or narcissistic. The drag queen is also the literal embodiment of the ageless aspiration on the part of men and women – particularly women – to escape the ruthless decrees of nature. Modern technology and medicine, as films like *Junior* acknowledge, are of course making this increasingly possible. Abortion, hormone replacement therapy, test-tube babies, genetic manipulation, transsexualism – with its litany of 'perversions' of nature, science has made all of us, in potential if not in fact, neither male nor female, but *cyborg*. Science has reduced the once irreversible edicts of sex to drag that can be donned or discarded. The modern drag queen announces the victory of artifice over nature and proclaims the Good News that anatomy need not, after all, be destiny.

In the words of RuPaul, the black American drag queen who led the way in 1993 with 'Supermodel': 'Once you believe you are what they tell you, you are lost . . . I think of myself as RuPaul, an extension of the power of the universe.' The cybernetic drag queen, calling on the magic of science, self-confidence and cosmetics, is something akin to a god; the ancients frequently worshipped hermaphroditic figures, knowing that true androgyny was the surest sign of deity (something Bowie tapped into in his creation of Ziggy Stardust).

Another, more practical explanation of why the drag queen has taken on godlike proportions is that her image is reflected in a thousand mirrors. In today's mediatised world she is possibly the most mediatised image – instantly and effortlessly cool, ironic, media-literate and thoroughly postmodern (after all, the drag queen reference points are not real women but Hollywood's version of them); the drag queen celebrates surface and signifiers glibly and without

253

shame in a way which lesser mortals imprisoned in hum-drum reality can only dream of. So it was inevitable that the drag queen would be appropriated by advertising – most notably in the TV commercial for Levi's, in which a New York taxi driver drools over the glamorous 'woman' in the back of his yellow cab before 'she' ostentatiously starts smoothing 'her' chin stubble with an electric razor. The ad exploits to the hilt the grace, attitude and ease of the world of the drag queen, contrasting it with the sweaty, realistic and repellent masculinity of the taxi driver, who thinks he's in control, but is shown to be woefully out of touch; ironically, but now somewhat conventionally, it is the female impersonator who is shown to have the 'balls'.

Nevertheless, despite wearing postmodernism like a mink stole, the drag queen is not herself superficial. Rather she is a deeply moral phenomenon, representing in herself the official religion of the late twentieth century – self-realisation; she is the glowing, shimmering, living Shangri-la of individualism and the cult of personality. The drag queen is the bastard child of the Eighties who sees to it that she nevertheless inherits that decade's legacy. The padded shoulders, the power dressing, the big hair, the bitching, the designer psychosis of the Eighties easily translated into drag, which is a continuation of these styles/addictions into parody (which nicely inoculates them against Nineties disapproval for Eighties habits) – the drag queen is Alexis Carrington in a cheater.

However, there are discontinuities. Where the Eighties was matt-black and desperately serious about money, the Nineties is lamé and desperately serious about wigs. Where the Eighties was about conspicuous consumption, the Nineties is about conspicuous transformation. But the most important feature remains constant: like the ambitious Eighties, the drag queen is nothing if not aspirational – she remains her own special creation.

Some male readers may consider this all very interesting, but rather irrelevant to their lives. 'We have no interest in putting on women's clothes,' you might protest. 'We are blokes who only wear clothes for blokes, thank you very much – none of that kinky stuff interests *me*.' Sorry, chaps, but there is no escape from the relentless forward mince of drag. Even dressing in the clothes of your own sex has become just another kind of transvestism. Mass consumerism has commodified gender to the extent that we have all become 'homeovestite' – masquerading as someone of the *same* sex.

Originally coined to pathologise and quarantine those who felt unsure about their masculinity or femininity and turned to clothes to consolidate their identity, the term has run rampant. As the famous American psychoanalyst Louise Kaplan has observed, 'Any person dressing in the clothes of his or her own sex could be a homeovestite.' The overstated femininity of Marilyn Monroe in her tight sweaters and hoop skirts, or the overdetermined masculinity of Marlon Brando in his tight jeans and motorcycle jacket, are easily recognisable as homeovestite. And of course, they and other stars have provided the uniforms and templates for the performance of masculinity and femininity on a mass scale.

As a result no male exposed to advertising and popular culture can buy clothes without buying into those 'perverse' fantasies and becoming himself homeovestite. The male consumer these days isn't just wearing clothes, he's wearing other men – but idealised, fetishised men that don't actually exist and cannot be allowed to.

It was naughty old Gore Vidal that couldn't resist pointing this out as far back as 1968 in his (then) scandalous sex-change novel *Myra Breckenridge*. He noted that society and industry had less and less use for real masculinity and that, in fact, it was becoming more and more unwelcome; consequently, 'the young men compensate by *playing* at being men, wearing cowboy clothes, boots, black leather, attempting through clothes (what an age for the fetishist!) to impersonate the kind of man our society *claims* to admire but swiftly puts down should he attempt to be anything more than an illusionist, playing a part.'

255

In other words, the male who doesn't impersonate females is doomed to impersonate men.

We're all hooked. We're all users. Like the babies of junky mothers we have been fed and nurtured in an environment spiked with drag before we were even born. And as children of mediatised age this is probably a practical adaptation. Drag is an inauthentic way of expressing something authentic in an inauthentic world – the only form of expression left in a world of surfaces. It is simply an intense signal in a universe of frantic noise where fetishism – of commodities, of images, of sex, of gender, of fame – is the only lingua franca. Most of all, drag is the drug that makes postmodernism bearable.

Oh, and it's fun.

Homme Plus, Spring 1995

INDEX

257